Writing Fiction
[in High School]

Bringing Your Stories to Life!

Also by Sharon Watson

Jump In: A Workbook for Reluctant and Eager Writers

The Lifeguard's Locker: A Parent/Teacher Manual for Jump In

(Middle school writing curriculum published by Apologia Press and available at www.apologia.com)

Writing Fiction [in High School]: Teacher's Guide

Writing Fiction
[in High School]

Bringing Your Stories to Life!

by Sharon Watson

www.WritingWithSharonWatson.com

Copyright © 2010-2011 by Sharon Watson.

All rights reserved. You know the drill. No part of this book may be copied, reproduced, or in any way transmitted, transmuted, or transmogrified without the prior, written consent of the author, except in conditions of "fair use."

Writing Fiction [in High School]: Bringing Your Stories to Life!
ISBN-10: 1463582080
ISBN-13: 978-1463582081

Writing Fiction [in High School]: Teacher's Guide also available
ISBN-10: 1463582285
ISBN-13: 978-1463582289

Printed in the United States of America

First printing July 2011

Examples in this course are meant solely for teaching purposes and in no way construe a recommendation of the complete book or story from which they are excerpted.

Cover photo copyright © 2011 by Esther Moulder, www.clickphotography.biz

www.WritingWithSharonWatson.com

To Terry,
the family,
and all the wonderful students
who have taught me

Table of Contents

1 FACTS ABOUT FICTION • 1

    The Power of Fiction • 1

    A Teeny-Tiny Grammar Lesson • 2

    About this Course • 4

    Good Writers Are Good Readers • 5

    Character Versus Person • 6

    Where Do Ideas Come From? • 6

    I Have an Idea. Now What? •7

    Make-Believe and Truths • 8

    Hook Your Reader • 9

2 POINT OF VIEW • 15

    The Nitty-Gritty of Point of View, Part 1 (1st and 2nd Person) • 17

    The Nitty-Gritty of Point of View, Part 2 (3rd Person) • 22

    Decisions, Decisions • 30

    A Common Point-of-View Mistake • 31

    A Word about Filters • 32

    Critiquing • 34

        For the Reader • 34

        For the Writer • 35

    Proofreading Marks • 36

    Optional Writing for POV • 39

3 FAIRY TALES • 41

    Another Tale, Another Prince Charming (Motifs) • 43

    The Power of Three • 44

4 CHARACTERS AND CHARACTERIZATION • 49

Leads, Genders, and Ages • 52

What the Character Says—Dialogue and Voice • 53

What He Thinks • 58

What He Does, Part 1 • 60

What He Does, Part 2: How to Show Character Emotion • 63

What the Character Looks Like, Part 1 • 66

What the Character Looks Like, Part 2: The Girl Wore a Coat • 68

This Is what I Look Like, Part 3 • 70

What Others Say/How Others React • 73

What the Author or Narrator Says about Him • 75

What's in a Name? • 75

The Telling Detail • 76

An Empathetic Lead • 78

How to Create an Empathetic Lead • 79

Character Motivation • 82

A Character Dies • 85

Be Specific • 86

The Antagonist • 87

5 CONFLICT • 91

The Conflict Menu • 92

Do Try this at Home, Part 1 • 94

Do Try this at Home, Part 2 • 96

Thirst • 97

Will Nemo ever Return Home? • 99

Death • 101

Tension •101

Character Arc • 106

Optional Writing for Conflict • 107

6 DIALOGUE • 109

    What She Says, What She Does • 110

    Conflict—Can't Get enough of It! • 115

    Subtext • 117

    Beware • 118

    Exposition • 119

    Other Formats for Dialogue • 121

    Speakers, Paragraphs, and Tags • 123

    Indirect Dialogue • 124

    Optional Writing for Dialogue • 126

7 DESCRIPTION • 129

    Description Has a Job to Do • 132

    Description Tools • 134

        Sensory Details • 134

        Figurative Language • 138

        Organic Imagery • 140

        Precise and Vivid Verbs • 141

        Direction • 143

        Weather • 144

        Time • 145

        Animals/Nature • 146

        Show, Don't Tell • 147

        Specificity • 149

        Character Reaction • 150

        Synesthesia • 151

        What to Avoid • 152

    Settings • 153

    Moving from One Location to the Next • 156

    Description Checklist for All Writers • 160

    Optional Description Writing • 161

8 WORDS, WORDS, WORDS • 163

Audience and Word Choice • 163

Connotation • 165

Contractions • 166

Verb Tense • 167

Sentence Impact • 169

Active/Passive • 171

Parallelism • 172

The Poetry of Prose • 174

Exclamation Points and Capitals • 176

Style • 176

A Word of Caution • 178

9 THEME • 179

Three Problems with Theme—And How to Fix Them • 182

Problem 1 • 182

Problem 2 • 185

Problem 3 • 189

Optional Writing for Theme • 192

10 PLOT • 195

The Hero's Journey • 199

La Ronde • 206

11 SCENES • 209

This Is *not* a Scene • 209

This *Is* a Scene • 210

Pat the Dog • 213

Yes? No? Maybe? • 214

The Scene's Guts • 219

Narrative Summary • 223

Narrative Summary and the End of a Scene • 224

Some Common Scene Mistakes • 227

Flashbacks • 232

Mirror Scenes • 237

Optional Writing in Scenes • 240

12 BEGINNINGS AND ENDINGS • 243

A Recipe for a Great Beginning • 244

Hook Your Reader • 244

Genre, Rules of the Story, Setting, and Tone • 246

Protagonist and Protagonist's Voice • 250

An Interesting Situation • 251

The Promise of Future Conflict • 253

Backstory • 254

Endings • 256

What Readers Expect from Endings • 258

13 GETTING PUBLISHED • 261

Revising • 261

Avenues to Getting Published • 263

What the Manuscript Looks Like • 272

Should You Read while You Write? • 274

Pen Names • 275

Rejection Letters • 275

BIBLIOGRAPHY • 279

1: FACTS ABOUT FICTION

Jane Austen, author of *Pride and Prejudice*, wrote her first novel at age fourteen. Christopher Paolini began his rough draft of *Eragon* when he was fifteen. Mary Shelley wrote of horrors in *Frankenstein* when she was nineteen.
    Now it is your turn.

THE POWER OF FICTION

    Alan Alda, an actor and writer, reveals in his memoir *Never Have Your Dog Stuffed* how he discovered the power of his written words:

> On the night of the first preview [of an Off Broadway revue], I stood in the wings and watched the opening sketch I had written. I heard actual laughs coming from the audience. This was the first time I had heard an audience laugh at something I had written, and a cocktail of sweet, tingling hormones shot through my brain. I was suddenly aware of

what an astonishing power there was in words. Once you set a thought in motion, it went on its own. You could write something on Tuesday, and they would laugh at it a week from Friday.

Plato, too, knew the impact poets, playwrights, and storytellers had on audiences. In fact, he seemed to advocate either running them out of town or censoring them, especially when their stories ran counter to the mores of the day.

Upton Sinclair's *The Jungle* had an impact, but an unexpected one. He wrote it to expose and improve the incredibly poor conditions of workers in the U. S. meat-packing industry in the early 1900s. Instead of a public outcry on behalf of the workers, however, readers focused on meat-inspection procedures and tainted meat, and pushed legislation which became the Pure Food and Drug Act of 1906. That was over a century ago; fiction still has not lost its power.

Readers become attached to characters. When Arthur Conan Doyle killed off his famous Sherlock Holmes, readers became so agitated that he brought the sleuth back to life. When the Harry Potter series came to an abrupt end in 2007, *The Miami Herald* printed an article filled with advice from doctors on how parents can help their children cope with the grief they may experience from the deaths in *Harry Potter and the Deathly Hallows*.

> Talent is helpful in writing, but guts are absolutely necessary. Without the guts to try, the talent may never be discovered.
> —Jessamyn West, author of *The Friendly Persuasion*

Even God used the power of fiction when He instructed the prophet Nathan to confront King David about the double sin of adultery and murder (2 Samuel 12:1-10). Nathan's job was to tell David a story that revealed unfair dealings and thievery; when David heard Nathan's made-up story, he was cut to the heart.

Fiction cannot be dismissed as unimportant. It's not "just a story."

A TEENY-TINY GRAMMAR LESSON

Before we get to your first assignments, let's clear up a confusing topic: Why is kiwi the name of a fruit *and* an animal?

Or maybe we should just review the use of italics and quotation marks in titles.

When should you use italics in titles? When should you use quotation marks? These burning questions are nowhere near the same level of importance as the kiwi enigma, but they bear examination.

Italics: Titles of books, magazines, newspapers, works of art, TV shows, movies, epic poems (the long, long ones), and ships (who knew?) are italicized. When writing them out by hand, underline them; when putting them on the computer, skip the underlining and go straight to the italics. Here are some examples:

A book:	*The Picture of Dorian Gray* by Oscar Wilde
An epic poem:	*Paradise Lost* by John Milton
A play:	*Hamlet* by William Shakespeare
A movie:	*Stranger than Fiction*
A TV series:	*The Mentalist*
A book series:	The Lord of the Rings series [Surprise! When referred to as a series, a title does not use italics or quotation marks.]

Quotation Marks: Titles of short stories, book chapters, articles from magazines or newspapers, episodes from TV shows, and short poems use quotation marks. One way to remember the difference between italic and quotation mark usage is that chapters, articles, and episodes are all pieces from longer works (books, magazines, newspapers, and TV shows). The "pieces" get the quotation marks; the original, whole work gets the italics.

A short story	"Everything that Rises Must Converge" by Flannery O'Connor
A chapter:	"First Day Finish" [from *The Friendly Persuasion* by Jessamyn West]
A short poem:	"The Bells" by Edgar Allan Poe
A TV episode:	"The Thin Red Line" from *The Mentalist*

1.1 All Writers and Discussion

Discuss these questions with your group:

> › Who are your favorite authors?
> › What are your favorite books?
> › What books or short stories do you dislike?
> › Figure out why these are your favorites and unfavorites.

1.2 All Writers

Write a letter to a living author you like to read. Authors like positive, specific feedback, and they sometimes enjoy answering questions about their work, especially if you mention you are a student. You will find the address of the publishing company (or an address or Web site for the author) near the copyright page or at the back of the book.

End of today's lesson

Report to the group when you receive a letter from your author.

About This Course

This course will teach you how to write fiction in the form of **short stories** and **novels**.

It will be helpful to know four things about this course:

1. It has two tracks. The first track is for **all writers**, no matter what your experience or skill level. The second is an optional **manuscript track** for those who have written the manuscript of a short story or novel or who are writing one.

   > **manuscript:** an unpublished work, whether in first draft form or ready for the publisher. Abbreviation: MS or ms. Plural: MSS or mss.

2. It works best when done with a group. You will write on your own, of course, but discussing ideas, submitting your work to the group for critiques, and critiquing others are important when learning to write fiction. If you don't have a group (classmates, homeschool group, friends, etc.), find or create one. Meet once a week. The benefits will be worth the work.

3. It uses a wide variety of short stories, novels, and movies to show effective or ineffective writing. *However, this course does not necessarily endorse any of the stories in their original form.* Their use in this course is simply as examples.

4. You will be assigned one novel and some short stories to read and a few movies to watch at specific times in the text. The novel, *The Last Book in the Universe* by Rodman Philbrick, is easy to read and, in fact, is below your reading level. This way you can focus on its writing and techniques but not be obliged to struggle with it.

The rest of the course is self-explanatory and easy to follow.

1.3 All Writers and Discussion

Make a list of three to five things you want to learn in this course. For example, do you want to know how to create interesting characters? How to create suspense? To write about a theme without having it stick out a mile?

Discussion: Discuss your list with the group.

GOOD WRITERS ARE GOOD READERS

If you want to be a good writer, be a good reader. But what does it mean to be a "good reader"?

Read books from many genres, time periods, and cultures. This broadens the scope of your learning and shows you what has been done in the past, how it developed, and what is possible for you to do with your writing.

genre: [ZHAHN rə] the kind of story, i.e., historical fiction, adventure, mystery, western, suspense, literary, etc.

C. S. Lewis, author of the Narnia tales, was an avid reader. He loved fairy tales and greatly admired the work of Kenneth Grahame (*The Wind in the Willows*) and George MacDonald (*Phantastes*, *Lilith*, and *At the Back of the North Wind*). Their influence is evident throughout Lewis's work. J. R. R. Tolkien's extensive knowledge of Germanic and Anglo-Saxon literature (think *Beowulf*) bleeds into *The Hobbit* and the Rings trilogy. When Dean Koontz, a modern suspense writer, was asked about favorite childhood memories, he began his reply with, "Going to Mars with Ray Bradbury." They—and you—are standing on the shoulders of literary giants. Get to know the giants.

Read with an awareness of what you are reading. Watch how the author structures his plot, handles point of view, or uses the conventions (guidelines) of his specific genre. When you find a compelling passage, copy it out by hand or type it into a computer file and then pick it apart to see how it was created. Imitate it by writing your own passage based on the original one.

CHARACTER VERSUS PERSON

People are real. *Characters* are invented, no matter how real they seem to readers. It's a nit-picky differentiation but an important one, especially when you discuss stories. For instance, instead of saying, "I thought this person's motivation was weak," try saying, "I thought this character's motivation was weak."

WHERE DO IDEAS COME FROM?

Ideas can come from anywhere—your subconscious, a crazy vacation, the Internet, a newspaper or magazine article, a friend's casual comment, a sermon point, a personal experience, books filled with story prompts, or a novel you happen to be reading. Anywhere and everywhere.

Ray Bradbury's *Fahrenheit 451* was born of two ideas that collided. Late one night when Bradbury was walking with a friend, a policeman gave them a warning for walking out late. Bradbury was so peeved he wrote "The Pedestrian." Later he wondered what it would be like if firemen did not put out fires but created them. From this came "The Fireman." And both of these ideas later influenced *Fahrenheit 451*.

In *Zen in the Art of Writing*, Bradbury recommends writing about what irks you, about how you wish things could be different. It works for him. It might for you.

E. B. White became interested in a spider in his barn on his new farm and he couldn't help but become attached to her. Her name? Charlotte. You can read about her in *Charlotte's Web*.

> Where does this stuff come from? Wish I knew.
> —Sue Grafton, mystery writer

When Leo Tolstoy saw a woman crushed to death under a train in 1872, he was overcome with emotion. She had thrown herself under the train because of a broken relationship, and Tolstoy had known her. From his grief, he fabricated the story of *Anna Karenina*, a married woman who has an unhappy affair.

Frankenstein, on the other hand, owes its life to a summer of inclement weather and the writings of Dr. Erasmus Darwin (the not-yet grandfather of Charles), who wondered if it were possible to use electricity to bring inanimate objects to life. So why not try corpses? thought young Mary Shelley.

Mystery writer Agatha Christie has a simpler secret to gathering ideas: "The best time for planning a book is while you're doing the dishes."

An idea is not a story, but it is the kernel that gets the story growing.

Get into the habit of writing down your ideas when they hit you. Keep a notebook nearby. Cut out that crazy newspaper article and keep it in a file for future reference and inspiration.

1.4 All Writers and Discussion

Comb through a newspaper for story ideas and make a list of three interesting things you find. Read the whole thing, even all the ads and personals. For instance, think of the stories you could invent from these six words (sometimes attributed to Ernest Hemingway): "For sale: baby shoes, never worn."

End of today's lesson

Discussion: Share your finds with the group.

I HAVE AN IDEA. NOW WHAT?

Here are some common methods for writing fiction:

> › You have no idea what you are going to write, but you sit down and write.
> › You have an idea, so you sit down and write.
> › You have an idea and a nebulous plan, so you sit down and write.
> › You have an idea and an organized outline, so you sit down and write.

Notice the common clause in all this: "You sit down and write."

All of these methods have worked for successful writers.

Which is best for you? Only you can tell.

Try different methods. Your learning style, left-brain/right-brain balance, personality, experiences, and habits will allow you to find the method that works best for you—**if you sit down and write.**

> If my doctor told me I had only six minutes to live, I wouldn't brood. I'd type a little faster
> –Isaac Asimov, author of *I, Robot*

Here's the "formula":

>Step 1: Write
>Step 2: Shape
>Step 3: Rewrite
>Step 4: Shape
>Step 5: Rewrite
>Steps 6-51: repeat steps 2 through 5 endlessly
>Step 52: Proofread and polish, polish, polish

Your process may be different, but you get the idea. Writing is not simply writing. It also involves follow-up work. And gluing your seat to the chair.

> There are three rules for writing a novel. Unfortunately no one knows what they are.
> --Somerset Maugham, author of *Of Human Bondage*

You'll learn many things in this course, but as you write your rough draft, forget about all of it and simply write. Use the creative right side of your brain to write your first unshapely mess. Then go back and use the formal left side of your brain (where your internal editor lives) to rewrite, shape, and polish.

MAKE-BELIEVE AND TRUTHS

Good stories are an intricate blend of make-believe and truth. For instance, it is not possible, to my knowledge, to walk through the back of a wardrobe and discover a land filled with dwarves, dryads, and talking animals. It's all invented, but it is grounded in such reality—believable characters, feelings, reactions, truths about life, settings, and so forth—that it comes alive in readers' imaginations.

You can invent a wise-cracking rabbit who stands upright and says, "What's up, Doc?" but no one will believe in him if you don't give him human reactions and feelings and make some honest observations about human nature and life—in Bugs Bunny's case, that if you are the underdog, it pays to be wily.

> The difference between fiction and reality? Fiction has to make sense.
> –Tom Clancy, best-selling author

If you write about a person—oops! character—betraying a friend, be honest about the friend's reaction (anger, fear, self-doubt, loneliness, etc.) or you will lose credibility with your readers and then you will lose your readers. And readers can smell a dishonest reaction as far as they can smell skunk spray on a windy night.

Speaking of credibility, Franz Kafka begins "The Metamorphosis" with this totally unbelievable event:

> As Gregor Samsa awoke one morning from uneasy dreams he found himself transformed in his bed into a gigantic insect. He was lying on his hard, as it were armor-plated, back and when he lifted his head a little he could see his dome-like brown belly divided into stiff arched segments on top of which the bed quilt could hardly keep in position and was about to slide off completely. His numerous legs, which were pitifully thin compared to the rest of his bulk, waved helplessly before his eyes.

Who can believe this situation? No human wakes up as an insect. The premise is completely make-believe. However, Gregor Samsa's *feelings*, his family's *reactions* and dealings with each other, his worry about his job—all of these are very honest and believable, and, therefore, the story is credible.

Your whole story, as you have written it down, is an invention. It never happened exactly that way. That's why it's called fiction. But you will make it *seem* as real as the world around you. You will build your story with believable and vivid details, honest emotions and reactions, and a cause-and-effect pattern (more on this in chapter 11: Scenes). This will cause your readers to willingly put their disbelief on hold and enter into the fictional world you create.

> I want you to know why story-truth is truer sometimes than happening-truth.
> —Tim O'Brien, "Good Form"

1.5 All Writers and Discussion

End of today's lesson

Make a list of five "lies" (or inventions) and five truths in movies, short stories, and novels of your choosing. If something is unbelievable, discover what makes it so.

Discuss the above with the group.

HOOK YOUR READER

Who has not been lured by this time-honored method of beginning a tale: "Once upon a time . . ."? Those four words hold so much promise and delight,

> I'm writing a book. I've got the page numbers done.
> —Steven Wright, comic

and, like a balloon filled with water, you can almost feel their heft in your hand as you anticipate the rest of the story.

First impressions are important in fiction. You have only a few minutes to **hook** your reader. A hook is just what it sounds like: Those first sentences or paragraphs that hold such enticing bait in front of a hungry reader that he'll bite and keep reading your story.

Here's the first sentence from Nicholas Sparks' *A Walk to Remember*:

> When I was seventeen, my life changed forever.

What was the event? How did his life change forever? Readers want to know! Check out this one from Charles Dickens' *A Christmas Carol*, which throws us into the middle of a grave situation (bad pun intended):

> Marley was dead: to begin with.

Sometimes the best hooks surprise us and make us ask questions. Consider how Dickens begins *A Tale of Two Cities*:

> It was the best of times, it was the worst of times.

With these contrasts, Dickens sets up the opposites and ironies that appear throughout his story and makes us ask, "How could this be?"

Nicolae, written by Tim LaHaye and Jerry B. Jenkins, borrows Dickens' hook in order to make a stark point:

> It was the worst of times; it was the worst of times.

Ray Bradbury uses a hint of violence in *Fahrenheit 451* to create curiosity:

> It was a pleasure to burn.
> It was a special pleasure to see things eaten, to see things blackened and *changed*.

If an author plants questions in the reader's mind, it becomes his job to answer them or at least address them in his story, which Bradbury does.

Here's part of the hook for Rodman Philbrick's *Freak the Mighty:*

> I never had a brain until Freak came along and let me borrow his for a while, and that's the truth, the whole truth.

How can you borrow someone's brain? How did the narrator get along without a brain? Does he mean it literally or figuratively? What's so freaky about Freak? When he says it's the truth, does he mean it or is he stretching things? Believe it or not, *all* those questions are answered in the book.

You may be familiar with this famous opening:

> It was a dark and stormy night.

Those words, so often imitated and parodied, begin Edward George Bulwer-Lytton's *Paul Clifford*, written in 1830. What suspense! What atmosphere! What sense of foreboding! Then he completely unplugs the electricity with how he handles the rest of his first sentence, which was perfectly acceptable to readers and editors of that time:

> It was a dark and stormy night; the rain fell in torrents—except at occasional intervals, when it was checked by a violent gust of wind which swept up the streets (for it is in London that our scene lies), rattling along the housetops, and fiercely agitating the scanty flame of the lamps that struggled against the darkness.

Was the rain falling or wasn't it?

Until recently, writers could take many chapters to hook readers, but this will bore today's readers. How many great classics have left you cold simply because they took so long to get to the meat of the story?

> Publishing houses hire professional readers, often college or graduate students, to read submissions. These young men and women have hundreds of stories to read and, most likely, will not finish yours unless you hook them early. For short stories, this means the first few paragraphs. For novels, the first pages.

There is a good reason why authors used to mosey through the first few chapters. People did not always have television, movies, or radio. The readers of *Robinson Crusoe* did not have shelves of books in their bedrooms. Stories came by way of plays, local storytellers, traveling professional storytellers, or an occasional book. In a world without constant bombardment, reading a book was a special treat, and, like a box of chocolates, was enjoyed when digested slowly.

But people don't read like that now. They are in a hurry. They expect the story to *get* to the story. In addition, they are accustomed to television shows that begin with one- or two-minute teasers—intentionally constructed to hook viewers—and movie previews that promise action, thrills, and adventure.

Here's the thing: You are not writing for people who lived one hundred years ago. Adjust your "hook" strategy for modern times.

Hooks can perform tasks other than catching readers and generating questions, such as:

> - Set the tone for the story
> - Let readers know what type of story they are reading (the genre)
> - Reveal tension
> - Introduce the main character and his or her major problem (the major dramatic question)
> - Foreshadow events to come
> - Predict (or give hints about) the ending

Keep this in mind: No cheating allowed. It isn't fair to begin your story with a stupendous bang that has nothing to do with what's really going on.

1.6 All Writers and Discussion

Discussion: Read the following hooks. What questions do they raise?

1. It looked like a good thing: but wait till I tell you. We were down South, in Alabama—Bill Driscoll and myself—when this kidnapping idea struck us. It was, as Bill afterward expressed it, "during a moment of temporary mental apparition"; but we didn't find that out till later. (from "The Ransom of Red Chief" by O. Henry)

2. "The most beautiful crime I ever committed," Flambeau would say in his highly moral old age, "was also, by a singular coincidence, my last. It was committed at Christmas." (from "The Flying Stars" by G. K. Chesterton)

3. There is no lake at Camp Green Lake. There once was a very large lake here, the largest lake in Texas. That was over a hundred years ago. Now it is just a dry, flat wasteland. (from *Holes* by Louis Sachar)

4. He should never have taken that shortcut. (from *Timeline* by Michael Crichton)

5. The funny thing about facing imminent death is that it really snaps everything else into perspective. Take right now, for instance. (from *Maximum Ride* by James Patterson)

6. It is a truth universally acknowledged, that a single man in possession of a good fortune must be in want of a wife.
    However little known the feelings or views of such a man may be on his first entering a neighbourhood, this truth is so well fixed in the minds of the surrounding families, that he is considered as the rightful property of some one or other of their daughters. (from *Pride and Prejudice* by Jane Austen)

1.7 All Writers and Writing Group

End of today's lesson

Create three hooks, put them into a hat with others from your writing group, and write a story from one you draw out. You need not write the whole story; simply write for ten or so minutes to see where you can take it—or where it takes you. Read results aloud, if desired.

1.8 Manuscript Track (for those who have written or are writing a short story or novel manuscript)

Read the opening sentences of your story. Do they grab the audience? Do they hint of things to come? Do they bring up essential questions?

Rewrite your hook until it is effective at capturing your audience. Then share it with the group and evaluate each other's hooks.

> The last lesson of the chapter →

1.9 All Writers

Enough of talking about writing! It's time to write a story. Your story will have only 26 sentences, one for each letter of the alphabet. Your first sentence will begin with a word starting with "A," your second with a "B" word, and so forth. For example: *A*uctions make me queasy. *B*oxes of plates, hangers, and rare books lie derelict among a quilt with special family history imbedded in its pattern and dressers missing knobs. *C*onfusion reigns, but it's all that is left of my family. (And so on.) Make sure to hook your readers early.

Type your story in a plain, size-12 font. Double-space your work. Put your name and page number at the top of each page (in a header). This is how you will submit all your work because this is how publishers expect it to look.

Proofread your work before handing it in.

Group: Exchange your story with someone in your group and read each other's stories. If your group is small enough and if you have time, bring enough copies for everyone to read your story (and you will read theirs). Find something positive to say about each one you read.

What you studied in this chapter:

- ✓ The power of fiction
- ✓ Italics and quotation marks
- ✓ Good writers are good readers
- ✓ Character vs. person
- ✓ Where ideas come from and what to do with them
- ✓ Make-believe and truth in fiction
- ✓ Hooks

1.10 All Writers

Begin reading *The Last Book in the Universe* by Rodman Philbrick. Finish it by chapter 4.

2: POINT OF VIEW

Who is going to tell your story? Obviously, *you* will write it, but who will *tell* it? Through whose eyes will your story be told?

What difference does it make who tells the story? Think of "Jack and the Beanstalk" told not from Jack's perspective but from the giant's. How would the story change? Who would be the hero—Jack or the giant?

Below are excerpts from two stories a real sister and her younger brother wrote. Both people, now adults, are remembering the same incident from their childhood; it happened in the 1940s in an unused chicken coop. Notice the difference between the two perspectives. First, the sister:

> My brother was squishing slow-moving flies on the windows and I was sweeping the dirt floor when a shadow covered the screen door. We heard mocking laughter and saw a tall, bulky boy click the hook outside, locking us in. We ordered him to let us out but he just laughed at us, his latest victims, and then disappeared through a stand of trees and bushes to his backyard. We hollered and then hollered some

more, but no one came. Finally my brother did the unthinkable: He tore the screen, reached his hand through, and unlocked the door. He grew up to be an engineer.

Now, the younger brother, as he remembers it:

> We were in a treasure cave loading the burros with gold and silver artifacts when the opening of the cave suddenly darkened. Someone rolled a large bolder in front of the cave entrance and blocked our exit. Trapped! We had no way out and the air was getting thinner with each breath and, to make matters worse, there were large spiders everywhere.
> After dealing with the arachnids, I was able to glean some charcoal from a previous fire, no doubt from a native religious ceremony, and some sulfur from a deposit in the cave wall. The cave was also inhabited by thousands of bats, whose guano is high in ammonium nitrate. I mixed the ammonium nitrate with the charcoal and sulfur to make the gun powder I used to blow open the cave entrance.

It's clear to see that the choice of the story's narrator makes all the difference.

In "A Crazy Tale" by G. K. Chesterton, a character relates some things that frightened him. All actions and ideas are filtered through his lens. Read this condensed excerpt and guess what this character is remembering:

> I heard a great noise out of the sky, and I turned and saw a giant filling the heavens.
> He lifted me like a flying bird through space and set me upon his shoulder. With the giant was a woman, and after I had lived some little while with them, I began to have an idea of what the truth must be. Instead of killing me, the giant and giantess fed and tended me like servants.
> One day, as I stood beside her knee, she spoke to me; but I was speechless. A new and dreadful fancy took me by the throat. The woman was smaller than before. The house was smaller: the ceiling was nearer.

> . . . A disease of transformation too monstrous for nightmare had quickened within me. I was growing larger and larger whether I would or no.

What very normal thing is this character talking about? Take a few guesses before looking at the top of the next page for the answer.

What is your first memory? Most likely, you remember it because the event had a strong emotion attached to it: fear, excitement, happiness, anger, confusion, etc. Perhaps you remember getting into trouble, getting lost, trying to walk, or meeting a younger sibling for the first time. Or maybe you remember the day you first noticed that people were not statues but beings who could move. How far back do you remember?

2.1 All Writers

End of today's lesson

Write down your earliest memory as a child. Be as complete as possible. Then put it aside for use in another assignment later in this chapter.

THE NITTY-GRITTY OF POINT OF VIEW, PART 1

It will be helpful to be familiar with some basic types of point of view (POV) so you can make informed decisions about which is best for your story. If you have taken a foreign language, you are familiar with the following pronoun chart:

	Singular Pronouns	Plural Pronouns
First person	I, me, my, mine	we, our, ours
Second person	you, your, yours	you (formal—ye), y'all
Third person	he, she, him, her, his, hers	they, them, theirs

There are a few more pronouns, but you get the point. This chart, also used in the English language, shows the archaic, formal "you" ("Hear ye! Hear ye!").

> Answer to "A Crazy Tale": This character is remembering what it was like to be a young boy. The giant is his father; the giantess, his mother. He is frightened when he sees he is growing up and they are no longer of gigantic, and therefore reassuring, proportions.

So, why the chart?

Here's why. The names of the POVs come from the pronouns and are named accordingly: first person, second person, and third person.

Before getting acquainted with your point-of-view choices, take a peek at the following character definitions, just for reference:

› **Protagonist:** the main character or lead, the one readers are cheering on, the one whose problems and desires are driving the story
› **Secondary character:** not as important as the lead; issues/desires are not as large or problematic as lead's
› **Antagonist:** another main character or a force, the one who keeps the protagonist from reaching his/her goal; sometimes the "bad guy"
› **Viewpoint character:** the character through which readers see the scene, chapter, or story; usually one of the protagonists

Now, *finally*, here are your most common POV choices. The first ones are in this lesson; the last ones are in the next.

First Person: Information is given through one character's eyes, and he becomes your narrator or guide. The narrator is usually the protagonist.

> Point-of-View Choices
>
> **First person**
> First-person peripheral
> Unreliable narrator
> Epistolary
> First-person plural
>
> Second person
>
> Third-person omniscient
> Third-person single vision
> Third-person multiple vision
> Third-person objective

Here's an example of a main character, Hank, telling his own story in *A Connecticut Yankee in King Arthur's Court* by Mark Twain:

I wanted to try and think out how it was that rational or even half-rational men could ever have learned to wear armor, considering its inconveniences; and how they had managed to keep up such a fashion for generations when it was plain that what I had suffered today they had had to suffer all the days of their lives.

The use of "I" in the narrative is a dead give-away that it is in first person.

In *The Great Gatsby* by F. Scott Fitzgerald, Nick Carraway is the story's first-person narrator. However, he is a secondary character; the story isn't about him. Gatsby is the main character, but everything we know about him is filtered through Nick's eyes. (Think of the Sherlock Holmes stories in which everything is told by and filtered through Doctor Watson.) This kind of POV is called **first person peripheral**. Here is Nick telling us of the first time he sees his neighbor Gatsby as they both stand in their yards at night:

> I decided to call to him. Miss Baker had mentioned him at dinner, and that would do for an introduction. But I didn't call to him, for he gave a sudden intimation that he was content to be alone—he stretched out his arms toward the dark water in a curious way, and, far as I was from him, I could have sworn he was trembling. Involuntarily I glanced seaward—and distinguished nothing except a single green light, minute and far away, that might have been the end of a dock. When I looked once more for Gatsby he had vanished, and I was alone again in the unquiet darkness.

Point-of-View Choices

First person
First-person peripheral
Unreliable narrator
Epistolary
First-person plural

Second person

Third-person omniscient
Third-person single vision
Third-person multiple vision
Third-person objective

The first-person narrator, no matter what kind he is, can tell us only what *he* is thinking, feeling, seeing, and experiencing. If he wants to reveal how another character is feeling, or how he *thinks* another character is feeling, he has to relate it by what he observes. Notice that Carraway can only relate what he sees Gatsby doing; he may surmise emotions and motivations from this, but he can only guess. So instead of writing "Gatsby was deeply troubled," Nick can only write "he was trembling."

How reliable is the first-person narrator? In truth, each story is colored by the viewpoint character and his or her perspective.

Near the beginning of *The Great Gatsby*, the narrator Nick Carraway admits he is "one of the few honest people" he has ever known. And we have to decide if he is telling the truth.

When there is a disparity between what the narrator says and what readers can guess is true, that narrator is called an **unreliable narrator**. A fun example of this is in Ring Lardner's *You Know Me Al*. Jack, the lead who is writing to his friend Al, has just teased his new wife by saying he is writing to two of his former girlfriends. Not too bright. A tiff ensues, which Jack reports to his friend Al in very ungrammatical terms:

Point-of-View Choices

First person
First-person peripheral
Unreliable narrator
Epistolary
First-person plural

Second person

Third-person omniscient
Third-person single vision
Third-person multiple vision
Third-person objective

Then she says If you don't tell me I will go over to Marie's that is her sister Allen's wife and stay all night. I says Go on and she went downstairs but I guess she probily went to get a soda because she has some money of her own that I give her. This was about two hours ago and she is probily down in the hotel lobby now trying to scare me by makeing me believe she has went to her sister's. But she can't fool me Al and I am now going out to mail this letter and get a beer. I won't never tell her about Violet and Hazel if she is going to act like that.

                                                          Yours truly, JACK

Where do you think his wife really went?

> **Point-of-View Choices**
>
> First person
> First-person peripheral
> Unreliable narrator
> **Epistolary**
> **First-person plural**
>
> Second person
>
> Third-person omniscient
> Third-person single vision
> Third-person multiple vision
> Third-person objective

A very early novel was largely in the form of letters from a young woman to her family. This technique of telling a story in letter-writing form is called **epistolary** (ee-PIS-toh-LER-ee). The book, *Pamela: Virtue Rewarded*, was written by Samuel Richardson in 1740.

First Person Plural: Information comes through an unknown, unnamed character as though the action is happening to the whole group. First person plural uses pronouns like *we* and *us*.

One example of this rare POV comes from *Then We Came to the End* by Joshua Ferris, a novel about a group of office workers undergoing lay-offs in an ad agency. Readers are never introduced to the narrator because everything happens to "us." In this excerpt, "we" have just been asked by "our" boss how the cold sore ads are coming along:

> We were in the process of coming up with a series of TV spots for one of our clients who manufactured an analgesic to reduce cold sore pain and swelling. We took in Joe's question kind of slowly, without any immediate response. We might have even exchanged a look or two. This wasn't long after his second promotion. Doing okay, more or less, we said, in effect. And then we probably nodded, you know, noncommittal half nods.

Ferris names specific employees and includes stories about them, and through them we develop empathy for their lives lived on the edge of frustration, heartache, goofiness, and impending lay-offs. But the narrator never steps up and identifies himself.

Second Person: A narrator tells what "you" said and did. Second-person POV is often used in tandem with the present tense, which gives it a snappy tone.

This example of second-person POV is taken from a student's paper. His assignment, like yours, was to write his earliest memory:

> Point-of-View Choices
>
> First person
> First-person peripheral
> Unreliable narrator
> Epistolary
> First-person plural
>
> **Second person**
>
> Third-person omniscient
> Third-person single vision
> Third-person multiple vision
> Third-person objective

> You're going ice skating tonight, with your dad as your training wheels. It takes a while to get your skates on, but it's worth the effort once you're on the ice. Your dad pushes you around and all you have to do is stand there and feel the need for speed. Suddenly, the speed stops, and you feel a mass pushing against you, very top heavy, falling on you and pushing you towards the smooth ice. That would be your dad tripping on his skates, falling like an old pine tree. You don't remember much after that. Some crying might have been involved; all you know for sure is that you end up in a bathroom, slightly dizzy, with a lump on your head, covered with ice, this time in the form of a cold pack.

Second-person POV can be interesting to read in a short story but tires readers when used in a novel.

It's time for a review. Below are the first-person and second-person POVs we've covered so far, plus an example of each:

First person: I flew from the uneven bars and nailed the landing.

First-person peripheral: I watched Jamal on the rings. His routine was fluid, looked effortless. The only thing that gave away his nerves was the tic under his left eye, but judges don't take off points for tics.

Unreliable narrator: I ditched my coach's choreography and used my own at the last minute. I was superb! No one ever conquered the balance beam like I did. I danced. I fluttered. I bounced like a bedspring. The audience watched in awed silence. Of course, the judges didn't know what they were doing. Because of their low marks, I didn't even place.

Epistolary: Dear Paige, I wish you could have come to my meet. I was fantastic!

First-person plural: We knew the routines. We had the crowd. Oh, sure, we were uncertain of ourselves and we shook before our turns came, but nothing could stop us from winning the gold.

Second Person: You stand at the edge of the mat, arms outstretched like a salute to the vast blue in front of you, and you feel the pulse of your heart pinging in your cheeks, in your toes. This reminds you to uncurl your toes because, although you know every move by heart, it is the little things that can undo you.

2.2 All Writers and Writing Group

Now you try it. Write a sentence or two for each POV listed below, just as in the examples above. Make up your own characters and situations.

> › First person
> › First-person peripheral
> › Unreliable narrator
> › Epistolary
> › First-person plural
> › Second person

End of today's lesson

Share your results with your writing group.

THE NITTY-GRITTY OF POINT OF VIEW, PART 2

In this last part of POV choices, let's look at third person— *he, she, they,* and so forth.

Third Person Omniscient—Information is given through the narrator's all-knowing pen. He sees everything and knows everything and is not a character in the story. Here's an example of third-person omniscient from *The Tragedy of Y* by Ellery Queen writing as Barnaby Ross, where readers meet the police consultant Drury Lane, a former Shakespearian actor who is now deaf, and Dromio, a very minor character who is in his employ. Lane is the first "he":

> Point-of-View Choices
>
> First person
> First-person peripheral
> Unreliable narrator
> Epistolary
> First-person plural
>
> Second person
>
> **Third-person omniscient**
> Third-person single vision
> Third-person multiple vision
> Third-person objective

Without hesitation he opened the door of the clothes closet and slipped inside. He brought the door to before him, and made sure that there was a crack wide enough to permit him to see into the room. The corridor, the whole floor, the room itself were entirely soundless. The room was rapidly growing dark, and the air in the closet was stifling. Nevertheless Lane burrowed more deeply into the nest of feminine clothing behind him, drew what breath he could, and composed himself for a long vigil.

> Omniscient switches from Drury Lane in the closet to Dromio behind a door and back to Drury Lane, giving information to readers that Lane does not have. Also, the narrator writes the room is "entirely soundless," something the deaf Drury Lane would not know.

The minutes passed. At times Dromio, crouched behind the door of the guest-room, heard voices from the corridor and fainter ones from downstairs; Lane had not even this awareness of the outside world. He was in complete darkness. No one entered the room in which he lay hidden.

This POV is out of fashion now but was popular in many of the older classics you may read for school. The narrator in third-person omniscient POV takes you into the minds and hearts of many characters in the story, sometimes many in each scene. The narrator in *Peter Pan*, for example, gets into the minds of Mrs. Darling, Peter Pan, Wendy, the boys, and Hook and even includes some passages directly from the narrator to the reader. While there is nothing inherently wrong with this, it is too scattered for the modern reader, who prefers to focus on one or two characters. Modern publishers, too, take a dim view of this POV.

> **Point-of-View Choices**
>
> First person
> First-person peripheral
> Unreliable narrator
> Epistolary
> First-person plural
>
> Second person
>
> Third-person omniscient
> **Third-person single vision**
> Third-person multiple vision
> Third-person objective

Third Person Single Vision (or third person limited)—Information is given through one character but not in an "I did this/I saw this" manner. Readers know what is going on in the story because they are looking at the events through the perceptions of one character or because the invisible narrator chooses to focus only on one character's thoughts, feelings, and life.

One example of third-person limited POV comes from Tony Earley's *Jim the Boy*, where the ten-year-old Jim Glass is waiting to visit his schoolmate Penn:

The front door opened and a woman Jim took to be Penn's mother walked down the steps and across the yard. She smiled broadly and waved. She wore a sky-blue dress and a white apron. Her copper-colored hair was tied loosely behind her neck. Jim waved back. When she got closer, he saw that, while she wasn't as pretty as Mama, something in her face made her nicer to look at. She was wildly freckled, and her smile, which was a little crooked, made Jim want to smile back. She took his right hand in both of hers and held it while she studied him. Her hands were warm and soft. Jim felt himself blush.

"Jim Glass," she said, in a pleasant, although strange, accent, "I am so pleased to meet you. Penn speaks of you with great fondness."

Everything readers know about Penn's mother comes from Jim's perspective. She's nicer to look at than his mama, and her accent is strange only because Jim thinks it is so. Also, readers assume this is Penn's mother only because Jim "took [her] to be Penn's mother."

Incidentally, this passage is from inside Jim's skin because the narrator relates that Jim "felt himself blush." That's a feeling that comes from the inside. If, as a writer, you want to stand back and tell the story from a distance, you might write, "Jim's cheeks turned red." You will have to decide how close to your character you want the narrator to be: in his skin, at his side, or at a distance. It will make a difference in how you tell your story.

Notice how, in Jane Austen's *Persuasion*, even the **sensory information** changes as the protagonist Anne Elliot bows her head and doesn't look up again. She is in this situation because eight years ago she broke off her engagement to Captain Wentworth and

> **Sensory information:** Information obtained by the senses—sight, sound, taste, feel, and smell.

this is the first time she meets him since then:

> Her eye half met Captain Wentworth's; a bow, a curtsey passed; she heard his voice—he talked to Mary, said all that was right; said something to the Miss Musgroves, enough to mark an easy footing: the room seemed full—full of persons and voices—but a few minutes ended it.

Instead of visual clues, all we get are auditory ones because Anne's head is down: She "heard" Wentworth talking to Mary and her friends, and the room "seemed" full of people and "voices."   Through Anne's perspective, the narrator relates what Anne hears, not what she sees.

Third Person Multiple Vision (or third person serial limited): As in third person limited, an invisible narrator relates what characters think, feel, see, do, and experience. The difference is that, instead of one viewpoint character, there are two or more. However, the narrator gets into only one mind at a time, and the characters through which we view the story are very few (or limited).

This POV is useful when you have characters that are different from each other or who have differing ways of looking at the world.

From *Tears of the Giraffe*, one of the books in The No. 1 Ladies' Detective Agency series by Alexander McCall Smith, here is Mr. J.L.B. Matekoni thinking about his new fiancée, Precious Ramotswe :

> Point-of-View Choices
>
> First person
> First-person peripheral
> Unreliable narrator
> Epistolary
> First-person plural
>
> Second person
>
> Third-person omniscient
> Third-person single vision
> **Third-person multiple vision**
> Third-person objective

> But then, on that noumenal evening, sitting with him on her verandah after he had spent the afternoon fixing her tiny white van, she had said yes. And she had given this answer in such a simple, unambiguously kind way, that he had been confirmed in his belief that she was one of the very best women in Botswana.

And here's his maid, who, because she will have to find a new job after the marriage, sees the same woman through a very different lens as she interacts with her employer, Mr. J.L.B. Matekoni:

The maid's eyes had opened wide and were staring at Mma Ramotswe with ill-disguised venom. Her nostrils were flared with anger, and her lips were pushed out in what seemed to be an aggressive pout . . . .

"I am finished now. You are finished too if you marry this fat woman . . . ."

. . . The situation was serious enough to merit desperate action, but it was hard to see what she could do. There was no point trying to reason with him; once a woman like that had sunk her claws into a man then there would be no turning him back.

You've learned that two people can perceive the same event or person very differently. The same is true for fictional characters.

Stay with one character for each scene. Choose the character with the most at stake and write it from her perspective. When switching from one character to another, wait for a scene break (indicated by a break in the text) or the end of a chapter. Then, to keep readers tracking with you, indicate early which character starts the new scene or chapter.

Watch how this happens in Michael Crichton's *Timeline*. At this point in the story, Chris, Marek, and Kate—all from the present—are in fourteenth-century France. Chris is being chased by knights and is following a boy to safety, he thinks. He is separated from Marek and Kate, who have earpieces to communicate with the rest of the group:

> The story from Chris's perspective

The black knight bellowed something. Chris didn't understand it.
They came at last to the edge of the clearing. Without hesitation, the boy leapt into space.
Chris hesitated, not wanting to follow. Glancing back, he saw the knights charging him, their broadswords raised.
No choice.
Chris turned and ran forward toward the cliff edge.

> A visual break between viewpoint characters

*
*

> The story from Marek's perspective

Marek winced as he heard Chris's scream in his earpiece. The scream was loud at first, then abruptly ended with a grunt and a crashing sound.
An impact.
He stood with Kate by the trail, listening. Waiting.
They heard nothing more. Not even the crackle of static.

> Nothing at all.
> "Is he dead?" Kate said.
> Marek didn't answer her.

It is very clear when Crichton moves from one character to another because he uses a visual marker and then uses the new viewpoint character's name in the first sentence. When it is Chris's scene, everything comes from his perceptions, and we even hear his thoughts (*No choice*). When it is Marek's scene, he is the one who winces from the noise.

Charles Dickens enables readers to keep up with him in *A Tale of Two Cities* by beginning each chapter with the distinct viewpoint character and location:

Start of chapter 9:

> It was a heavy mass of building, that chateau of Monsieur the Marquis, with a large stone court-yard before it, and two stone sweeps of staircase meeting in a stone terrace before the principal door.

Start of chapter 10:

> More months, to the number of twelve, had come and gone, and Mr. Charles Darnay was established in England as a higher teacher of the French language who was conversant with French literature.

Start of chapter 11:

> "Sydney," said Mr. Striver, on that self-same night, or morning, to his jackal; "mix another bowl of punch; I have something to say to you."

This technique is so effective that it is still being used today.

Another way of keeping track of multiple viewpoint characters in a novel is through the use of tense. Use past tense with one character and present with another. Dean Koontz does this effectively in *One Door Away from Heaven*, juggling four lead characters. Here is Micky Bellsong in one of her chapters (past tense):

> Wednesday, after a fruitless day of job-seeking, Micky Bellsong returned to the trailer park, where much of the meager landscaping drooped wearily under the scorching sun and the rest appeared to be withered beyond recovery.

The ten-year-old lead, called Curtis Hammond, checks into all his chapters with the present tense:

> Down through the high forest to lower terrain, from night-kissed ridges into night-smothered valleys, out of the trees into a broad planted field, the motherless boy hurries. He follows the crop rows to a rail fence.
> . . . The fence, old and in need of repair, clatters as he climbs across it. When he drops to the lane beyond, he crouches motionless until he is sure that the noise has drawn no one's attention.

Typically, tense changes and multiple viewpoint characters are reserved for novels, as in the example above, not short stories.

Point-of-View Choices

First person
First-person peripheral
Unreliable narrator
Epistolary
First-person plural

Second person

Third-person omniscient
Third-person single vision
Third-person multiple vision
Third-person objective

Switching her skirt: flicking a fold of her skirt back and forth, as a cow switching her tail. This may indicate she was enjoying her notoriety.

Third Person Objective (formerly called dramatic, sometimes called third person cinematic; are you confused yet?)—The narrator of this POV acts as a reporter, standing outside all the characters and simply relating the actions and dialogue of the story's characters. This POV has the feeling of watching a play: The narrator tells only what can be seen on the stage.

An example of this comes from Shirley Jackson's "The Lottery":

"Nancy next," Mr. Summers said. Nancy was twelve, and her school friends breathed heavily as she went forward, switching her skirt, and took a slip daintily from the box. "Bill, Jr.," Mr. Summers said, and Billy, his face red and his feet overlarge, nearly knocked the box over as he got a paper out. "Tessie," Mr. Summers said. She hesitated for a minute, looking around defiantly, and then set her lips and went up to the box. She snatched a paper out and held it behind her.

The narrator views the proceedings from the outside, but it is clear to us that Nancy's friends are nervous by their actions ("breathed heavily") and that Billy, too, is nervous ("his face red" and he "nearly knocked the box over"). How is Tessie feeling?

It's time for another review. Below are the third-person POVs we've studied in this section, along with examples of each.

Third-person omniscient: Hillary saw the brand name on the side of the tent and was happy because it was the same as her name. She thought it was the perfect way to begin her first camping trip. Carter wondered if Hillary knew the tent was named after a male.

Third-person single vision: Carter felt a pulsing pain in his bandaged hand. It hurt worse when he forgot to keep it in an upright position, which was always. The pain brushed his upper lip with sweat and shrank his world to the size of his hand. He slowly pulled the duct tape away from the cut and examined the swollen red edges that ran from the tip of his first finger to his palm. He expected Hillary to be grossed out, but she must not have been because she moved closer and peered at his hand. *What a ghoul*, Carter thought.

Third-person multiple vision: Hillary guessed that Carter would need help gathering sticks for the fire, so she set out on her own, marching into the undergrowth. She swatted away limbs at eye level and broke through spider webs with one swoop. Just as she heard Carter call her name, she noticed a thick patch of plants with groups of three leaves. She thought they were very pretty with their red berries.

***

"Hillary!" called Carter. "Come back! Don't leave me alone!"
He saw that the duct tape was coming loose again and wondered how far it was to a ranger station. What if he developed blood poisoning? What if he couldn't stand up long enough to wave a red handkerchief in the air for the rescue helicopter? Did he even bring a red handkerchief? And was there such a thing as a rescue helicopter? Those shows on TV always had one, didn't they? His eyes felt heavy. His hand throbbed. His breathing became shallow.

Third-person objective: Hillary emerged from the woods carrying a small load of broken sticks and a fistful of green leaves. She stepped over a snake in her path.

"Look what I brought you," she said. She smiled and held out her arms to Carter.

Carter looked in her direction and squinted. Then he collapsed to the ground.

"Carter, wake up! Did you faint?" Hillary dropped the sticks and leaves, ran to his side, knelt down, and slapped his cheek.

2.3 All Writers

Now you try it. Write a few sentences for each POV listed below, just as in the examples above. Make up your own characters and situations.

› Third-person omniscient
› Third-person single vision
› Third-person multiple vision
› Third-person objective

Share your results with the group.

2.4 All Writers and Discussion

Review a favorite short story or novel and determine its POV. List the viewpoint characters. Then study a few passages to see how close or far away the narrator is standing (anywhere from in the character's skin to a great physical or time distance).

End of today's lesson

Discuss your findings with your writing group.

DECISIONS, DECISIONS

With all these choices, how do you decide how to tell your story? Which point of view should you choose? Which character should tell the story?

Beginning writers will most likely benefit by using first-person or third-person limited POV. But you know your story and characters. You know the effect you want to make. And if you don't, do not lose heart. Simply experiment. Write it now; change it later!

When pondering point-of-view and viewpoint-character decisions, ask these questions:

> Whose story is this anyway? Who is the protagonist? Who has the most to lose if things go badly?

> Would the story be more interesting told from another character's perspective other than the protagonist's?

> Would part or all of the story gain anything if told from the antagonist's perspective?

> If I tell this in first person, how will I convey important information or events that happen outside the realm of the viewpoint character's knowledge?

A Common Point-of-View Mistake

Choose your point of view. Choose your viewpoint character(s). Then stick to them. Avoid the common mistake of, say, beginning with third person limited (one character) and then sliding into third person multiple vision (more than one character) unaware. Here's an example of that mistake:

> Avi glared at JJ across the back of her horse. How dare he take Blackie without asking! Avi stamped her foot and fought for breath. Her arms shook against Blackie's hot and heaving side. JJ smiled at Avi and patted Blackie's back. He remembered the exhilarating pace Blackie had set and knew he would take her again in a heartbeat.

If Avi is your viewpoint character, change the last two sentences to something like this:

> Avi watched JJ pat Blackie as though he owned her, and she guessed he would take the horse again if given half a chance.

A WORD ABOUT FILTERS

Filters are phrases that indicate the information is coming from your viewpoint character. Here are some taken randomly from Elizabeth Peters' *The Summer of the Dragon*:

> I had the idea that...
> I was forced to the conclusion that...
> I wondered why...
> I had the feeling that...
> I knew...
> I noticed that her hands...
> I suspected...
> I concluded that...

The next sentence, complete with filter, comes from the same Peters' book (filter underlined):

> His eyes were twinkling with <u>what I could only regard as</u> inappropriate amusement.

How does her observation change if it reads this way:

> His eyes twinkled with amusement. Very inappropriate.

A character cannot look into another character's heart and know what is going on there; he can only guess by observing outward signs. These outward signs are often reported by the viewpoint character: I noticed that . . ., I suspected . . . .

P. D. James' *The Children of Men* has helpful filters in third person. The story moves back and forth between Theo's first-person diary accounts and third person single vision, where Theo is still the viewpoint character. In this passage, Theo can only guess what is in the mind of Julian, the young woman who is asking him for a favor (filters underlined):

> The appeal in her voice was unmistakable, simple and direct, and, suddenly, <u>he thought he understood why</u>. It had been her idea to

approach him. She had come with only the reluctant acquiescence of the rest of the group, perhaps even against the wish of its leader. The risk she was taking was her own. If he refused her, she would return empty-handed and humiliated. <u>He found</u> he couldn't do it.

Some writers don't like to use these kinds of phrases as filters; they believe filters are extraneous and only clutter up the story. Who's right? It's your call.

However, filters are more than phrases. You learned this when you read the personal narratives written by the sister and then the brother at the beginning of this chapter. Everything written in most of the first- and third-person POVs is filtered through the life and lens of your viewpoint character(s).

Harper Lee's *To Kill a Mockingbird* is written in first person, through the filter of Scout, a young girl at the time the story events occur. Scout tells the story, but it is obvious she is not telling it as a young girl; she is telling it as she looks back and remembers those summers. Notice the word choices in this sentence:

> Mrs. Dubose lived two doors up the street from us; neighborhood opinion was unanimous that Mrs. Dubose was the meanest old woman who ever lived.

A young girl of six or seven would not write that "neighborhood opinion was unanimous," but would more likely report that "everyone thought that Mrs. Dubose was the meanest old woman who ever lived."

Be aware of how you are telling your story and how the information is getting from the viewpoint character to the reader.

2.5 All Writers

> Read the following paragraphs from Louis Sachar's *Holes* and write down the filters, the phrases that show that the information is coming through Stanley's perspective.

Excerpt from *Holes*. We join Stanley Yelnats—tired and thirsty from his desert sojourn—as he notices an object on the dry lake bed and decides to check it out:

There was no point in heading toward Big Thumb, he decided. He would never make it. For all he knew it was like chasing the moon. But he could make it to the mysterious object.

He changed directions. He doubted it was anything, but the fact that there was *something* in the middle of all this *nothing* made it hard for him to pass up. He decided to make the object his halfway point, and he hoped he hadn't already gone too far.

He laughed to himself when he saw what it was. It was a boat—or part of a boat anyway. It struck him as funny to see a boat in the middle of this dry and barren wasteland. But after all, he realized, this was once a lake.

End of today's lesson

CRITIQUING

Critiquing: evaluating another's work, usually based upon a stated criteria

Critiquing is an important skill. The word may conjure up images of being critical and negative, but in this case it simply means to evaluate and remark upon. The aim is not to be *critical* but to be *helpful*. When you critique someone else's work, look for the effective things they did and identify some places for improvement.

You will learn best how to write if you critique the work of your writing group *and* the work of published writers. Pick any book off the library shelf and critique it. What has the author done well? Do you like her POV choice? How can she improve? Other than the Bible, no book is sacred—not even the classics—and each book is open to careful scrutiny.

Consider the following guidelines when critiquing the stories or assignments of your writing group members.

FOR THE READER:

1. Keep in mind the focus of the critiquing session. For instance, the assignment might be to determine how well the writer revealed character emotions. Comment only on the stated objective. (The teacher or your assignment will tell you what the objective is.)
2. Use the universal proofreading marks (in the chart on page 36) and a colorful pen.
3. Be positive. State two things you like about the work or what the writer has done well.
4. Then state two questions, places for improvement, or corrections in a polite manner.

5. Be specific. For example, don't say, "I don't like your story," but say, "The hero's motivation is unclear," or, "Most of your story is from Jack's perspective, but this paragraph is from Ian's. Did you mean to do that?"
6. Write your name on the classmate's paper so when you return it, he or she will know who made those suggestions.
7. Remain quiet when others are critiquing. You will have your turn.

FOR THE WRITER:

1. Double-space your homework and put your name and page number at the top of each page.
2. Bring enough copies of your story/assignment for everyone in your group.
3. Listen politely to the critiques.
4. Ask questions for clarification. Avoid defending yourself or arguing.
5. You need not change everything the readers suggest. This is *your* story. Go with your gut instinct.
6. Try not to cry (!).

Proofreading Marks

Mark	What it means	How to use it	The results
ℯ	Take it out	Give it it to me.	Give it to me.
ℯ	Take it out	Use a picture, or school ID.	Use a picture or school ID.
⌒	Close the gap	ab out	about
⌒	Close the gap	proof read	proofread
≡	Capitalize	Sydney Opera house	Sydney Opera House
/	Make lowercase	the President's job	the president's job
∧	Add	"No" she said.	"No," she said.
/	Add a letter	acknowledgment	acknowledgement
∧	Add word(s)	When I my head (nod)	When I nod my head
∪	Transpose	There is it again.	There it is again.
—	Italicize	The Scarlet Letter	*The Scarlet Letter*
¶	New paragraph	at night. ¶The next day,	at night. The next day,
no ¶	No new paragraph	sometimes. He threw	sometimes. He threw
⃝ sp	Check spelling	(imput) sp	input
⃝	Spell out	(Gen.) Black	General Black

2.6 All Writers and Group Critique

Below is a passage from C. S. Lewis's *The Magician's Nephew*. Choose Digory or Polly (the children who are in a remote attic room), or Uncle Andrew as your viewpoint character and rewrite the passage in third person single vision, from that character's perspective. You may use your own words, but stay true to the character's feelings, as found in the excerpt. Information about the other characters' thoughts and emotions must be filtered through your viewpoint character's observations and dialogue.

Group Critique: Bring enough copies (double-spaced) for everyone in your group. Critique and discuss as many as you have time for. What is the aspect of the assignment you are critiquing? This question: How well does this writer keep the passage in third person single vision, making all character thoughts and possible feelings come through that selected character's perspective?

Excerpt from *The Magician's Nephew*, as Uncle Andrew traps Polly and Digory in the attic room:

> Digory was quite speechless, for Uncle Andrew looked a thousand times more alarming than he had ever looked before. Polly was not so frightened yet; but she soon was. For the very first thing Uncle Andrew did was to walk across to the door of the room, shut it, and turn the key in the lock. Then he turned round, fixed the children with his bright eyes, and smiled, showing all his teeth.
> "There!" he said. "Now my fool of a sister can't get at you!"
> It was dreadfully unlike anything a grown-up would be expected to do. Polly's heart came into her mouth, and she and Digory started backing toward the little door they had come in by. Uncle Andrew was too quick for them. He got behind them and shut that door too and stood in front of it. Then he rubbed his hands and made his knuckles crack. He had very long, beautifully white, fingers.

End of today's lesson

2.7 All Writers and Discussion

Earlier in this chapter you wrote down your first memory. Get it now and answer these questions:

> What point of view did you use?

> How close to that child is your retelling—in the skin or outside looking at yourself?

> Did you tell it as though you were that age or from the distance of your current age, looking back?

Now rewrite your memory. Use a different POV from the one you originally used. Decide whether you want the narrator to be inside looking out or outside at a distance. Decide also if your narrator will see the event as it unfolds or be looking at it from a distance of years.

Discussion: Discuss which version you like better. Discuss, too, what you had to change for your new POV and distance.

2.8 Manuscript Track

Review your point-of-view choices and ask yourself these questions:

- ☑ Am I happy with my POV strategy, viewpoint character(s), and distance?
- ☑ Is this the best way to tell my story?

Choose one of your chapters (or short story passages) and comb it for consistency. Have you stayed in the chosen viewpoint character's perspective? Is everything filtered through his or her perspective? Rewrite the chapter or passage as needed.

Make enough copies of your new version for your group members. Critique each others' work to provide helpful feedback.

OPTIONAL WRITING FOR POV

1. *You Know Me Al* by Ring Lardner, *Pamela: Virtue Rewarded* by Samuel Richardson, *The Screwtape Letters* by C. S. Lewis, and the clever "Marjorie Daw" by Thomas Bailey Aldrich are all stories written in letter form (epistolary stories). Write your own short story in the form of letters. The letters may be one-sided, as in *You Know Me Al*, or they may be an exchange of letters (or e-mails or texts) as in "Marjorie Daw."

2. Write a passage (about 500 words) of a story using an unreliable narrator.

3. Find a passage in a book. Change the POV and rewrite the passage. Be aware of what you have to change to make the passage work.

4. Rewrite "The Prodigal Son" (Luke 15:11-32) from another character's POV (it is originally in omniscient). You may use the original characters or create a new one to be your viewpoint character.

5. Rewrite a fairy tale from another character's POV.

What you studied in this chapter:

✓ The "lens" of the viewpoint character coloring the story
✓ POV choices
- First person
- First-person peripheral
- Unreliable narrator
- Epistolary
- First-person plural
- Second person
- Third-person omniscient
- Third-person single vision
- Third-person multiple vision
- Third-person objective

✓ Filters
✓ Critiquing

3: FAIRY TALES

Long before Jacob and Wilhelm Grimm collected fairy tales, adults told these stories to each other and to their children. The tales have been "cleaned up" for modern sensibilities and seem tame to us today, but to those parents and children, they were the stuff of a hard life. "Little Red Riding Hood," for instance, was most likely intended to warn young girls about predators of the two-footed sort. Just how dangerous was it to be alone in the woods? What could a young girl do when approached in a suspicious manner? Even today children are warned about strangers.

Fairy tales occur in all cultures and touch on universal issues. Consider the child who has lost a parent. What happens when a parent remarries? Will the daughter be cared for and loved by her stepparent, or will she be seen as an irritation, an interruption, or an extra mouth to feed? How many fairy tales deal with this very issue? And who today, having lost a parent, has not wondered these very things?

> Good fiction concerns itself with the real problems and values of men.
> –John Gardner, author and professor

Perhaps it is this universality of themes and troubles that makes fairy tales resonate with readers. They touch a chord, a nerve.

Let's look at some characteristics of tales, of which fairy tales are a subgroup. These points are derived from *The Forms of Fiction* by John Gardner and Lennis Dunlap [examples added]:

› The setting is "in a land far away" or "a long time ago." ["Once upon a time, in a land far, far away . . ."]
› The circumstances are remarkable or far-fetched. [A king holds a contest to see who can make his daughter laugh.]
› The characters may possess supernatural powers, but, nonetheless, have very human emotions. [The jealous queen puts a curse on a rival; a frightened young peasant girl talks with woodland creatures.]
› The events are extraordinary, whether natural or supernatural. [A fish grants three wishes.]
› The laws governing the story make perfect sense within the story. [If you make the princess laugh, you get to marry her.]
› Good and evil are clear-cut. [The fairy-godmother is good; the fire-breathing dragon is bad.]
› The ending has a ring of finality to it. ["And they all lived happily ever after."]

3.1 All Writers and Discussion

Read fairy tales from a variety of cultures.

Discussion: Compile a list of the types of characters found in fairy tales (knight, giant, fool, etc.). Be as complete as you can; you will use this list later. Discuss these questions:

› How do these character types differ from tale to tale?
› Why are stepmothers often wicked in these stories?
› How do the protagonists overcome their difficulties?
› What magic or supernatural powers are used?
› What are common elements in the tales?
› Tales vary from culture to culture. Identify some differences.

End of today's lesson

ANOTHER TALE, ANOTHER PRINCE CHARMING

Ever notice that some of the same elements occur in many tales? For instance, the idea that a young girl has to love an unlovable man or creature appears in "The Beauty and the Beast," "The Black Bull of Norroway," and "The Princess and the Frog," to name a few. Dark woods appear in many tales, as do characters who give magical assistance, or young men sent on a quest for treasure or wisdom.

> Fairy tales are more than true; not because they tell us dragons exist, but because they tell us that dragons can be beaten.
> —G. K. Chesterton

These recurring elements, characters, and situations are called **motifs**. Think of how many times dark woods are used in stories: "Snow White," *The Wizard of Oz* movie, "Hansel and Gretel," and Mirkwood in *The Hobbit* come to mind. Often these woods are a time of mental confusion for the protagonists and can also be a place of testing. Snow White, for example, is tested in the woods: Will she be kind to the animals? When she shows them her kind nature, they reward her by helping her along the path to the dwarves' cottage. For Bilbo Baggins, the darkness of Mirkwood is a place of confusion and testing. He and his companions are lured away from the path, and Bilbo must come up with a plan to rescue them. When he is successful and passes the tests, he is rewarded with these things: He acquires some self-confidence ("He felt a different person, and much fiercer and bolder") and the powerful sword *Sting*, and his companions see him in a more favorable light ("they saw that he had some wits"). These are all important rewards for being successful in testing.

The dark woods, the testing, and the reward are all common and powerful motifs in literature, perhaps because they reflect real life.

Magic mirrors, maidens locked up in towers, dragons guarding gold, impossible tasks, gifts with supernatural powers, donors who first test the candidate to determine his or her worthiness, characters fated to wander so they can become wiser, wicked stepmothers, the clever trickster (Bugs Bunny, Brer Rabbit, and Pan), characters who are not as they seem (shape-shifters such as a queen who turns into a witch), and, yes, even the gallant prince charming are all motifs found in many tales across many cultures.

> Bugs Bunny is who we'd most like to be; Daffy Duck is probably who we are.
> —Cartoonist Chuck Jones

When you come across a motif in your reading, consider two things about it:

(1) Historically, what does it mean in tales?
(2) What is the new spin the current tale puts on it?

The answers to both questions will be revealing and will show you the story on a deeper level.

Motifs can be found in many kinds of writing. When you use a motif in yours, respect its meaning but add your own unique perspective to it, as your story demands.

THE POWER OF THREE

Another fun thing often found in fairy tales is the number three. A genie grants three wishes, a king has three daughters, a hero tries for success three times. Fairy tales are rife with the rhythm of three.

Why is the pattern of three so enticing, so embedded in our story structures? Consider the three-in-one God who made us: Father, Son, and Holy Spirit. Consider, too, that "God created man in his own image" (Gen. 1:27). These facts of origin may hold the answer to our fascination with threes in our literature.

Threes may appear as **parallel phrases** (underlined normally below) or **single words** (underlined with wavy lines) as in "Probably Shakespeare" by Jessamyn West:

> Melinda took her hand off Milton's shoulder and watched the sea that <u>lifted ships</u> and <u>stirred old bones</u> and <u>separated lovers</u>.
> They had come to the booths and shops and stands; the many eyes hunting customers, the many voices shouting wares. Melinda looked at the faces, lined, puffed, waiting.

The rhythm of three can be written into a **progression of phrases**, as in this example from a student's paper:

> Something made a noise. A noise somewhat like a giggle. A giggle from a little boy.

"Noise" in the first sentence is repeated in the second, which sets up the "giggle" for the next sentence. This has the delightful effect of creating a little suspense and anticipation.

Lemony Snicket's *The Wide Window* contains many patterns of three. Below is one pattern of three constructed of **complete sentences** (underline of key words added). Notice how the use of the underlined words and the contrast built into the passage heightens the effect of the horror as Violet, Klaus, and Sunny watch their aunt's house plunge into Lake Lachrymose:

> My own research <u>tells me</u> that the children watched in mute amazement as the peeling white door slammed shut and began to crumple, as you might crumple a piece of paper into a ball. I <u>have been told</u> that the children hugged each other even more tightly as they heard the rough and earsplitting noise of their home breaking loose from the side of the hill. <u>But I cannot tell you</u> how it felt to watch the whole building fall down, down, down, and hit the dark and stormy waters of the lake below.

Did you find the other set of three in that passage? (The answer is on the next page.)

Threes can be used in **dialogue**. Here is an example from G. K. Chesterton's "The Dragon at Hide-and-Seek," as the outlaw knight Sir Laverok tries to make a point. The Chancellor speaks first:

> "But, my good Sir," said the Chancellor, pausing in the act of trying to creep into a rabbit burrow, "the dragon can grind castles to powder with his heel. I regret to say that he showed not the least embarrassment even in approaching the Law Courts."
> "I know of a castle which he cannot reach," said Sir Laverok.
> "The offensive animal," said the Lord Chamberlain, poking his head for a moment out of a hole in the ground, "actually entered the King's private chamber without knocking."
> "I know of a private chamber that he cannot enter," replied the outlaw knight.
> "It is very doubtful," came the muffled voice of the Lord High Admiral from somewhere underground, "whether we shall even be safe in any of the caverns."
> "I know a cavern where I shall be safe," said Sir Laverok.

There are four other sets of threes in that short passage. Can you find them? (The answer is on the next page.)

Jesus uses a pattern of three **characters** in "The Good Samaritan." Three men walk by the victim. First comes the priest, then the Levite, and then the Samaritan. Notice the progression Jesus builds into the story. He begins with a revered member of society, moves down to a respected member, and ends with a hated one, which, ironically, is the hero of the story.

The power of three comes from Jesus' progression from reverence to respect to revulsion. Can you feel his listeners squirming as He leads them through the story toward the ending they do not want to hear?

When you use a pattern of three, make it count for something, as Jesus did. If your hero must accomplish three **tasks**, make the first one hard, the second one harder, and the third one impossible. This creates tension and excitement for the reader. Or use the first two to **contrast** with the final idea, as with the Lemony Snicket passage.

Whether the pattern is made of single words, phrases, sentences, dialogue, or events, a judicious use of threes could make your story richer and more interesting.

Answer to *The Wide Window* excerpt: down, down, down.

Answer to G. K. Chesterton passage:
- Three characters challenge the knight.
- They give three locations, all beginning with "c."
- There is a downward progression of locations for the speakers:
  1. At the lip of the rabbit burrow
  2. Poking a head out of the ground
  3. From underground
- And the titles of the speakers progress upwards in importance:
  1. Chancellor
  2. Lord Chamberlain
  3. Lord High Admiral

This makes Chesterton's point and adds irony.

3.2 All Writers and Discussion

Make a list of all the patterns of three you can think of in life, the Bible, and literature, especially in fairy tales.

Discussion: Compare your list with those of your writing group.

3.3 All Writers and Discussion

Watch the movie *The Princess Bride*.

Discussion: Discuss the motifs and patterns of three you find there. How did they enhance your enjoyment of the movie?

3.4 All Writers and Group Activity

Write your life as a fairy tale. You may write your life as a whole or only a slice of it (a time of great trouble, testing, or growth, perhaps). Refer to the list of characters you compiled earlier in this chapter when you consider characters to include in your story.

Think about the motifs available to you, and put your own original spin on any you use.

Use a pattern of three.

Your tale may be anywhere from serious to humorous in tone.

For this exercise, YOU are the hero of your own tale. You may be the Trickster, the Fool, or the Maiden in Distress, but you are still the hero—the protagonist, the lead—of your story. You are not a passive bystander.

Group Activity: Bring enough double-spaced copies of your tale for everyone in your writing group. Read each others' tales. No need to critique although you may ask questions of the writers.

3.5 Manuscript Track

Mull over your manuscript and ask yourself these questions:

☑ If I have used any recurring images, characters, or situations (motifs) found in other literature, have I respected what they mean in that body of literature but also added my unique spin that has meaning within the context of my story?

☑ Have I used any patterns of three?

☑ Have I used them effectively? In other words, have I used them to add a pleasing rhythm to the story, magnify a contrast, highlight a growing tension, and so forth?

☑ Have I used them sparingly so they will have the best effect?

READER ALERT: We will be using *The Last Book in the Universe* throughout the next chapter. Please finish reading it, if you have not already done so.

What you studied in this chapter:

- What a fairy tale is
- Fairy tale characters
- Motifs
- The power of three

4: CHARACTERS AND CHARACTERIZATION

READER ALERT: This is the chapter in which you begin to use *The Last Book in the Universe* in discussions and assignments. If you have not already done so, finish reading it now.

Who can forget Tarzan, the Wicked Witch of the West, Scrooge, or Anne Shirley? Each is such a definite, clear-cut character that seems to leap off the page with a life of his or her own. You, too, can create characters as loved, feared, and alive as these are.

Your characters most likely are composites of you, people you know, and fictional characters. Bits and pieces of scavenged personality traits and quirky habits are patched together much as Dr. Frankenstein sewed his creation, and that's okay. In fact, it is more desirable to create this way than it is to render a real person onto the page for your fiction purposes. First, it gives you more room for creativity, and second, if your characters are truly fictional, you can't be called in the middle of the night by an angry friend who has just recognized herself in your story!

How do you get ideas for characters?

Study people. One great place to study people is in an airport. Many nationalities, cultures, shapes, sizes, ages, and idiosyncrasies come through airports, more so than in a mall. Become a people watcher. Begin writing your own *Field Guide to Humans*.

Be a keen observer of people—their appearances and inner workings. Your subconscious will cough them back up when you need them.

Read stories. Examine how other writers put characters together and present them on the page. From this you will learn what works and what doesn't, what is old and trite, and what is fresh yet keenly honest. Thornton Wilder, author of *The Bridge of San Luis Rey*, admitted that he did not have many life experiences from which to write. Instead, he drew upon his knowledge of history and literature.

Think about yourself. Yes, you. Are you quiet and shy? Boisterous? You'll know how to create a character with these traits. Do you wish you were adventurous and bold? Put your fervent longings to use when creating characters with these qualities.

After you consider all these people, what are you supposed to do with them? Transmute them into characters, which come in all varieties. Here are a few:

Primary characters or leads—These are your main characters, your protagonists. You want to fully flesh out any primary characters, make them three-dimensional. These characters are driving the plot because they have the strongest desires and goals. They also have fears, hopes, a birth order, and, perhaps, rotting cheese in the fridge. Readers will invest emotional energy in these characters' successes and failures.

Antagonists—These folks are agents of change and can be benign, malignant, or anywhere in between. They thwart your lead or have goals that keep your lead from his/her goals. Sometimes they're the "bad guys." (In another chapter, we'll deal with antagonistic forces that are not characters.)

Secondary characters—These folks are not quite as important to the plot as the leads, but they make the story richer. They may be friends of the lead, sidekicks, co-workers, family members, classmates, members of a guild, or fellow travelers on a journey. They, too, have desires, goals, fears, and hopes, and maybe rotting cheese, but they remain secondary to the plot. Readers will be mildly curious about these characters.

Tertiary characters—These characters fill out a story: the partygoers, the man at the gas station, the warriors in the attacking army, the volleyball players on the beach. In movies, these characters are called extras, and they remain unnamed, for naming them would give them a significance they do not have. And no one cares about their rotting cheese.

Do you plan out a character fully before you write, or do you simply start typing and see what happens to a character?

Here are two authors with widely opposing views on the matter. The first one is from John Cheever, author of short stories and novels. He disdains those who do not plan:

> The legend that characters run away from their authors—taking up drugs, having sex operations, and becoming president—implies that the writer is a fool with no knowledge of his craft. This is absurd . . . . The idea of authors running around helplessly behind their cretinous inventions is contemptible.

The second is from Ray Bradbury, author of, you guessed it, short stories and novels. He delights in *not* planning:

> Find out what your hero or heroine wants, and when he or she wakes up in the morning, just follow him or her all day.

Which one is right? Both are. Cheever's method of writing is perfect for Cheever, and Bradbury's method fits Bradbury. Which method of creating characters is right for you? You won't know until you write often and discover which one works for you. If you find yourself and your characters languishing, take a break and try the other method.

Either way—planning or being spontaneous—your characters may become as alive to you as John Steinbeck's:

> It would be a great joke on the people in my books if I just left them high and dry, waiting for me. If they bully me and do what they choose I have them over a barrel. They can't move until I pick up a pencil. They are frozen, turned to ice standing one foot up and with the same smile they had yesterday when I stopped.

4.1 All Writers

Take a moment now to identify the leads, one antagonist, two secondary characters, and three tertiary characters in *The Last Book in the Universe*.

> Leads
> One Antagonist
> Two Secondary Characters
> Three Tertiary Characters

End of today's lesson

LEADS, GENDERS, AND AGES

When reflecting on the character you are inventing, you may want to use a character questionnaire to give you ideas about your new creation. One can be found at www.writingclasses.com. Under the Resources tab, go to Writer's Toolbox, and there you will find two character questionnaires along with other great information.

Get to know the characters you create. Know their past, their families of origin, their favorite car, the thing they feel most proud of, where they want to take their next vacation, etc. You may never use all of this in your story, but it helps to know your character in depth.

If you wrote your character's personality as a weather report, what would the report be like?

Something to consider—the gender and age of your leads. This information may be helpful to you when creating characters:

Chapter 4: Characters and Characterization   53

- The majority of book readers are female.
- Female readers will read a story about a female or a male.
- Male readers tend to read stories about males and avoid stories about females.
- Teens prefer reading about characters of their age or slightly older.
- Stories for children should have leads in the audience's age range.
- If you want to have more readers, consider creating both a female and a male lead.
- There's some controversy about this one, but here goes: Sci-fi readers tend to be male; fantasy readers tend to be female. You may want to consider the gender of your characters accordingly.

There are exceptions of all sorts to the above list, but editors pay attention to these things because they want the books to sell. And so do you.

A variety of techniques are at your disposal to move characters out of your head and onto the paper (more information on each appears in the next lessons):

- What the character says
- What he thinks
- What he does
- What he looks like
- What others say about him
- How others react to him
- What the author or narrator writes about him

WHAT THE CHARACTER SAYS—DIALOGUE AND VOICE

We'll study dialogue more fully in a later chapter, but for now, remember that each character must sound like himself. There is no doubt in readers' minds that this next speaker, from Bette Greene's *Summer of My German Soldier*, is from the American South:

> Reveal a character by…
> 1. What the character says
> 2. What he thinks
> 3. What he does
> 4. What he looks like
> 5. What others say about him
> 6. How others react to him
> 7. What the author or narrator writes about him

"Then you figger the POW was fixin' to join up with them eight saboteurs?" asked Mr. Jackson.

> **Syntax:** how the sentence is constructed, the order of the words and parts of speech

Greene's use of vocabulary, sentence fragment, and **syntax** fit Mr. Jackson perfectly.

On a related topic, readers understand characters by their **voice**. Voice is not only the words a character speaks but also how the character narrates his or her story. It is how a character or narrator *sounds* to the reader and is achieved by a combination of things: vocabulary; sentence structure, length, and syntax; figurative language; paragraph length, and so on. Not to worry. You've probably been doing this with your characters and didn't know it.

Let's look at a few examples of voice. The first one is from Robert Lawson's *Mr. Wilmer*, in which readers meet a man who discovers he can talk with animals. Toby is the lion, whom Mr. Wilmer found to have a toothache. Can you tell which speaker is the Zoo's Keeper and which is the Director of the Zoo by how they sound?

[One speaker]
> "Mr. Wilmer, it seems, by his own account, was enabled to accomplish this remarkable diagnosis by conversing with Toby in the private form of language with which very few humans are privileged to be conversant. In short, he talked to the lion and the lion told him what the trouble was."

[Another speaker]
> "Make room there and leave the gentleman get to his bed. It's completely exhausted he is, what with conversing all day with the animals and confounding the scientific world and all."

In *Mr. Wilmer*, the Director of the Zoo is characterized as educated and polite while the Zoo's Keeper is characterized as being less educated and of Irish descent. The Director is the first speaker; the Keeper is the second.

Voice is not always defined by dialogue. This next example of voice is from the narrative of *The Book Thief* by Markus Zusak. It is the story of Liesel Meminger, a young girl in Hitler's Nazi Germany during World War II, who, as we join her, has just lost not only her whole foster family and friends in a bombing raid but also an important journal in which she chronicled her life on Himmel Street. The story's narrator is Death (first-person peripheral POV), and it is his voice we hear in this example:

> Her book was stepped on several times as the cleanup began, and although orders were given only to clear the mess of concrete, the

girl's most precious item was thrown aboard a garbage truck, at which point I was compelled. I climbed aboard and took it in my hand, not realizing that I would keep it and view it several thousand times over the years. I would watch the places where we intersect, and marvel at what the girl saw and how she survived. That is the best I can do— watch it fall into line with everything else I spectated during that time.

Death's voice, as he tells Liesel's story, is formal. Note the phrases "at which point I was compelled" and "I spectated." The first sentence is longish but clear. The attitude is respectful.

Yet another example of voice in the narrative is from Margaret McMullan's *When I Crossed No-Bob*. Although the young girl Addy doesn't talk about herself in this first-person excerpt, her voice tells quite a bit about her as she views a wedding in the U. S. South just after the War Between the States:

> This big man is walking Irene to her beau, who is a tall man with sandy hair, and he looks happy-scared, his eyes crinkly from smiling. I know him to be the schoolteacher. His name is Mr. Frank Russell and both he and Miss Irene are lucky because they're getting married and they have all their teeth.
>   . . . Miss Irene's uncle gives her away because her pa died in the war. Her uncle must weigh as much as a good cow and I wonder how Mr. Frank, who looks to weigh not much over 120, summoned the courage to ask that big man for his only niece's hand in marriage. What gave him that kind of brave?

But what if the narrative is not in the first person? Voice can still be conveyed. In *Tears of the Giraffe*, a book in Alexander McCall Smith's The No. 1 Ladies' Detective Agency series, Precious Ramotswe is the main third-person narrator. She is in her forties and is, as she describes, of "traditional build." The series takes place in Botswana in Africa. Notice the formality, the meandering, and the gentle irony in Mma Ramotswe's voice, all of which mirror the feel of the country (Note: The missing period after "Mr" is from the original text):

> Mma Ramotswe was a considerate driver and was ashamed of the bad driving which made the roads so perilous. Botswana, of course, was much safer than other countries in that part of Africa. South Africa was

very bad; there were aggressive drivers there, who would shoot you if you crossed them, and they were often drunk, particularly after payday. If payday fell on a Friday night, then it was foolhardy to set out on the roads at all. Swaziland was even worse. The Swazis loved speed, and the winding road between Manzini and Mbabane, on which she had once spent a terrifying half hour, was a notorious claimant of motoring life. She remembered coming across a poignant item in an odd copy of *The Times of Swaziland*, which had displayed a picture of a rather mousy-looking man, small and insignificant, under which was printed the simple legend *The late Mr Richard Mavuso (46)*. Mr Mavuso, who had a tiny head and a small, neatly trimmed moustache, would have been beneath the notice of most beauty queens and yet, unfortunately, as the newspaper report revealed, he had been run over by one.

Notice how the narrative wanders from one topic to a related one. Notice, too, the passive voice: "there were aggressive drivers there" and "was a notorious claimant of motoring life." Putting these two phrases into the active voice ("the many aggressive drivers would shoot you" and "claimed many lives"), while preferable in most writing, does not fit the feel and pace of this African country, story, and narrator.

These first- and third-person narrators interpret the story for readers. They interpret the events through their eyes and perceptions. They color the story by what they relate and how they relate it. Even their voice—how they sound to readers—is part of the story.

The narrator's voice and how he tells the story have a tremendous impact on your story. Remember the narrator Death from *The Book Thief*? Author Markus Zusak relates how he experimented with Death's voice:

> At first, though, Death was too mean. He was supercilious, and enjoying his work too much. He'd say extremely creepy things and delight in all the souls he was picking up . . . and the book wasn't working. . . . [S]ix months later I came back to Death—but this time, Death was to be exhausted from his eternal existence and his job. He was to be afraid of humans—because, after all, he was there to see the obliteration we've perpetrated on each other throughout the ages— and he would now be telling this story to prove to himself that humans are actually worth it.

Voice—how a character sounds or comes across to the reader—is so integral to the story that it sticks out when the author comes out of the character's voice. Can you imagine Spaz saying this to Ryter in *The Last Book in the Universe:* "Allow me to converse with the approaching Monkey Boys"?

4.2 All Writers and Discussion

Rewrite a passage of your choice from *The Last Book in the Universe* by choosing one of the following two options:

Option 1: Write the passage in Ryter's more formal voice. Ryter is your new viewpoint character; you may use either first- or third-person POV. Feel free to add any dialogue you wish that will add clarity to Ryter's voice.

Option 2: Create a new voice for Spaz in your chosen passage. In other words, make his words and observations sound different to the reader. Will he be less street-smart? More vulnerable? Angry? Cocky? Formal? Aloof? You choose.

Make enough copies for everyone in your discussion group.

Discussion: Read each others' work and discuss how this new viewpoint character and voice changes the story.

4.3 Manuscript Track

Read your short story or a large portion of your novel manuscript and ask yourself these questions:

- ☑ Is my narrator's voice consistent throughout the story?
- ☑ Is there any place where my narrator says words, uses syntax, or makes observations not in his or her voice?

End of today's lesson

☑ Is the voice helpful to my telling of this story, or do I need to change it as Markus Zusak did for *The Book Thief?*

After you make the appropriate changes, share the old and new versions with your critique group. See if they agree with your changes.

WHAT HE THINKS

> Reveal a character by...
> 1. What the character says
> 2. **What he thinks**
> 3. What he does
> 4. What he looks like
> 5. What others say about him
> 6. How others react to him
> 7. What the author or narrator writes about him

"What he thinks" is related to what your character says. In a first-person narrative, everything comes from the viewpoint character: his thoughts, interpretations of events, and dialogue. Notice how, in "Cathedral" by Raymond Carver, the unnamed husband relates his thoughts about his wife bringing a blind friend to the house:

> I saw my wife laughing as she parked the car. I saw her get out of the car and shut the door. She was still wearing a smile. Just amazing. She went around to the other side of the car to where the blind man was already starting to get out. This blind man, feature this, he was wearing a full beard! A beard on a blind man! Too much, I say.

"Just amazing," "feature this," and "too much, I say" are the husband's reactions or thoughts about what he sees. Readers hear his thoughts and interpretations of the events. Also, the narrator knows the blind man's name but is not using it here. That tells readers how he feels about the visitor—he doesn't yet see him as a real person.

It's easy to get inside your character's head when writing in first person. But what if you are using third person? Watch how Oscar Wilde records Dorian's thoughts in *The Picture of Dorian Gray*. The following passage occurs as young Dorian gazes at his now-finished portrait and bemoans the brevity of his youth:

> Yes, there would be a day when his face would be wrinkled and wizen, his eyes dim and colourless, the grace of his figure broken and deformed. The scarlet would pass away from his lips, and the gold

steal from his hair. The life that was to make his soul would mar his
body. He would become dreadful, hideous, and uncouth.

As he thought of it, a sharp pang of pain struck through him like a
knife, and made each delicate fibre of his nature quiver.

Wilde, at this point, is in Dorian's head so we can see Dorian's temptation at this critical point in his life. We are reading Dorian's thoughts in third person.

What a character thinks can be vastly different from what she says, as recorded by a first-person narrator here:

> I looked at Nellie's painting and was stunned. I had never in all my life seen anything so hideous. What could I say that wouldn't crush her?
> "It's beautiful," I told her.

Or how about this discrepancy to show a jealous character, as recorded in third person:

> Lila stood in front of Nellie's painting and evaluated it. *This is better than mine*, she thought. *For once I'd like to do something better than her.*
> "Nellie," she said, "paintings of horses are so old school. Grow up."

Here is Mma Ramotswe again, this time from *The No. 1 Ladies' Detective Agency,* as she thinks. Her thoughts are introduced instead of assumed:

> And she thought: I am just a tiny person in Africa, but there is a place for me, and for everybody, to sit down on this earth and touch it and call it their own. She waited for another thought to come, but none did, and so she crept back into the hut and the warmth of the blankets on her sleeping mat.
> Now, driving the tiny white van along those rolling miles, she thought that one day she might go back into the Kalahari, into those empty spaces, those wide grasslands that broke and broke the heart.

Notice the use of a colon to introduce her first thought.

Thoughts may be written out in normal font, as in the "Cathedral" passage:

Too much, I say!

Or they can be written in italics, as in this example from the Amish Leah's perspective in *The Sacrifice* by Beverly Lewis:

She wondered if Lizzie had ever stopped to think about her own future, back when she was Leah's age. *Was she at all like me when she was young? Did she think some of the same thoughts as I do now?* She tried to imagine Lizzie Brenneman wandering outside as a young girl, talking quietlike to a favorite dog—like Leah often did to companionable King—or looking up at the black night sky, speckled with bright stars, wishing she could count them, so many there were.

Whatever method you use, the idea is to alert readers early that they are reading a thought. Then they don't have to back up and read a section over again in an effort to understand it.

It can be confusing to readers to come to a thought in quotation marks because this punctuation usually signals spoken words. For this reason, avoid putting character thoughts in quotation marks.

4.4 All Writers and Discussion

Find two examples of "what he thinks" in *The Last Book in the Universe* and determine what this reveals about Spaz to the reading audience.

Discussion: Share your findings with your group. Do you agree with their findings and conclusions?

End of today's lesson

WHAT HE DOES, PART 1

Reveal a character by...
1. What the character says
2. What he thinks
3. **What he does**
4. What he looks like
5. What others say about him
6. How others react to him
7. What the author or narrator writes about him

What a character does may be the surest way to know him. Dialogue can give a false impression, thoughts can be unreliable, looks can be deceptive, and others' reactions to a character misleading.

But what a character does says a lot about him, which brings to mind Jesus' words, "By their fruit you will recognize them" (Matthew 7:16 NIV).

Readers know about Ryter in *The Last Book in the Universe* by what he does in the story: he befriends Spaz, he challenges him to make the quest to find his sister, and he accompanies him along the difficult journey, dispensing help and wisdom along the way. If you have to be stuck with a gummy, this is the one to be stuck with.

No one had to *tell* you Ryter is brave; the author *shows* Ryter acting in courageous ways and saying bold things, and you picked up the hints. If you learn anything from this course, let it be this: **Show, don't tell**.

Telling the reader can be insulting and is often considered poor writing. For instance, telling a reader that an old woman is self-centered is not nearly effective or suspenseful as, through dialogue and actions, *showing* the old woman working on her family to get her own way, ignoring a family rule, giving the wrong driving directions and not correcting the mistake, and being more concerned for herself than she is for her family when they meet with danger. This is the grandmother in Flannery O'Connor's "A Good Man Is Hard to Find," which you will read soon.

> The abstract is seldom as effective as the concrete. "She was distressed" is not as good as, even, "She looked away."
> –John Gardner

How do you show that a man is a miser? Write scenes in which he refuses to give his workers fuel on wintery days, is out of touch with his employees, and says of poor people they should die to "decrease the surplus population." This is how Charles Dickens writes of Ebenezer Scrooge in *A Christmas Carol*, and it is very effective.

Here is an example of how to show a trait, from Dean Koontz's *Dragon Tears*, in which readers meet Connie and Harry, two cops from the Multi-Agency Law Enforcement Special Projects Center in Laguna Niguel, California. Connie has just thrown an empty paper cup at the wastepaper basket but missed. Watch Harry and what he *does*:

> As [Connie] moved out of sight into the hall, he stared at the cup on *his* side of the room. With his foot, he nudged it across the imaginary line that divided the office.
>
> He followed Connie to the door but halted at the threshold. He glanced back at the paper cup.
>
> By now Connie would be at the end of the corridor, maybe even descending the stairs.

Harry hesitated, returned to the crumpled cup, and tossed it in the waste can. He disposed of the other two cups as well.

Koontz doesn't write "Harry was extremely neat" or "Harry liked his world to be orderly." He doesn't have to. Harry's actions speak for him.

Even the verbs you use to describe how your character walks, eats, drives, etc., *show* readers instead of *tell* them. Be specific—choose specific verbs. Instead of writing "She walked into the room," write "She staggered into the room" or "She ambled into the room." Notice the verbs P. J. Wodehouse (pronounced WOOD-house) uses as his famous valet Jeeves moves around in *Enter Jeeves: 15 Early Stories*:

| Give your main character a great entrance.
| –Sid Fleischman, author of *By the Great Horn Spoon!*

› Jeeves shimmered silently from the room.
› "Sir?" said Jeeves, kind of manifesting himself.
› He vanished.
› Jeeves projected himself into the room.
› . . . floated noiselessly into the room.
› Then he streamed imperceptibly toward the door and flowed silently out.
› Then he seemed to flicker, and wasn't there any longer.

All these verbs give readers the idea that Jeeves is a kind of magician, able to appear and disappear at will.

4.5 All Writers and Group Activity

Choose a character (your own or an existing one from literature or movies). Then choose a trait (selfish, generous, self-doubting, eager to please, organized, etc.). In a scene of about 500 but no more than 750 words, show a character displaying that trait. You are not allowed to write that trait or any of its synonyms in your scene but must show readers this trait through actions, dialogue, and specific verbs.

End of today's lesson

Group Activity: Read the scene to your writing group but don't tell them what trait you are showing. They are to guess the trait.

4.6 Manuscript Track

Examine your story to make sure you are *showing* character traits instead of *telling* them. Rewrite as needed. Share your old and new version of one passage with your critique group.

WHAT HE DOES, PART 2: HOW TO SHOW CHARACTER EMOTION

Characters need to feel emotions: fear, anger, love, anxiety, frustration, panic, happiness, and so forth. Make sure your lead does not skip blithely through the story because if the lead doesn't feel anything, neither will your reader. And if the reader does not feel any fear, anxiety, or excitement, the story will be declared boring and you will lose your reader.

> **Reveal a character by…**
> 1. What the character says
> 2. What he thinks
> 3. **What he does**
> 4. What he looks like
> 5. What others say about him
> 6. How others react to him
> 7. What the author or narrator writes about him

Your vast repository of life experiences will come in handy here. Sometime in your past, you came into a room just after someone had a fight there. What were the clues that the people in the room were angry or tense? Perhaps someone's arms were crossed or their lips were pressed together. Maybe they weren't facing each other or they stood closer than normal, leaning into each other. Maybe someone had a salt shaker poised above their head like a pitcher with a baseball. Without anyone saying a word, you knew that a tiff had just occurred simply by observing the people and the physical clues. And you hoped the tiff wasn't about you.

If a real-life person is experiencing an emotion, the emotion will be accompanied by physical clues. In the same way, if a character is experiencing an emotion, you will show it by writing physical clues.

Avoid *telling* the reader this:

Kevin was angry.

Instead, *show* Kevin in action:

> When Kevin struck out, he threw down his bat, kicked the umpire, and stomped back to the bench.

4.7 All Writers and Discussion

Remember a time someone was angry or perturbed with you and write a list of at least three physical clues that tipped you off to their emotion.

Then remember a time when you were angry with someone. What did you do? How did your body react (example—your face felt hot, your muscles felt tense, you slammed a door)? Write a list of at least three physical proofs that you were angry.

Discussion: Discuss your lists with your group. Compile a list of physical proofs of anger, both from inside one's body and from the outside looking on.

Then discuss how a writer can show the emotions indicated for each of the following sentences:

Anger: Josh stood by the side of the road and looked at his flat tire.

Excitement: Cassie just won the most important game of her life.

Frustration: T.J. wanted to go to the concert, but his mother wouldn't let him.

Sadness: Five-year-old Emmie stood on the sidewalk with her empty cone in her hand and looked at the ice cream splattered on the concrete.

Discussion again: Read the following six examples of the physical clues that describe an emotional state and determine which emotions the authors are aiming for.

1. Anyhow, I agree to have supper with Freak and his mom, even though the idea of it makes me feel tensed up, like there is a hand inside my stomach and the hand is, you know, making a fist. (from *Freak the Mighty* by Rodman Philbrick)
2. I refuse to smile, though I'm forced to bite a hole in my bottom lip to achieve this effect. There are lots of things I want to do. I'd love to bound onto the table and gyrate like an idiot football player in the end zone. I'd love to dash to the jury box and start kissing feet. I'd love to strut around the defense table with some obnoxious in-your-face taunting. I'd love to leap onto the bench and hug [Judge] Tyrone Kipler. (from *The Rainmaker* by John Grisham, after the lead learns the verdict went his way)
3. Sweat trickles down my neck and face. It is suffocating under this [orange] tree. Huge orange-tasting waves are slamming against the inside of my stomach. I crawl out from under the tree just in time to throw up every last bit of the fried chicken I had for dinner. (from *Devil on my Heels* by Joyce McDonald)
4. For at that moment a curious little procession was approaching—eleven Mice, six of whom carried between them something on a litter made of branches, but the litter was no bigger than a large atlas. No one has ever seen mice more _____ than these. They were plastered with mud—some with blood too—and their ears were down and their whiskers drooped and their tails dragged in the grass, and their leader piped on his slender pipe a melancholy tune. On the litter lay what seemed little better than a damp heap of fur; all that was left of Reepicheep. He was still breathing, but more dead than alive, gashed with innumerable wounds, one paw crushed, and, where his tail had been, a bandaged stump. (from *Prince Caspian* by C. S. Lewis) [The original word that fits in the blank is in the teacher's guide.]
5. Inspector Thumm reached his office in a lather of thought. He grunted at [his secretary], marched into his sanctum, hurled his hat across the room to the top of the safe, and threw himself into his swivel chair with a scowl.

    He put his large feet on his desk, and then after a moment drew them down . . . . He fumbled with his calendar. He rose and began to pound his floor. Then he sat down again and jabbed a button on the underside of his desk top. (from *Drury Lane's Last Case* by Ellery Queen)
6.   Madaya, Burma, 15.9.93
A day or two before I left headquarters I was enjoying my midday tub, when my [servant] came and announced that a big bear had been caught and was being brought up to me; I implored him not to do anything so rash but he went away saying "Master bringing, yes." The bathroom is comparatively small and I knew that if a large bear were introduced there would be unpleasantness. I hastily forgave my enemies and tried to say my prayers, but the only one I could remember was the prayer for fine weather. As it happened my [servant] meant bird when he said bear, having caught a large

sort of buzzard which naturalists have dignified with the name of hawk-eagle; so I left off praying for fine weather and unforgave my enemies forthwith. (Hector Munro—Saki—in a light-hearted letter to his sister in 1893)

4.8 All Writers

Set aside one day in which to track your emotions and emotional reactions. Create a chart and then record what emotion you felt, what triggered the emotion, and what physical clues accompanied the emotion (shallow breath, jumping up and down while clapping, heightened heart rate, and so forth). Do this for every emotion from mild to strong. If you want help identifying emotions or naming them, put "list of emotions" into your favorite Internet search engine and review the lists you get.

End of today's lesson

WHAT A CHARACTER LOOKS LIKE, PART 1

Reveal a character by…
1. What the character says
2. What he thinks
3. What he does
4. What he looks like
5. What others say about him
6. How others react to him
7. What the author or narrator writes about him

Congratulations. You have reached the middle item in a long list of great techniques you can use to reveal characters to your readers. Read on.

These things belong in the "looks like" category: physical attributes, mannerisms, and clothing. Agatha Christie always describes her Belgian detective Hercule Poirot as having an egg-shaped, balding head, which he tilts to one side. He also waxes his mustache and keeps it trim and luxurious. Rex Stout gives his large and reluctant detective Nero Wolfe the habit of moving his lips in and out when he is deep in thought. Sir Arthur Conan Doyle grants Sherlock Holmes a thin face decorated with a beak-like nose, and the habit of playing his violin when piecing together the clues.

Find Flannery O'Connor's "A Good Man Is Hard to Find" (http://pegasus.cc.ucf.edu/~surette/goodman.html) and read down to the sentence that begins with "In case of an accident." Then come back when you've finished that passage, and we'll chat.

***

O'Connor quickly and deftly paints pictures of all her characters in this short story. Look at how she describes John Wesley: an "eight-year-old boy" and "a stocky child with glasses." That's all you get of his physical description, but you have no trouble picturing him as he lies on the floor reading comics with his sister. O'Connor gives two short descriptions, and readers fill in the rest.

Readers know from Bailey's actions—he "didn't look up from his reading"—that he has been through this before. He has heard his mother scold him and try to get her way often, and he simply ignores her. But what do you know about him from his physical description?

These quick brushstrokes work well in short stories. In novels, you will take more time introducing main and secondary characters, feeding readers information as necessary, not in one large clump.

4.9 All Writers and Discussion

Answer the questions below and discuss your answers with the group:

› What is the one physical description of Bailey's wife?
› What is she wearing?
› What do these two things tell you about her?
› What is the mannerism O'Connor gives the grandmother when the old woman is "rattling the newspaper at [Bailey's] bald head"?
› When do you know any of the grandmother's physical attributes?
› In the car, what is she wearing?
› What does this tell you about her?
› What are Spaz's physical descriptions, mannerisms, and clothing in chapter one of *The Last Book in the Universe*?
› What are Ryter's in chapter one?

End of today's lesson

WHAT THE CHARACTER LOOKS LIKE, PART 2: THE GIRL WORE A COAT

> Reveal a character by...
> 1. What the character says
> 2. What he thinks
> 3. What he does
> 4. **What he looks like**
> 5. What others say about him
> 6. How others react to him
> 7. What the author or narrator writes about him

As you learned from the previous lesson, it is not necessary to tell readers everything about your character's eye and hair color, length and style of hair, shade of nail polish, height, weight, and shoe size—that is, unless some of these are important to your character's character and personality traits. Describing Bailey's wife as having a "face as broad and innocent as a cabbage" and her green kerchief as having "two points on the top like rabbits' ears" tells readers she is laid back, as innocuous as a bunny rabbit. Her physical attributes and her clothing show readers her inner self. Again, showing, not telling.

Choose carefully the exact **physical attributes**, **mannerisms**, and **clothing** that will imply something important about your characters.

Writing "The girl wore a coat" is bland and tells your readers nothing. We still know nothing about the girl. How does each of these sentences change the image of the girl in readers' minds:

> › The girl wore a full-length mink coat.
> › The girl wore a studded, black-leather jacket with chains.
> › The girl wore a too-large raincoat, dirty and torn.

God may look at the heart, but people judge by outward appearances (I Samuel 16:7b). Each item of clothing in the list above changes how readers feel about or perceive the girl. The clothing helps to characterize the girl.

In real life, appearance isn't always an indicator of inner character.

In fiction, though, it often is.

It used to be that when an author wanted to show a character as manly, he would describe him as being robust and having a square jaw. Or if a woman was feminine, she would have a heart-shaped face and violet eyes.

Clichés: [klee SHAYS] old, used, or worn out phrases, images, or situations.

Although writers may not use these descriptions today because they are **clichés**, descriptions of the outward man, in fiction, typically characterize the inward man.

In addition to clothing, you can use **setting** to characterize a character. In *The Great Gatsby*, F. Scott Fitzgerald describes a setting with lots of movement in it, and then he ends it with our first glimpse of one of the antagonists: "Tom Buchanan in riding clothes was standing with his legs apart on the front porch."

Soon afterward, Fitzgerald describes Buchanan's wife and her friend as "buoyed up [on the couch] as though upon an anchored balloon" with their dresses "rippling and fluttering as if they had just been blown back in after a short flight around the house." Lots of movement—and then in comes Buchanan:

> Then there was a boom as Tom Buchanan shut the rear windows and the caught wind died out about the room, and the curtains and the rugs and the two young women ballooned slowly to the floor.

This man is solid, stolid, immovable. He shuts the windows, stops the breeze, and the women cease their illusion of movement. This reveals his character and his role in the story.

John le Carré uses a description of a character's house to give readers insight into this character in *The Constant Gardener*. Here is Sandy Woodrow, a member of the British High Commission in Kenya, who, readers find later, is not as he seems:

> The newly completed building he was ascending was austere and well designed. He liked its style, perhaps because it corresponded outwardly with his own. With its neatly defined compound, canteen, shop, fuel pump and clean, muted corridors, it gave off a self-sufficient, rugged impression. Woodrow, to all appearances, had the same sterling qualities.

Le Carré uses the phrases "gave off...[an] impression" and "to all appearances" to show readers that the outward man may not match the inward one. Readers would do well to smell a rat.

That girl with the coat, incidentally, is standing still. How boring. No one wants to read a description of a paper doll. Describe your **character in motion**. Flannery O'Connor in "A Good Man Is Hard to Find" shows each character as he or she is doing something: Bailey is reading, his wife is feeding the baby, and John Wesley and June Star are on the floor reading the funnies. All are doing something very natural according to their intrinsic character, including the grandmother who shakes the newspaper at her grown son's head.

Describe your characters in motion or show them as they do something. It's time to fix that stiff, paper-doll girl in the coat.

4.10 All Writers and Discussion

Show each coat-wearing girl below in motion. Write three sentences, one for each girl. Make her movements or actions *mean* something; make them reveal her inner self. Make her motions characterize her.

> A girl with a full-length mink coat
> A girl with a studded, black-leather jacket with chains
> A girl with a too-large raincoat, dirty and torn

End of today's lesson

Discussion: Share your three sentences with the group. You may be surprised at the variety you discover.

THIS IS WHAT I LOOK LIKE: PART 3

> **Reveal a character by...**
> 1. What the character says
> 2. What he thinks
> 3. What he does
> 4. **What he looks like**
> 5. What others say about him
> 6. How others react to him
> 7. What the author or narrator writes about him

This is absolutely the last section in "What he looks like." I promise.

How can you get the lead's physical description across to readers if the story is in first person? It used to be that you could stand the lead in front of a mirror, reflective window, or, at the very least, the inside of a shiny spoon. But that method was used so much it has become, you guessed it, clichéd. What's a writer to do?

Here's how Sue Monk Kidd handles it in *The Secret Life of Bees* as her young protagonist Lily describes herself:

> My hair was black like my mother's but basically a nest of cowlicks, and it worried me that I didn't have much of a chin.... I had nice eyes, though, what you would call Sophia Loren eyes, but still, even the boys who wore their hair in ducktails dripping with Vitalis and carried combs in their shirt pockets didn't seem attracted to me, and they were considered hard up.

Lily identifies herself with her mother in this description. This is important to the theme of the book—the loss of her mother and Lily's desire for her. Describe your protagonist in a way that links the physical to the **story's meaning**.

Lily does not say, "I am considered ugly," but writes that even losers aren't interested in her. Sometimes it pays to be **indirect**.

Notice that she alludes to fashions of the day ("ducktails" and "Vitalis") so readers know the **time period** (1964, in Lily's case).

When you describe a character, whether in first or third person, make the physical attributes *mean* something in the life of the character and in the life of the story.

Self-description works well if you show your character in **motion**:

> I jump up, which is the only way I can reach the top shelf of my locker. In tenth grade, I am still fifth-grade tall and have heard every "short" joke known to geeks and jocks.

Physically, all that readers know about Spaz in *The Last Book in the Universe* is that he has epilepsy. Sometimes you don't need to describe many physical attributes. This gives readers more freedom to imagine the character.

Freak the Mighty, written by Rodman Philbrick, the author of *The Last Book in the Universe*, gives few physical attributes. Max, the lead, describes himself as "a big goon" who trips over everything, and he folds the fact that he is in an L. D. (learning disabled) class into a sentence about how kids call him names in school. This uses motion *and* indirectness.

Dialogue gives us another look at Max. The new neighbor kid says to him, "Hey you, Doofus! Yeah, you with the hairy face." And Max reports that his grandparents whisper that Max resembles his dad, who is in prison for murder. This last is related to the theme of the book—that Max *looks* like his dad but hopes he will not *be* like his dad.

Travis Jordan, in Frank Peretti's *The Visitation*, gives **no physical description** of himself but highlights his profession—or lack thereof:

> It was Monday, the typical pastor's day off. Kyle Sherman and I were sitting at my kitchen table with coffee cups and a bag of Oreo cookies between us. He was still in his twenties, dark-haired, wiry, a fresh horse ready to gallop. For the past four months, he'd been at this table in this little house several times, keeping in touch and trying to be a good shepherd.
>
> And hoping to keep some strays from straying further, I surmised. I know I caught his attention the moment he arrived to take over the pastorate. I was still the official pastor until I passed my mantle to him, but I was conspicuously missing. Antioch Pentecostal Mission had a pastor—a *former* pastor—who couldn't go near the place.

From these two paragraphs contrasting himself to Kyle, readers understand much about Travis, and they hear his voice—weary and a bit cynical.

If you want your readers to have a precise idea of some physical attribute, include it early, before readers have time to create their own image of your character.

Many short stories pass over self-descriptions altogether. If the personality and voice of the narrator carries the story, readers get an image of the narrator in their minds from those.

Description does not exist simply to describe. I know, I know. It sounds crazy, but it's true. Descriptions have more than one job: creating a mood, associating a physical attribute with something important in the story (as with Lily and her hair that is like her mother's), revealing an attitude about the self-describer, showing a personality trait, adding to a voice, etc.

If your character description is simply describing, you have only just begun.

4.11 All Writers and Discussion

Write a character's self-description by doing this: Choose a classmate or family member and then, from first person, write their description as though they were in a story. Be choosy about which attributes and facts you include. Let their personality shine through in this description.

Use your tools: movement/actions, dialogue, being indirect, something to represent time period or culture, outer description to reveal inner meaning, etc.

Discussion: Read your description to your discussion group. They are to guess who your viewpoint "character" is.

End of today's lesson

4.12 Manuscript Track

Study one character from your manuscript. Where can you use this character's physical appearance, mannerisms, and clothing to good effect? Have you used them to characterize your character or simply as random props?

Rewrite as needed and share the new version with your critique group. Bring enough copies for each member of the group and critique each others' work.

WHAT OTHERS SAY/HOW OTHERS REACT

You've seen it before: Someone enters a room and everyone ignores him; another enters and instantly is surrounded with admirers. You may react to the first person with indifference and to the second with interest because of how others are acting. Others' reactions can shape how you feel about people.

Movie directors know this and use a reaction shot in their films. When one character says something or when something happens, the camera cuts to another character to get that character's reaction. Audiences see a look of surprise, horror, fear, disdain, delight, and so forth, and then they know how to interpret the event. If the lead is happy with an event, chances are that audiences will be too. If the antagonist is happy with the event, audiences will not be. The next time you watch a movie, check out the reaction shots and be aware of how they shape the movie for you.

Reveal a character by...
1. What the character says
2. What he thinks
3. What he does
4. What he looks like
5. What others say about him
6. How others react to him
7. What the author or narrator writes about him

Written stories, too, need reactions from surrounding characters to more fully reveal other characters. In James Michener's *Hawaii*, Abner Hale, a young divinity student, is described by the narrator as "a thin, sallow-faced youth with stringy blond hair" and "emaciated." He comes from "an impoverished-looking farm" and a super-strict family. Readers have a negative impression of him from these, but then Michener imbues this character with even more negativity. When Abner and his roommate apply to be missionaries to Owhyhee (Hawaii), Abner learns that his roommate's application will take only a week while his will take two. He asks Reverend Thorn why. This is what happens next:

> Reverend Thorn wanted to blurt out the truth: "Because you're an offensive, undernourished, sallow-faced little prig, the kind that wrecks any mission to which he is attached. There's not a man on my committee that really thinks you ought to be sent overseas, but I have a niece who has got to get married one of these days. And maybe if I can talk to her before she sees you, possibly I can force her into marrying you. That, young man, is what requires two weeks."

This internal diatribe reveals a lot about Reverend Thorn, but it also gives Thorn's negative reaction to Abner. Readers react negatively to this "prig," even before he's done anything stupid.

4.13 All Writers and Discussion

Find an example of a character reacting to another one in *The Last Book in the Universe* or in another book. Discuss how this colors your reaction to the character.

Who gives you the creeps? What does he/she do, say, or look like that gives you that creepy feeling? How do you feel when you are around that person? On paper, describe the feeling as best you can. What do you think when you are around this person? How does your body react?

Discussion: Share your examples and ideas with the group.

End of today's lesson

WHAT THE AUTHOR OR NARRATOR SAYS ABOUT HIM

Sometimes the author or narrator simply has to *tell* instead of *show*. This may be in the interest of time. Or perhaps it is simply the best way to reveal information. Jack London uses this method in "To Build a Fire":

> Reveal a character by...
> 1. What the character says
> 2. What he thinks
> 3. What he does
> 4. What he looks like
> 5. What others say about him
> 6. How others react to him
> 7. What the author or narrator writes about him

> It was a clear day, and yet there seemed an intangible pall over the face of things, a subtle gloom that made the day dark, and that was due to the absence of sun. This fact did not worry the man. He was used to the lack of sun.

London tells us the man is not worried. We believe him and move on, but we expect the character to *act* not worried later on.

When you insert information from the narrator or the author, you most likely will need to prove it later.

WHAT'S IN A NAME?

Although real people may be named Rose Busch or Jim Shortz, avoid this treachery in your writing. It will detract from your story. Also avoid names like Dudley Do-Right (the good guy) and Snidely Whiplash (the bad guy) unless you are writing a comedy or a comic book. Terry Pratchett, in many of his Discworld books, uses humorous names like Captain Carrot, Sergeant Detritus, Mrs. Cake, and so on, but he does this on purpose to add to the fun.

Avoid overly descriptive names like Lucy Starbright or Buck Strongheart. This was popular a hundred years ago but can mark you today as an amateur.

Consider these lists of character names from C. S. Lewis's *That Hideous Strength* and guess which one is the list of good guys and which is the list of bad guys:

<u>List A</u>
Dr. and Mrs. Cecil Dimble
Canon Jewel
Mark and Jane Studdock
Mr. Fisher-King
Miss Grace Ironwood
Arthur Denniston
Mrs. Ivy Maggs
Mr. MacPhee
Dr. John Ransom

<u>List B</u>
Lord Feverstone
John Wither
Miss Hardcastle
Mr. Steele
Mr. Straik
Mr. Stone
Professor Frost

Connotation: an implied meaning

Lewis uses a preponderance of names to show meaning. Frost, Steele, and Wither all have negative **connotations**, as do Hardcastle and the harsh-sounding Straik. Contrast that to the positive connotations of Ransom and Jewel and the soft-sounding names of Dimble, Maggs, and MacPhee.

Why do you think Bilbo Baggins sounds so huggable? The sound of the name and its connotation really do matter when choosing character names.

Unless you are trying to be funny, avoid naming a large, bellicose, truculent, strident female character Tiffany. It simply doesn't work.

You may want to choose a name that corresponds to your character's age and ethnicity. This will help readers "see" her better. Edna, for instance, is of a different age and culture than Oksana, Ngaio, Zainab, or Bianca.

Buy a book of baby names or borrow one from the library. This will cut out hours of painful brain spasms.

Avoid using similar names in your story. Libby, Lydia, and Biddy are too close in form and consonant/vowel construction to use together, and readers will have a hard time keeping them separate from each other. Do your reader a favor and vary the names.

THE TELLING DETAIL

The telling detail is the detail that makes the character come alive for the reader, the detail by which the character is most known.

An example comes from *How Right You Are, Jeeves* by P. G. Wodehouse, in which we find a very loud Aunt Dahlia:

> She greeted me with one of those piercing view-halloos which she had picked up on the hunting field in the days when she had been an energetic chivvier of the British fox. It sounded like a gas explosion and went through me from stem to stern.

In other places, she "booms" or "bellows" but never simply "says." Her telling detail is her volume, which implies a certain level of energy and forcefulness.

Another example of a telling detail comes from Ray Bradbury's *Fahrenheit 451.* In a book that pits technology against nature, the almost seventeen-year-old Clarisse McClellan is described as having a "faint perfume" scent with the "wind and the leaves carry[ing] her forward." She watches birds, collects butterflies, deposits flowers and chestnuts on Montag's porch, and asks him if he's ever smelled leaves before. Each time she appears in the story, something of nature accompanies her, even if it is a dandelion. Every description of her uses a nature image.

Readers of *The Caine Mutiny* by Herman Wouk will most likely remember Captain Queeg by his irritating habit of clacking steel balls together in his hand.

Describe? No. Characterize.

4.14 All Writers and Discussion

If you were a character in a book, what would your telling detail be? What would you *want* it to be? Write these down.

Sometimes it is this disparity between who a character is and who he *wants* to be that generates an inner tension for him and for readers.

4.15 Manuscript Track

Examine the lead in a project you are working on and ask these questions:

- ☑ Have I described my lead in a variety of ways (action, dialogue, description)?
- ☑ Have I included enough information?
- ☑ Have I included too much?

End of today's lesson

☑ Have I spread out the description so it doesn't come in one large clump and in one method?
☑ Does the description of the lead have anything to do with the inner life of the character or the life of the story?

Make changes and present your new version (1-4 pages) to your group for their critique. Bring enough copies for all in your group.

AN EMPATHETIC LEAD

No, that's not a "pathetic" lead. There are plenty of those around. Read on to learn about an "empathetic" lead.

How many books have you stopped reading because the protagonist did not interest you?

When you have empathy for someone, you identify with him or her in some way. There is something about that person you understand or that interests you. In the same way, you want your readers to be interested in the lead, to identify with him and really care about what happens. You want them to keep turning pages to find out if he will be all right. How do you do that?

There are a number of good ways to do this.

But first, it's time to explore.

4.16 All Writers and Discussion

Think about the last movie you watched or the last book you read. What was there about the lead that made you cheer her on? Why were you on her side? Why did you care what happened to her? Make a list of reasons.

What does Philbrick do in *The Last Book in the Universe* to make Spaz an empathetic lead, even though Spaz's first act is to rob an old man?

Discuss, also, how writers make characters empathetic in movies and other books.

4.17 All Writers

End of today's lesson

Write about your first hero. Who was it? What qualities did your hero possess that made him or her so important and vital to you? Exploring this idea in depth will enable you to write a hero with believable qualities readers can connect with.

HOW TO CREATE AN EMPATHETIC LEAD

In creating an empathetic lead, consider giving your character some positive attributes:

- Courage of any kind
- Integrity (following his own rules, even when it hurts him)
- A sense of humor
- Cares for another character (dog, sister, grandmother, etc.)
- Competence in some area
- Not whiny about bad things in his or her life (exception: comedy writing)
- Is in danger/is threatened
- An interesting voice
- May be a victim but does not act like a victim

And include some "negative" attributes:

- Is the underdog in some area (birth order, social skills, physical prowess)
- Is flawed in some way
- Is alone
- May be missing family members to whom he was attached
- Is vulnerable in some way
- Was wounded in childhood (physically, mentally, emotionally, or spiritually)

If you watched *WALL•E*, you probably were rooting for the little robot early on, even though he speaks no words for about 25 minutes. Why did you root for him? What makes him empathetic to viewers?

He is alone and the last of his breed, works hard, is proficient in his tasks, is resourceful, takes care of a little bug, appreciates and saves items with which we are familiar, has childlike qualities in his movements, and longs for company and love. And he's cute. What's not to like?

Even thieves in caper movies must show themselves worthy to be liked. Take *The Italian Job* or *Ocean's Eleven*, for instance. The thieves are empathetic because someone is out to get them or has done them wrong (in other words, someone is worse than they are). In addition, some of them have positive relations with family or friends, they are competent at what they do, and they respect each other's roles in the heist.

Even an immoral character can be made to be empathetic. Edith Wharton does this in *Ethan Frome*. Ethan has an affair with a younger woman who is a servant in his house. How does Wharton engage readers' empathy for him? Here's how:

> › Ethan is quiet and uncomplaining about his lot in life.
> › He feels sorry for his mother and takes care of his ailing parents until they die.
> › His acquaintances and folks from his village are sympathetic toward him.
> › His wife is characterized as large, sickly, whiny, faultfinding, manipulative, and controlling. [Note: If his wife were kindhearted, readers would not have positive feelings toward Ethan.]
> › The author describes Ethan's wife as being a "bloodless old woman," an "alien presence," and an "evil energy."
> › Ethan feels like a prisoner in his own house and feels that his manhood is compromised.
> › The method he chooses to gain happiness and escape his reality only makes things worse.
> › The narrator (the man who relates the story) clearly feels sympathy for him.

How does Charles Dickens make the selfish miser Ebenezer Scrooge an empathetic character in *A Christmas Carol*? First, he is the viewpoint character. By default, this elicits some empathy. But Dickens has to work to keep readers' empathy. So we find Scrooge alone and friendless, even though it is his own fault. Next, through the ministrations of the Ghost of Christmas Past, we learn that Scrooge wasn't always a "Scrooge." We see him as a lonely schoolboy who, for the most part, is abandoned and friendless. We watch him as a young worker, competent in his profession. Then we read of the failed relationship with his fiancée. Last, we learn his possible fate through the Ghost of Christmas Yet to Come and, more important, Tiny Tim's possible fate. At this crucial point, we see how Scrooge reacts to both of these fates. These things are what shaped Scrooge, and we champion him and wish him well.

However, this takes a whole book. What if you only have four minutes?

Tony Stark, the lead in the movie *Iron Man*, is a selfish, arrogant, self-aggrandizing womanizer who develops, manufactures, and sells weapons. How can viewers possibly like this character? How do the writers win them over in less than four minutes? Here's how:

> - Stark is the viewpoint character; this gains some reader empathy.
> - He has a sense of humor, even if it is dry.
> - He has a good rapport with the young soldiers, both male and female, who are transporting him through enemy territory, and it is clear that they like him or, at least, are awed by him.
> - Even his rude, sexist remark is deflected for viewers by the female driver's smile (the reaction shot).
> - And last, he comes under attack. His armored vehicle suddenly is barraged with enemy fire. With his own weapons. The ones that bear the name of his company on them. In other words, he gets smacked down almost before his story begins.

This last irony, along with watching him bleed, seals the deal. Viewers suddenly care about Tony Stark or are curious enough to keep watching.

After you gain empathy for your lead, you will work to retain reader empathy. How? Your lead will meet problems and story complications head on, even if he or she hesitates in the beginning. And your lead will be active in his or her own story, trying to figure out what to do next and how to get around the next hurdle set up by the forces of antagonism.

4.18 All Writers and Discussion

Write the first scene of a story, about 500 words but no more than 750. In it, create and reveal an empathetic lead. Use a combination of actions, dialogue, and description. Show, don't tell.

Use first or third person.

End of today's lesson

Discussion: Read your scene aloud and listen to the group's responses. Were they on your character's side? Did they feel empathy for him or her? Give feedback to other readers.

CHARACTER MOTIVATION

Empathetic characters are, for the most part, not completely motivated by things like greed, revenge, fear, jealousy, pain, or a lust for power. Leave those negative motivations for the antagonist. Protagonists need something to get them going, some motivation to get them into the story. Here are some positive motivators for your empathetic lead:

- Self-preservation
- A desire for adventure or freedom
- Protecting or rescuing someone
- Curiosity (this may be a good one to begin with but will not sustain a story)
- Friendship
- Loyalty
- Love

Duty used to be a strong motivator but is rarely used in stories today because it feels too sterile, too unfeeling. When modern readers enter Jane Austen's *Persuasion*, for example, they are not convinced that a heroine would throw away the love of her life and break an engagement simply because her aunt advises her to. In the book, the heroine is motivated by duty to her elders and to convention, but plenty of other motivations exist for today's writer.

If you use duty as a motivator, use it for a secondary character, as with the knight protecting the Holy Grail in *Indiana Jones and the Last Crusade*. Or combine it with a stronger motivator like love.

Choose a combination of positive motivations and, to make a fully three-dimensional hero or heroine, sprinkle in a few not-so-worthy ones that get blasted out of the character as he or she moves through the story.

Think of George Eliot's *Silas Marner*, in which we meet a miser motivated by an unhealthy sense of self-preservation due to a betrayal and emotional wounding. When the crunch comes, though, Marner steps up and is motivated by his desire to protect another from the hurts life has given him. Marner is later threatened by a neighbor who wants to take Marner's adopted daughter Eppie away, and Marner is filled with complementary motivations that help him fight for her good. In fact, he has come so far from the self-preserving miser we met earlier that he lets Eppie decide what she wants for her life, even though it is tearing him apart.

That's the large-scale, story-sized motivation. But every small decision needs a logical motivation too. In Orson Scott Card's *Ender's Game*, six-year-old Andrew ("Ender") Wiggin is attacked by bullies whose leader is Stilson. As Ender wonders how to handle the situation, this goes through his head:

> This would not have a happy ending. So Ender decided that he'd rather not be the unhappiest at the end. The next time Stilson's arm came out to push him, Ender grabbed at it.

And then Ender lets him have it. His motivation in this scene, that of not wanting to "be the unhappiest at the end," is clear and makes sense based on his vulnerable character.

Many beginning writers make the mistake of letting their characters sit around and think their way into a decision. Don't let this happen to you. Although decisions are made every day in real life by pondering them, they are not made this way in fiction. Push your characters. They must be motivated to make a decision or to change. How? H. G. Wells' *The Invisible Man* shows us how to use an event to motivate a character.

Scientist Griffin, the evil genius of the story, has been experimenting on live cats. As any modern reader of sci-fi knows, the scientist begins on bunnies or cats and then moves up through the larger animals, finally experimenting on humans but certainly not himself. So something has to happen in Griffin's life to catapult him from making cats invisible to trying the experiment on himself. What is it?

One of the house's renters brings her suspicions about the cats to the landlord, who bangs on Griffin's door to complain about missing cats and loud laboratory machines. To make matters worse, Griffin is months behind in his rent payments and is afraid that the landlord will one day seize the lab equipment and all of Griffin's scientific secrets. Here is what Griffin reports:

> But this brought matters to a crisis. I did not know what he would do, nor even what he had power to do. To move to fresh apartments would have meant delay; all together I had barely twenty pounds left in the world,–for the most part in a bank,–and I could not afford that. Vanish! It was irresistible.

His decision is not based on thinking alone. It is based on events and his reactions to it. Because Griffin feels the squeeze of suspicion and lack of money, his decision to "vanish" feels believable.

4.19 All Writers and Discussion

Find one motivation for Spaz going on his adventure with Ryter. Find one motivation for Ryter going with Spaz.

Discussion: Share your findings with the group. Do you agree with the motivations others in your group assign to the characters? Do you think the character motivations are strong enough and logical for the character?

End of today's lesson

4.20 Manuscript Track

Review your story and check your lead's motivations. Ask yourself these questions:

☑ Are the motivations that plunge my lead into the story believable?
☑ Are they strong enough to carry my lead through the story?

☑ Are they mostly positive for the protagonist and mostly negative for the antagonist?
☑ Do the motivations for my protagonist match his/her personality and history?
☑ Do even the smallest choices my leads make have clear, believable motivations or are they just making decisions because I want them to or because they need to for the sake of the story?

Make any adjustments you need to and report your changes to the critique group for discussion.

A CHARACTER DIES

Your story may contain a character who dies, but that character's death will be in vain unless you can make your reader care about him first.

If readers see the character in a loving relationship, they will care more deeply when that character dies. The movie *The Italian Job* begins with a thief. There is no question he is a thief, and soon viewers see him stealing something. But [plot spoiler alert] this guy is going to die. How do the writers make viewers care about him and his death?

> He is in a loving relationship with his daughter. He is seen calling her and sending her an expensive gift. Even over the phone it is clear that he loves her and that she reciprocates that love.
> He mentors a younger thief to whom he is officially passing the reins.
> He respects the younger thief's abilities; the younger thief respects his wisdom and considers him a father-figure.
> He cares for his team and respects each member's place on the team.
> His death comes as a betrayal at the hands of a team member.
> Last, we see the reactions of the team members when he dies. The lead holds him on his lap and mourns for him, reluctant to let him go.

Many of these techniques overlap with those of how to create an empathetic character. Other techniques include making the reader feel fear for the character by putting the character in jeopardy, putting another character on location to witness the death and/or mourn the death, and showing how the death of another character negatively affects the lead's life—like the lead now being alone.

Here's the thing: If someone in the story does not love or care about the character that dies, the reader will not care, either. Minor characters can be picked off and no one will care. After all, expendable crewmen come and go. But to enable readers to care about the death of an important character, you will need to lay a little groundwork.

4.21 All Writers and Discussion

Think of a book or movie in which a character dies. Write a list of at least three things the writers do to make the audience care about the character's death.

Discussion: Discuss the book or movie you chose and how the writers make you care about the character's death. Compile a list of techniques from your discussion. Also, discuss this question: How does Rodman Philbrick make readers care about Ryter's death?

End of today's lesson

BE SPECIFIC

Good guys aren't good all over the place and in every way. Bad guys aren't bad through and through. Be specific about the good guy's "goodness" and the bad guy's "badness."

Ryter, in *The Last Book in the Universe*, is a good guy, but his goodness is focused. He cares about Spaz. He wants to help Spaz discover Spaz's story. This is the essence of his goodness.

Billy Bizmo is an antagonist who forces Spaz to do things he doesn't want to do and who hides Spaz's true story from him. But he isn't bad all the way through. It is Billy who, upon occasion, looks out for Spaz because he is Spaz's father.

Is your character good because he is truthful? Courageous? Self-sacrificing? Then focus in on that goodness and enlarge upon it. Is your antagonist bad because he is a cheater? Violent? Greedy? Then capitalize on this trait and make it work for the story.

THE ANTAGONIST

You likely know that the antagonist is the force for change in a story. In *A Christmas Carol*, the antagonists are **internal** (Scrooge's miserly, hard heart) and **external** (the three ghosts). The ghosts, though kind and helpful, are antagonists because they are agents of change.

Most antagonists aren't that kind and helpful.

In this section, we are going to discuss only antagonists who are characters, not forces (like *nature* or *greed*). So we're thinking of characters like Darth Vader, Lex Luther, Doctor Octopus, the Joker, the Sheriff of Nottingham, Hook, the wicked stepmother, the human varmint in a western, the double-crosser in a spy novel, and the murderer in a mystery.

4.22 All Writers and Discussion

Pause and discuss this question with your group: Why are the antagonists so much more fun—and compelling—than the leads?

You may want to create an antagonist who, in value, is the **opposite** of the lead. For instance, if the lead values honesty, make your antagonist act out deception, lies, and prevarication. Does your lead value hard work? Make your antagonist value self-indulgence and laziness. Or make him value working hard toward an unworthy goal. What is your lead's major trait? Create the opposite trait in your antagonist. In this way, they can be more fully pitted against each other—and the lead's good trait can *mean* something.

> Only a writer who has the sense of evil can make goodness readable.
> —E. M. Forster, author of *The African Queen*

Or make your lead and antagonist value the **same thing** but want to achieve their goals in opposite ways. If the lead is lonely and wants to find mother love, create an antagonist who also is lonely and wants to find mother love, but she does it in negative ways.

Perhaps your lead was emotionally wounded in childhood. Give your antagonist a **similar childhood wound**, too, but show how she deals with it in unhealthy ways. Instead of coping and trying to find help and healing, she lashes out or tries her hand at retribution.

Whatever the case, the lead and the protagonist are linked together. *Because* your lead is good in one way, your antagonist will be bad in that same way. *Because* your lead values something, your antagonist will value the opposite.

Because you gave your lead a wound in childhood, your antagonist will have a similar wound. These two characters should be inextricably linked.

We'll deal with this topic more fully in the chapter on conflict, but for now, be aware that the size of the antagonist's badness has the potential to display the size of the lead's goodness. The hero is only as good as the antagonist is bad.

Create an antagonist to bring out, develop, or show off your lead's good qualities.

> There is no man alive who is not the darling of himself, and that's enough for all practical purposes. And he will do the necessary, as the saying is, to spread that radiance to the less fortunate."
> –William Saroyan, author of *My Name Is Aram*

Understand this: The antagonist is the hero of his own story. In *his* story, *he* is the good guy. He has a goal, and the protagonist is keeping him from it. Every nasty thing he does is justifiable in his mind and, as you may have discovered in your discussion, he doesn't live by the rules the lead makes for himself. While the lead most likely is self-sacrificing (at the right time in the story), the antagonist may be selfish and ego-centric, choosing to destroy rather than save. But in his mind, the end justifies the means.

4.23 All Writers and Discussion

Write a few journal entries or letters from an antagonist. This may be an antagonist you make up on the spot, have already written in one of your projects, or borrow from a published book (like Madame Defarge in *A Tale of Two Cities* or the White Witch in the Narnia series). Have the antagonist describe his or her home life, history, desires, goals, methods for reaching those goals, and justification for using those methods. In the journal or letters, the antagonist is explaining himself to you. No need to get fancy. Simply divulge these things from his or her point of view and in his or her voice.

Discussion: Discuss how this journal or letter from the antagonist changed your view of the character. What else has it changed? If you created a new antagonist, how will your knowledge of the antagonist help you write him or her in a story?

End of today's lesson

What you studied in this chapter:

- ✓ Character types
- ✓ Techniques to reveal characters
    - What he says (dialogue and voice)
    - What he thinks
    - What he does (including character emotions and specific verbs)
    - What he looks like (and how to describe a first-person narrator)
    - What others say about him
    - How others react to him
    - What the author or narrator writes about him
- ✓ Character names
- ✓ The telling detail
- ✓ How to create an empathetic lead
- ✓ Character motivation
- ✓ A character who dies
- ✓ Creating an antagonist

5: CONFLICT

You have been taught to be kind to people, but now that you are a writer, you can ignore that advice—at least when it comes to how you treat your characters. Here's what Vanessa Grant, a romance writer, says about the topic:

> Forget everything you ever learned about being nice to people. To be a good storyteller, you must treat your characters terribly, throwing their worst fears in their faces.

Are you ready to get nasty?

The word *conflict* may conjure up images of angry fighting. But let's look at some other words for *conflict*, words that may more closely resemble how you write or what your own character comes up against: troubles, struggles, issues, difficulties, problems, stresses, attacks, tension, hostilities, resistance, obstacles, disappointments, or battles.

Whatever word you use for conflict, the point is that your character's desires and goals are pulling him through the story, and the forces aligned against him are pushing him back.

THE CONFLICT MENU

A writer has many choices when considering the types of conflicts characters will experience. A character may struggle with . . .

> › Him/herself
> › Another character
> › A society, civilization, law, mindset, or worldview
> › Nature
> › Technology
> › God

A short story may be centered on one character, event, or conflict, but novels have room for the many forms of conflict, both **internal** (against him/herself) and **external** (the rest of the list).

The character who battles wizards, dragons, evil geniuses, armies, friends who betray, storms, journeys through caves, and giant spiders must also wrestle with his own inner demons. These may be self-doubt, past failures, a negative belief about himself, a quick temper, a longing for fame, an emotional wound, or a whole host of other personal ills.

> You cannot run away from a weakness; you must sometimes fight it out or perish.
>
> —Robert Louis Stevenson

When a character battles an internal issue, his battle must eventually become external. He makes choices, he acts, he puts things in motion. For example, the younger brother in Jesus' parable of the prodigal son might have felt inferior to his older brother or he might have craved pleasure and adventure. Whatever the internal woe, he made it external by demanding his inheritance of his father. Suddenly he is plunged into acres of external conflicts against his father, his brother, his friends and acquaintances, his boss, the pigs, and society's expectations for him as well. Find a way to make your lead's internal battles become external, thereby affecting others. Vanessa Grant says it this way:

If your characters don't experience internal conflict, you're telling the reader that the issues in this story aren't important enough to worry about. Internal conflict is essential, but external conflict generates excitement. Whenever a character experiencing internal conflict acts in response to that struggle, it becomes externalized and may create conflict with other characters.

Conflict in stories exists for these reasons:

- To show off or highlight your character's good qualities
- To create an opportunity for your character to learn something, grow, or change
- To temporarily thwart his goals and desires
- To gain further empathy for the character
- To create tension and suspense for the reader by capitalizing on his fears on behalf of the character

Be selective about the conflicts you will submerge your lead in. Make them tailor-made for your character, based on his personality, temperament, needs, inner demons, history, goals, and desires.

What better conflict can you have for a little girl whose father was wrongly imprisoned than for her to grow up and watch her fiancé also be falsely accused, wrongly imprisoned, and on his way to the guillotine? You can find this story in *A Tale of Two Cities* by Charles Dickens.

If your character accidentally kills his young daughter by backing his car over her, what better conflict can you devise for him than to immerse him in a battle to save the life of the only woman who has been able to conceive a child in the last 25 years? You can read about him in the futuristic *The Children of Men* by P. D. James.

> We are all faced with a series of great opportunities brilliantly disguised as unsolvable problems.
>
> –John W. Gardner

These conflicts pick at the scabs, so to speak, of the protagonists and open up their old wounds. Now they must not only battle outside forces rallied against them but also the internal pain exposed by these forces and situations.

Characters are defined and shaped by the conflicts they encounter. The worse the conflict, the better your character's character will be revealed, especially when you custom-fit the conflicts to the character. Pressurize your character. Squeeze him to bring out his true nature.

English author and dramatist John Galsworthy writes this: "A man of action forced into a state of thought is unhappy until he can get out of it."

Find out what makes your lead unhappy and then throw it at him.

5.1 All Writers and Discussion

Using all the categories in the conflict menu, identify Spaz's conflicts in *The Last Book in the Universe*.

Discussion: Share what you find about Spaz and his conflicts. Other than having epilepsy, what is his wound and how has Philbrick capitalized on it? Also, discuss the conflicts in other books and in films with which you are familiar.

End of today's lesson

5.2 Manuscript Track

Review your story and identify the conflicts you have thrown at your lead. Ask yourself these questions:

- ☑ Are the conflicts varied?
- ☑ Do the conflicts give my lead a chance to shine in his strength?
- ☑ Do the conflicts open past wounds?
- ☑ Are the conflicts tailor-made for my lead's personality, goals, and desires?
- ☑ Are the conflicts important and believable enough to engage my reader's empathy and fear?

Examine one chapter or passage and rewrite one conflict as needed. Discuss your changes with your critique group and listen to their feedback.

Do Try This At Home, Part 1

In this lesson, let's examine one way to create conflict in your protagonist's life. The next lesson covers four more ways.

Use your character's fear. As Vanessa Grant says at the beginning of this chapter, "[T]hrow their worst fears in their faces." Is your character afraid of heights? Construct the plot in such a way that she has to climb a ladder, stand on a roof, or jump from a cliff. Is she afraid of flying? Put her on an airplane. Is she afraid of being ridiculed? Put her in the rain and make her mascara run in front of the person she most wants to impress.

Warning: Plot Spoiler Ahead! Who can forget poor Winston Smith in George Orwell's *1984*? He's being tortured, but in a break in his "treatment" meant to make him "sane," he asks the question everyone wants to know: "What is in Room 101?" His torturer replies, "You know what is in Room 101, Winston. Everyone knows what is in Room 101."

Days of torture later, Winston's torturer adds, "The thing that is in Room 101 is the worst thing in the world."

Then he elaborates further as a guard brings in a wire basket: "The worst thing in the world," said O'Brien, "varies from individual to individual."

O'Brien moves aside so Winston can see his worst fears squirming in the cage: rats. Yes, folks. Rats. Readers know from traveling through the story with Winston that he is afraid of rats. Despite the needles, the electrocutions, the starvation, the sicknesses, the mental mind games and agonies, the apex of his torture is rats in a cage being forced, quite literally, in his face (and onto his head).

So, what's in *your* Room 101?

5.3 All Writers

Write down one of your fears. Then write about how it began or developed. Include incidents where you have had to confront it or ways you have avoided it. Also write about how you feel when confronted with this fear or are made to do the thing you fear most. Don't write "afraid," but write how it affects you physically. How does your body act and react when in the presence of this fear?

Writing about this fear and your reactions to it will help you write more honestly about your character's fear.

End of today's lesson

DO TRY THIS AT HOME, PART 2

Below are four more methods you can use to create conflict in your characters' lives.

Put your character where he doesn't want to be. Think of Jimmy Hawkins kidnapped by the pirate Long John Silver in Robert Louis Stevenson's *Treasure Island*. Think of Tom Hanks' character Chuck Noland ("no land"—get it?) in the movie *Cast Away*, a man who lives by the clock but is now on a deserted, timeless island. And think of lonely Nemo in the movie *Finding Nemo*, who is in a dentist's fish tank far from home. Far from home is a good place for your characters to be.

These examples happen to be undesirable locations, but you can stick your character in undesirable situations too. Johnny Tremain is in a revolution and doesn't want to be (*Johnny Tremain* by Esther Forbes). In *The Princes Bride*, Princess Buttercup is engaged to Prince Humperdink against her will. Devise locations and situations that will trouble your lead.

> I would never write about someone who is not at the end of his rope.
> —Stanley Elkin

Bring someone to town. How many westerns begin with a stranger coming into town? This new character, whether innocently or because he is a snake in cowboy clothing, stirs up a heap o' trouble for the whole town and for specific characters. *The Hobbit* by J. R. R. Tolkien begins this way, with the wizard coming into the shire. So does Jane Austen's *Pride and Prejudice*. So does *Pudd'nhead Wilson* by Mark Twain. So does Sarah Orne Jewett's "A White Heron." And, of course, there's P. L. Travers' Mary Poppins character. And don't forget . . . well, you get the idea.

Send someone out of town. The narrator in Joseph Conrad's *Heart of Darkness* goes on a journey of discovery. Frodo Baggins leaves the shire on a mission in The Lord of the Rings trilogy. Westley leaves Buttercup in *The Princess Bride* so he can make his fortune and become worthy enough to marry her. Pinocchio leaves town ostensibly to have fun and be independent, but it is really to make him wiser. Spaz leaves the Urb on a quest to see his sister before she dies.

Disrupt a routine. When you begin your story by showing a character's interesting or unusual routine, you set up future events that will disrupt the routine. The events you set in motion for your character will knock him off center, and he may spend the rest of the story trying to regain his balance in his new situation. The movie *Matchstick Men* with Nicholas Cage begins this way. Cage's character is a con man, Roy Waller, who suffers from an obsessive-compulsive disorder. To try to deal with life as he knows it, he has developed certain routines, including closing doors three times. You can be sure that, not too far into the movie, his orderly life is going to be disrupted. Richard Adams' *Watership Down* begins with the main characters going about their daily routine of eating together and complaining about the bullies just before their lives are turned upside down.

5.4 All Writers and Discussion

Use one of the above ideas (or one of your choosing) and write a scene of approximately 500 words, immersing a character in trouble. You do not need to develop it into a story at this point or resolve anything. Simply practice putting him off balance. And have fun being mean!

Discussion: Tell the group which method you used to immerse your character into a conflict and how you did it. Comment on the ideas group members used.

End of today's lesson

THIRST

Every character thirsts for something. Read novelist Kurt Vonnegut as he gives his advice on the matter:

> When I used to teach creative writing, I would tell the students to make their characters want something right away—even if it's only a glass of water. Characters paralyzed by the meaninglessness of modern life still have to drink water from time to time.

Your main character has to have a strong desire. This strong desire is going to drive the story. And this strong desire is going to be thwarted during the story, thus creating conflict. The kinds of conflicts your lead encounters depend entirely upon his desire.

What does your lead desire? "Make sure your main character wants something, and make sure somebody is keeping him from getting it," writes Lavonne Mueller, a playwright and author. This is the heart of your conflict. Boy wants girl; boy can't get girl. Girl wants a mother's love; girl can't get a mother's love.

What does Spaz yearn for? He wants to belong. He has no home, no family group. He used to, but he doesn't any more. What is keeping him from his desire? His foster father, his epilepsy, the Bully Bangers, the Enforcers and Masters in Eden, and a host of other forces.

An abstract desire, say, love, should be represented by something concrete like an object or a person. Spaz wants to belong, which is abstract and hard to describe, so Philbrick puts him on a journey to his sister Bean, the concrete embodiment of belonging. J. R. R. Tolkien uses a ring as the concrete representation of power. If your character wants to be respected, choose something solid and concrete to represent that respect. Perhaps she will search for an important archeological artifact or work hard in her new job or try to impress members of her cheerleading squad. Choosing love, happiness, or respect for a desire is vague. Create a specific object or character to visually represent your character's deep desire. Be specific.

> I don't measure a man's success by how high he climbs, but how high he bounces when he hits bottom.
>
> –General George S. Patton

After you have developed your lead's desire, figure out how your lead is going to express this desire. Sure, he has a desire—to become rich, say. But what is his goal? What is his desire going to look like in the story? To work hard? To plan a heist? To con his rich aunt? To create a new company based on his newest invention? To unearth lost Mayan gold?

Make sure your lead's goal is large enough and important enough to carry the story. Les Edgerton, author of *Hooked*, calls this the **story-worthy goal** because it has to pull your character through the whole story.

Of course, your protagonist doesn't have to reach his goal. Sometimes the story is better if he doesn't. For instance, he may not get the money but he gets the girl. Or he finds the treasure but, now wiser, gives it away.

When you know your lead's deepest yearning, you can intelligently devise the right conflicts for him. When you know his goal, you can work to keep him from it by putting obstacles in his way.

One device that leads to greater conflict and depth is to have the character's desire and the goal oppose each other. Frodo Baggins experiences this in The Lord of the Rings trilogy. He wants to be rid of the ring because it is causing all kinds of trouble, but to get rid of the ring, he must journey through Mordor and throw the ring into the fires of Mount Doom—two things he very definitely does not want to do.

Another way to add depth to your character is to load him up with opposing desires, one he is aware of and one deep in his subconscious. This, too, is true of Frodo, who, after chapters and chapters of slogging through places he does not want to be in order to get rid of a ring he does not want to have, he becomes so attached to the ring that he slips it on his finger and cannot throw it into the fire. In fact, his subconscious desire for the ring is so strong that he can only be free of it when Gollum bites off his finger. That's a powerful subconscious desire.

You may find it helpful to state your protagonist's and antagonist's goals in the form of infinitives: to see . . . , to find . . . , and so forth.

WILL NEMO EVER RETURN HOME?

When readers begin stories, they are quick to pick up on the lead's desire and/or goal. They form questions in their minds, and you want them to do this. Will the lead be respected? Will she find her mother? Will Frodo get to Mount Doom in one piece and with the ring? Will Elizabeth Bennet find happiness in the person of Mr. Darcy? Will Pinocchio become a real boy? Will Westley come back for Buttercup?

The question that readers develop as they get into the story is called the **major dramatic question** (MDQ). Everything in your plot will focus on this question. In fact, if something in your story is not related to the MDQ or will not help answer it, consider deleting it, no matter how much you love it.

Readers will react to your story, in part, by how you answer the major dramatic question. If the story begins with "Will he get to know his family and find his place in it?" but ends with "Will he get the girl?" audiences will be confused and disappointed by the story. This happens in the movie *Elizabethtown*, which begins with the first MDQ about the family but answers the second about the girl. Very unsatisfying to audiences. However, if the story begins with "Will Indiana Jones find a more grown-up relationship with his father?" and it is quite clear by the end of the story that Jones does or does not, audiences will have a more fulfilling experience and will not feel cheated.

> The greater the difficulty, the more glory in surmounting it.
> –Epicurus

You may have guessed by now that the answer to the MDQ can be "yes," "no," or "maybe." Even in these seemingly straight answers, there may be deviations. "Yes," Indy finds the Ark of the Covenant but loses it to the government. "Yes," Pinocchio becomes a real boy though not by anything he set out to do. "No,"

Benjamin Franklin Gates does not get to keep the treasure in the movie *National Treasure*, but he gets the girl. And a resounding "no" goes to Ethan Frome, who will never find happiness.

Avoid drawing a rabbit out of your hat near the ending to manufacture a "yes" answer. Groundwork must be laid for the final solution earlier in the story. When *deus ex machina* ("god out of the machinery") is employed, that is, when you use a last-minute coincidence to save your hero, readers feel cheated. Coincidences are frowned upon in fiction. Let your hero battle it out and get himself out of the last and greatest event of his story.

5.5 All Writers and Discussion

Discuss a few books and movies of your choice and determine the lead's desire and goal for each. Also, identify each major dramatic question and how it is answered.

5.6 Manuscript Track

Ponder your story and answer these questions:

- ☑ What is my lead's most burning desire?
- ☑ What concrete object or character represents that desire in my story?
- ☑ Do my character's desire and goal oppose each other?
- ☑ Does my character have a subconscious desire that wars with his conscious one?
- ☑ What is my lead's major dramatic question?
- ☑ Do I effectively answer it by the end of the story?

Make enough copies of your first chapter (or the first section of your short story) for your critique group. Read each others' beginnings and guess what the major dramatic question is in each. If readers have a hard time figuring yours out, rewrite as needed.

DEATH

While most readers want to avoid death in real life, they like reading about it in stories. As suspense writer Dean Koontz writes, "The fear of death and the explicit threat of death lie at the thematic core of nearly every novel."

There are many types of death when you consider that death is a loss of some sort. Of course, there is the physical death but also the death of a dream, of a relationship, a business venture, a reputation, an emotional death brought on by betrayal or grief, and the list goes on.

How many times does Spaz face physical death, either his or someone else's? What about other kinds of death? What about Westley and Buttercup in *The Princess Bride*? Is either of them threatened with death, whether physical, emotional, or otherwise?

Something has to be **at risk** for the protagonist or his choices will mean nothing to him or to the reader. Spaz risks losing his sister, his friend Ryter, a family and place in Eden, and even his life. What is at risk for your character?

5.7 All Writers and Discussion

End of today's lesson

Is Dean Koontz right? Check it out. Discuss various books and movies to find "the fear of death" and "the explicit threat of death," whether physical, emotional, or otherwise.

TENSION

Tension is a kind of nervous energy or excitement, and that's one of the reasons people pick up a book and read it. They want that low-level intensity or an edge-of-the-seat thrill. And you had better give it to them.

Every story will have its unique level of tension based on the characters, the action, and the genre expectations. A short story character sketch contains less tension than an adventure or spy story.

Jessamyn West's "The Buried Leaf," for instance, is about Mattie, a bored teenage Quaker girl in the 1860s in southern Indiana. She is sick of her name, her life, and her family. The action of the story is no more than digging up a page from the Bible a relative had buried long ago. But through dialogue and interaction with her parents and brothers, and through

> The best stories don't come from "good vs. bad" but "good vs. good."
> —Leo Tolstoy

hearing the story of the people who buried the page in the first place, Mattie has a change of heart. The MDQ is "Will Mattie be reconciled to her lot in life?" and the answer is "yes." The tension is low-level. No one bleeds, no one dies, no one even yells. The thematic element of death is expressed in Mattie's relationship with her father: Will that relationship die, or will Mattie forgive her father for being the average Joe he is?

Edgar Alan Poe's "The Tell-Tale Heart," on the other hand, is loaded with tension. The viewpoint character has just killed his neighbor and hidden the body under the flooring. Add a few policemen to the mix, and you have a story with a lot of nervous energy. The character is tense, and the story is too.

How do you create tension in your own stories?

Make it perfectly clear what will happen **if your lead fails**. If Spaz fails in *The Last Book in the Universe*, he risks losing his chance to see Bean, his chance to live with Bean in a family situation, and even his own life. Make sure the risks and the possible failures are plain to readers and meaningful to the lead.

Even though you may begin the story by dropping your lead into the middle of a conflict (*in media res*), your early conflicts will be less torturous for him than the later ones. As the story proceeds, the antagonistic forces will be more powerful. In other words, **escalate** the difficulties the lead encounters. This is covered more fully in the chapter on plot, but for now, keep in mind that conflicts can be graded based on how much they affect the lead.

How much does the event or situation mean to the character? If it means little, your story will have little tension. If it means much, your story will have more tension. When you keep the story centered on the major dramatic question and **how the situation is affecting the character emotionally**, the tension can be acute.

Tension also comes from **jeopardy**. Jeopardy is the idea that your character could suffer pain or loss. He should be in jeopardy of losing the things that mean the most to him. The more the jeopardy (potential physical pain, loss of family, reputation, life), the more important both the antagonist and the lead become in the eyes of the reader. Jeopardy intensifies their size, so to speak, in the story. Of course, if you keep threatening to hurt your character but never do, the story will feel flat. Deliver on some of those threats.

In the movie *The Music Man*, Marian the librarian has the goods on the con man Harold Hill. She knows something about him that could get him into a lot of trouble with the mayor and the townspeople. Even though Hill doesn't know this, the audience knows it and feels the jeopardy he is in. When Marian decides not to divulge the damaging information, along comes a salesman who knows the wily Hill and can get him into deep trouble. And he sets out to do just that. When your character is not in trouble, the reader has to be made to feel that he *could* be in trouble at any minute.

Orson Scott Card, author of *Ender's Game*, suggests in *Characters and Viewpoint* that writers ask these questions about jeopardy:

› Does your character feel jeopardy?
› Does your audience know of the jeopardy, even if the hero doesn't?
› What are the jeopardies your hero faces?

Consider establishing a **time limit**. The "ticking time bomb" is an honored method of adding tension to a story: Characters must defuse the bomb before it blows them up. But other examples abound. Phileas Fogg and his valet Passepartout have to make it around the world in eighty days to win a bet in *Around the World in Eighty Days* by Jules Verne. The slave girl Florens has to find the blacksmith who knows a thing or two about medicine before her mistress dies of small pox in *A Mercy* by Toni Morrison. Kidnappers demand ransom by a certain time or they'll kill the victim. Stranded motorists in the desert must find help before they die of dehydration. This ratchets up the tension for character and reader.

Now would be a good time to mention the **classical unities**, so named because these principles were used in ancient Greek plays:

> **Time:** Many ancient Greek plays had a story time of no more than 24 hours. Likewise, the story times of today are as short as is needed to adequately tell the story. The action in some stories occurs in just a few hours; in others, it takes years. If you have a gap of time that does not contribute to the story or its tension, consider closing the gap and shortening your story.
>
> **Place:** Originally the plays had only one setting. Now we like variety but still prefer our stories to occur in as few places as needed. The mystery genre, for example, prefers most of the action to happen in only a few settings (think of Agatha Christie's *And Then There Were None*, with the bulk of the action on an island).

Action: The old plays contained only one plot. Similarly, we still keep the story focused on the main action with as few subplots as possible. Any subplots should add to the meaning of the main plot, as should all of the story's events.

What do the classical unities have in common? They all put limits on certain story elements. Limits, if used strategically, can add to your story's tension.

Short sentences can add to tension if applied at a critical time. Here's an example of this from Michael Crichton's *The Lost World*:

> Then he heard it clearly—a low rumbling growl, almost a purr. It was coming from beyond the foliage ahead. It sounded like the biggest jungle cat he had ever heard. And intermittently, he felt a slight vibration, hardly anything, but enough to make the car keys clink against the steering column. As he felt that vibration, it slowly dawned on him: It's walking.
> Something very big. Walking.

Or use very **long sentences** at a pivotal moment, as in this example from Ray Bradbury's "I Sing the Body Electric!" We join the action just as Agatha, eleven years old, runs out of the house. Agatha is not physically blind but blind with anger:

> Blind, Agatha made the curb, wheeling about, seeing us close, all of us yelling, Grandma way ahead, shouting, too, and Agatha off the curb and out in the street, halfway to the middle, then in the middle and suddenly a car, which no one saw, erupting its brakes, its horn shrieking and Agatha flailing about to see and Grandma there with her and hurling her aside and down as the car with fantastic energy and verve selected her from our midst, struck our wonderful [grandma] even while she paced upon the air and, hands up to ward off, almost in mild protest, still trying to decide what to say to this bestial machine, over and over she spun and down and away even as the car jolted to a halt and I saw Agatha safe beyond and Grandma, it seemed, still coming down or down and sliding fifty yards away to strike and ricochet and lie strewn and all of us frozen in a line suddenly in the

midst of the street with one scream pulled out of all our throats at the same raw instant.

How many sentences are in that paragraph? Note, too, all the **powerful verbs** that add to the motion and energy of the action.

The **active voice** aids in creating tension:

Passive: Zeke was hidden behind the Dumpster.
Active: Zeke hid behind the Dumpster.

Using the passive voice subtly conveys that the character is not active in his situation but is a victim of his circumstances. Prefer the active voice.

Consider using more than one **viewpoint character** in your novel. From time to time, use a chapter or section to show what the antagonist is up to, from his perspective. When readers see his plans but the protagonist does not, readers fear for the protagonist in jeopardy, and they feel tension from the situation.

Even when characters have the same goal, **put them at odds** with each other. If two characters are tied together and want to escape, make them disagree about their method of escape. Now they are not only struggling against their assailant but also against each other.
All characters, no matter how much they like or love each other, should be at odds with each other at one time or another during the story; the more the better. While this doesn't make a happy life, it can make an exciting story.

Use **dialogue** to create conflict and show tension between characters. Chapter 6 covers this more fully.

Tension benefits from **moments of calm**. If the whole story is full of tense, emotional scenes, your reader will lose interest. Give the story a break so you can ramp up again. A great example of this is when Spaz and his sister Bean are eating apples in the apple trees. The name of the chapter, "When They Come for Us in the Apple Trees," reminds readers of the tension, but it is a back-burner tension because of the relaxed events of the chapter. Readers get a breather—just in time to get on the roller coaster again. Pace yourself.

CHARACTER ARC

You've got conflict. You've got antagonistic forces and tension. You've got subconscious desires and opposing goals. So what?

Well, here's what: Squeezed through the garlic press of antagonistic forces, your lead is going to change. The more the squeeze, the more the possibility for change.

> The real glory is being knocked to your knees and then coming back. That's real glory.
> –Vince Lombardi, coach for which the NFL Super Bowl trophy is named

The amount of change a character experiences from the beginning of his story to the ending is called a **character arc**. It is an imaginary curve that shows how much the character changed. Some character arcs are flat, as with Peter Pan who refuses to grow up. Some have a mild arc, as with young Mattie in "The Buried Leaf." And still others have a rainbow-shaped arc, like Scrooge. When a bow is strung and ready for the arrow, it is under a great amount of tension and has a noticeable arc to it. Something similar may be true of your characters: The more the personal tension and change from the beginning of the story to the ending, the more the character arc.

How much is your character going to change? How is the pressure going to change him or her?

5.8 All Writers and Discussion

On the topic of tension: Read "The Tell-Tale Heart" by Edgar Allan Poe. It can be found at http://www.poemuseum.org/works-telltale.php. Write down three of the tension devices you find there. Share your results with the group.

End of today's lesson

On the topic of character arc: Compare the Spaz you find in the beginning of *The Last Book in the Universe* to the Spaz you find in the end. In what ways has he changed? What made the changes?

5.9 All Writers, Discussion, Critique

The last lesson →

Write a tension-filled scene of about 500 words. Choose three devices you learned in this chapter to create the scene. Write the names of the devices on the back of one of your pages. Bring enough copies for your group. Read and critique.

OPTIONAL WRITING FOR CONFLICT

1. Write a short story that begins with your character far from home. Put him where he doesn't want to be. Will he return? If so, how?

2. Write the beginning of a story to show a character in his or her routine. Make it of interest to the reader. Then write a list of ways to knock him/her off center and disrupt the routine.

What you studied in this chapter:

Being nasty to your characters
The types of conflicts you can throw at your character
Ways to introduce conflict
- The character's fears
- The character where he doesn't want to be
- Someone comes to town
- Someone goes on a journey
- A disrupted routine

The character's strong desires and goals
The MDQ (major dramatic question)
Death and the level of risk
Methods for creating tension
Character arc

6: DIALOGUE

Dialogue (or if you prefer: *dialog*) is simply conversation between characters. You know how to speak. You've heard people talk. So what's the big deal? Why a whole chapter dedicated to dialogue?

"The main purpose of dialogue is to reveal character and to move the story along." So writes Sol Stein, an author himself. Again, so what?

Here's the thing: Dialogue has a job to do.

The following example of dialogue from *A Girl Named Zippy* by Haven Kimmel reveals character. We join Zippy, age 10, as she tries to avoid going to church by "losing" her pink New Testament. What do you learn about Zippy from the words she says? What about her dad?

> . . . Dad reached down under his chair and pulled out my missing Bible.
> "Where did you find that?" I asked, genuinely perplexed.
> "In the bathroom trash can."

"You're kidding! How odd. I must have totally accidentally without even knowing it thrown it away with my old church bulletin last week. How silly of me!"

"Accidents happen," he said, handing it to me.

A side note: Unlike real life where everyone talks at once, dialogue typically occurs between only two characters at a time. Occasionally other characters can be in on the dialogue, too, but new writers are advised to limit dialogue to two characters at a time.

6.1 All Writers

Discussion: Use three words to describe Zippy. What kind of a man is her father?

Find one place in *The Last Book in the Universe* where a character's words reveal something about himself/herself. Discuss with the group.

End of today's lesson

WHAT SHE SAYS, WHAT SHE DOES

You will remember from chapter four on character and characterization the many tools you have at your disposal to reveal characters to readers (what she says, what she thinks, what she wears, and so forth). In this section, we are going to explore more fully the character's words (what she says) and actions (what she does) as they relate to dialogue.

A character may say this:

"I'm going home now."

Those bland words will not help reveal character or the character's emotional state. Readers will gain a better understanding of the character if she says

"I can't wait to get out of here."

or

"You people are nuts. I'm outta here."

Make the **words** inside the quotation marks indicate the state of the speaker.

Avoid using adverbs to show the speaker's state of mind (adverbs underlined below):

"I'm going home now," she said <u>nervously</u>.
"Give me your arm," the nurse said <u>piercingly</u>.
"I've never crashed a plane yet," the pilot said <u>laughingly</u>.

Adverbs tell instead of show, and you want to avoid that.

The **words and syntax** a character uses can reveal much about him. Here is Mr. Myers, who is trying to convince the teenage Alfred (the "Mr. Kropp" below) that Alfred's loser uncle is the man for the job, taken from *The Extraordinary Adventures of Alfred Kropp* by Rick Yancey:

> As I told your uncle, Mr. Kropp, I need someone to retrieve the sword for me. A man of consummate skill and discretion. A man who is incorruptible, untouched by the temptations of evil men. I need someone who is indefatigable, Mr. Kropp. A man who will not give up or falter when all odds are against him. In short, I need someone who will lay down his life to recover a treasure that is beyond any value mortal men may place on it.

Mr. Myers is very formal in his syntax and word choice. He is also being ironic in his little speech because he knows that Alfred's uncle is none of those things. In fact, the uncle is just the opposite. In this way, readers know not to trust Mr. Myers—his words do not match what readers know about the characters.

Make each character sound like himself/herself.

Read your dialogue out loud. This is a reliable way to determine if it sounds natural or stilted.

dialect: words, phrases, and spellings written as they sound, usually indicating an accent, locale, or cultural group

A word about **dialect**: Use it sparingly. Here's an example of dialect from Joel Chandler Harris's "Mr. Fox Is Outdone by Mr. Buzzard," a Brer Rabbit tale:

> Mr. Buzzard flapped his wings and scrambled around right smartly, he did, but it weren't no use. Brer Fox had the advantage of the grip, he did, and he held him right down to the ground. Then Mr. Buzzard squalls out, sezee:
> "Lemme 'lone, Brer Fox. Tu'n me loose," sezee. "Brer Rabbit'll git out. You're gittin' close at 'im," sezee, "en 'lebm mo' licks'll fetch 'im," sezee.

In case you didn't get the words of Mr. Buzzard, here's a translation: "Leave me alone, Brer Fox. Turn me loose," says he. "Brer Rabbit will get out. You're getting close to him," says he, "and eleven more licks [chops of the ax] will fetch him," says he.

Even "Brer" is dialect for "Brother."

Although this dialect is totally appropriate for the narrator to use, it is hard for some readers to interpret. Consider your audience. If they will understand the dialect, use it. If they won't, think about adapting it into a readable style for them. After all, you are writing your story so someone will read it.

In Amy Tan's "Rules of the Game," the nine-year-old chess champion Waverly Jong, living in San Francisco's Chinatown but born of Chinese parents, is clearly embarrassed by her mother. Is her mother's English hard to understand?

> "Aiii-ya. So shame be with mother?" She grasped my hand even tighter as she glared at me.
> I looked down. "It's not that, it's just so obvious. It's just so embarrassing."
> "Embarrass you be my daughter?" Her voice was cracking with anger.

No matter how hard a speaker's words might be to understand in real life, make sure they are quite easy to understand on your story's page, as Tan does with her story. This way the reader is not distracted by the words but stays engaged in your story.

What are the characters doing when they speak? Certainly they aren't standing around looking like cardboard cut-outs of themselves. They move. They gesture. These actions are called **narrative actions** (or **beats**).

An example of narrative actions comes from *Devil on My Heels* by Joyce McDonald, in which we see the maid Delia in action:

> "Delia, let me help."
> She slams the tray on the table so hard one of the cups topples over, spilling coffee. "Help! How you gonna help?" She throws a dishtowel at the tray. Within seconds it's a soggy brown.

How is Delia feeling? If you guessed "angry," you are correct. How do readers know Delia is angry? By her actions woven into the dialogue. The specific verbs are helpful too: "slams" and "throws."

If you strip away the original narrative actions and replace them with others, you can give Delia a different emotional response. Using narrative actions to reveal character can be potent.

Another example of narrative action comes from a student's retelling of the Cinderella story. Notice how Drizelda, her sister (the narrator), and their mother are not simply standing still and talking but are moving and gesturing:

> I looked in my mirror again. I almost started to cry, but Drizelda bustled into the room holding three huge dresses. "Which one should I wear?"
> I let out a fake sneeze so she would not think anything of my watery eyes. When I looked up, I examined the dresses she had laid out carefully on my bed.
> Drizelda turned to me. "What do you think?"
> I pondered the three dresses and pointed to the yellow dress with the tiny pink pastel flowers sprinkled everywhere. "Wear this one."
> Drizelda gave a squeal of delight. "That's the one I wanted to wear too!" She grabbed the gown off the bed and ran back to her room to put it on. I sighed.
> When I was done getting ready, I ran downstairs where mother was waiting. Mother crossed her arms and tapped her foot. "What is she doing?"

I pulled my gloves on using my teeth. "Drizelda? I don't know," I said through my teeth. Just as I answered, a door slammed upstairs and Drizelda emerged. How she had squeezed her form into that narrow space I will never know. She teetered downstairs in the highest heels I had ever seen her wear, and, when she reached the bottom of the staircase, she twirled. "How do I look?"

The narrative actions woven throughout the scene show readers what kind of women these characters are. They also make the characters come alive as readers see them in action.

When you do this in your writing, you draw the curtain back and reveal your characters as though they were on a stage.

Random fact: Most readers enjoy reading dialogue rather than long paragraphs of narrative, and dialogue creates more white space on the page—something readers respond to positively.

6.2 All Writers and Discussion

Write a scene of about 500-750 words in which two characters speak and act. Reveal something—anything—about these characters to your audience. Your two characters can already exist in literature or movies, be made up, or be two people you know. This exercise works best if you choose two characters that are very different from each other. Make them speak. Give them narrative actions (beats).

End of today's lesson

Discussion: Bring enough copies for all members of your discussion group and read each others' work. Then make guesses as to what the writer is trying to reveal about the characters.

6.3 Manuscript Track

Check one passage or chapter of your manuscript and ask yourself these questions:

☑ Have I used my characters' words and syntax to reveal their personalities?
☑ If I have used any dialect, is it easy for the reader to understand?
☑ Have I used narrative actions or beats with my dialogue to show emotion, action, or personality?

CONFLICT—CAN'T GET ENOUGH OF IT!

Dialogue reveals character. It moves the plot along. And, according to Jerry B. Jenkins, co-author of the Left Behind series, it also does this:

> Almost every conversation in a novel should be an argument, or reveal deceit, or show tension.

Does he take his own advice? Let's look at a passage of dialogue in *Nicolae*, one of the Left Behind books. In this scene, Leon Fortunato has just informed the plane's pilot, Rayford Steele, to get ready to fly again. Steele tells Fortunato it is against international aviation rules for him to fly again within twenty-four hours, but Fortunato isn't having any of it:

> If you want to get to know your characters better, ask yourself: "How would they behave in a quarrel?"
> –Barnaby Conrad

"Nonsense," Fortunato said. "How do you feel?"
"Exhausted."
"Nevertheless, you're the only one qualified to fly this plane, and you'll be flying it when we say you'll be flying it."
"So international aviation rules go out the window?"
"Steele, you know that international rules on everything are embodied in that man sitting on that plane. When he wants to go to New Babylon, you'll fly him to New Babylon. Understood?"
"And if I refuse?"
"Don't be silly."

How did Jenkins do?

Fortunato asks Steele, "How do you feel?" and Steele gives a **direct answer**: "Exhausted."

Later, Steele asks of Fortunato, "And if I refuse?" and Fortunato, instead of telling Steele what will happen if he refuses, gives an **indirect answer**: "Don't be silly."

Much of movie dialogue is indirect. It can add to tension and keep the dialogue from being boring. In fact, studying movie dialogue can be helpful when writing your own stories.

Incidentally, if you want to have a philosophical discussion in your story, try weaving it into a scene of tension or when the characters don't know they are in jeopardy but the readers do. What better time is there to make two characters discuss their ideas about life than when they are careening down a steep hill in a little red wagon headed toward the cliff? Bill Watterson does this often in the comic strip *Calvin and Hobbes*. If Calvin simply talked to his stuffed friend Hobbes while playing with blocks on the floor, no one would read the strip. The dangerous action layers the discussion with more meaning.

In Disney's *Tangled*, Flynn Rider and Rapunzel share their secrets only when they face death by being drowned in a watery cave. Because of the danger, their secrets take on a special meaning.

For the most part, though, you will let the story's events and the characters' actions and choices make the philosophical point for you.

6.4 All Writers

Write a scene of approximately 500 words in which two characters want the same thing. It can be a job, a boyfriend, a pair of shoes, the last spot on the basketball team—anything. You need not resolve the issue. Simply write what happens between the two.

Discussion: Read your scene to the group. Comment helpfully on how the other members handled their conflict.

End of today's lesson

SUBTEXT

There's a rich life lying just below the characters' words. Often characters—and people in real life—don't say what they really mean. When Chase Tully, a character in Joyce McDonald's *Devil on My Heels*, tells the main character Dove, "You make me crazy," he is really saying, "I love you." Dove knows this and, after Chase drives off, responds with "I love you too."

The following example of subtext comes from Lemony Snicket's *The Slippery Slope*. Two of the three siblings, who lost their parents in a freak house fire, are trying to decide if they should dig a pit in which to trap one of their antagonists, Esmé Squalor:

> Violet reached her hand down to the ground. The dirt was very cold, but quite loose, and she saw that they could dig a pit without too much trouble. "Is this the right thing to do?" Violet asked. "Do you think this is what our parents would do?"
>
> "Our parents aren't here," Klaus said. "They might have been here once, but they're not here now."

The subtext of Klaus's response may be something like this: "I'm angry because we have to make this important decision alone, and we'll probably choose something our parents would not approve of."

The next example of subtext comes from Tony Earley's *The Blue Star*, the story of Jim, a high school senior in North Carolina during World War II, who might be in love—or very strong like—with Crissie. In this passage, Jim and Crissie have found an abandoned house and pretend they are two old people:

> "Old man," she said, "I can't believe you ate all the walnuts."
> Jim blinked rapidly, then smiled. Once again he felt sunshine pouring out of his mouth. "Old woman," he said in a gruff voice, "I didn't eat *all* the walnuts. I just ate *most* of the walnuts."
> "You didn't leave me enough to make a cake."
> "Well, I don't know what you expect me to do about it now. You know I flat love walnuts."

Subtext: It's not about the walnuts; it's about the relationship and the two of them trying out what it would be like to be an old, married couple.

BEWARE

Dialogue is not real conversation. If it were, you would bore your readers to death:

"Hey, Jackie, I haven't seen you in a while. What have you been doing?"
"Nothing much. I had the flu."
"The stomach kind or the sore throat kind?"
"Neither. I just had a fever for three days and couldn't get out of bed. You know, aches all over. I couldn't even eat."
"You look like you've lost some weight."
"My mom made chicken soup. Had to sip it through a straw."

And on and on, *ad nauseum*. Who cares? Use your new dialogue tools to give meaning to the interchange.

One thing that is true for both real conversations and made-up dialogue: People rarely use each others' names in conversations, and writers rarely use character names in dialogue. Here's how NOT to do it:

"I say, Holmes, hadn't you better take her case?" said I.
"Watson, I can't think of a more boring case," said Holmes.
"But, Holmes, she's the duke's daughter."
"Watson, I deduced as much. Her left earlobe was very instructive, wouldn't you say, Watson?"
"I can't say as I noticed her left earlobe, Holmes. I was more interested in her auburn hair."
"Watson, that is exactly why you will never be the detective I am."

You get the idea. Listen to people talk. Hear how many times they use—or do not use—their names in the conversation.

Dialogue is the *illusion* of real conversation. Writers streamline their dialogue and make it *do* something in the story: reveal character, move the plot, and show argument, tension, and deceit.

EXPOSITION

It's tempting to cram **exposition** into your dialogue.

Some technical information or backstory (something that happened before your story begins) may be unavoidable. Here's a sample of necessary exposition between a mother and her seven-year-old daughter, taken from Michael Crichton's *Airframe*. The first speaker is the daughter:

> **exposition:** explaining, telling, or teaching something

> "What's quart?"
> "Quart? It's a measure of liquid."
> "No, Mom, *Qua-urt*," she said.
> Casey looked over and saw that her daughter had picked up her new laminated plant ID badge, which had Casey's picture, and beneath that C. SINGLETON and then in large blue letters, QA/IRT.
> "What's *Qua-urt*?"
> "It's my new job at the plant. I'm the Quality Assurance rep on the Incident Review Team."

Here readers learn some abbreviations that Crichton will use often in the story, so it's important to get them in early.

Whenever possible, put the exposition and backstory into a context to keep it from being boring, as when Spaz, in *The Last Book in the Universe*, says he used to belong to a family unit but doesn't want to talk about it now. It makes readers curious.

Here's an example of how NOT to use exposition:

> "I love that skirt!"
> "What? Do you mean this green one with the pink flowers?"
> "Yes. I love the wide shirring on the band. You know shirring is another word for lots of little gathers made in parallel lines by using elastic thread in the bobbin."

Yuk! What awful dialogue! Don't let it happen to you.

Dole out the information piece by piece, at the point where the reader needs it. And try to **interrupt it** with other characters or with action. Using a combative character can be helpful during exposition, as shown in this passage from the Christian suspense novel *Night Light* by Terri Blackstock. Kit Arboghast, the mayor, is explaining why nothing of an electrical nature is working during an earth-wide calamity:

> "First of all, the government has been able to conclusively determine that this event, which they're calling the Pulses, is global and is caused by a pulsar, which is a rotating neutron star. This pulsar was created from a supernova that occurred in 1999."
>
> "Speak English," someone yelled. "I don't know a supernova from super*man*."

The technical information the mayor reveals could be boring to the reader because of its content and because it stops the forward motion of the plot. But Blackstock intersperses the exposition with shouts from the town members gathered to hear the mayor. The interruptions, in this case, are questions readers might also be asking and so might keep the readers' interest.

Aldous Huxley uses a similar strategy when the Warden of the Savage Reservation lists facts about the reservation to Bernard and Lenina (and readers) in *Brave New World*. About the time the Warden mentions the "current from the Grand Canyon hydroelectric station," Bernard remembers that he left a tap turned on at home in London; he obsesses about it throughout the rest of the recitation, calculating how much it is costing him. Huxley alternates the Warden's dialogue with Bernard's troubled thoughts.

Generally, most authors prefer to keep exposition out of their dialogue by folding it cleverly into the narrative.

6.5 All Writers

Choose a scene from a movie and transcribe it. That is, write down all the dialogue and the narrative action.

Then determine the dialogue's purpose in the story. Is it there to reveal character? To advance the plot? To argue, deceive, or to create tension? Write the

Chapter 6: Dialogue   121

End of today's lesson

dialogue's purpose and how the writers accomplished it.

What is the subtext? In other words, what are the characters *really* saying?

6.6 All Writers

New lesson →

Insert the correct punctuation (commas and quotation marks) for the sentences below. Write them by hand or type them onto a computer and print them out to hand them in. If needed, study the dialogue in *The Last Book in the Universe* to see how Philbrick does it.

1. Jane, I don't love you anymore   said Tarzan.
2. You were always more interested in your stupid elephants   said Jane   than you were in me.
3. Tarzan said   I find their conversation more interesting.
4. I'm going back to my mother in England   said Jane. I'm taking my leopard-skin outfit with me.
5. And I   said Tarzan   am keeping the tree house. There are plenty of baboons who will be glad to share it with me.

OTHER FORMATS FOR DIALOGUE

Let's look at a few unconventional ways published writers have written their dialogue. Here's Florens, the first-person narrator and young, black slave girl in Toni Morrison's *A Mercy*:

Soon as I knock a woman opens the door. She is much taller than Mistress or Lina and has green eyes. The rest of her is a brown frock and a white cap. Red hair edges it. She is suspicious and holds up her hand, palm out, as though I might force my way in. Who hath sent you she asks. I say please. I say I am alone. No one sends me. Shelter calls me here. She looks behind me left and right and asks if I have no protection, no companion? I say No Madam. She narrows her eyes and asks if I am of this earth or elsewhere? Her face is hard. I say this earth Madam I know no other. Christian or heathen, she asks. Never heathen, I say. I say although I hear my father may be. And where doth he abide, she asks. The rain is getting bigger. Hunger wobbles me. I say I do not know him and my mother is dead. Her face softens and she nods saying, orphan, step in.

How does Morrison's method affect you? What might it do for the reader? What do Florens' words and Morrison's format reveal about Florens?

Cormac McCarthy uses no punctuation marks in dialogue in *The Road*, and sometimes he doesn't even use apostrophes in contractions. In this passage, the unnamed lead, who is the boy's father, has just sewn his leg up after being shot with homemade arrows. The lack of apostrophes is normal in the original text:

> That hurt, didnt it, the boy said.
>   Yes, it did.
>   Are you real brave?
>   Just medium.
>   What's the bravest thing you ever did?
>   He spat into the road a bloody phlegm. Getting up this morning, he said.

And here's yet another example of unconventional dialogue mechanics, this time from Terry Pratchett's fantasy *Reaper Man*. In this passage, Death, who has been laid off and now calls himself Bill Door, has found a new employer and is working as a farmhand for Miss Flitworth. He and Miss Flitworth are visiting in her formal parlor where he is having trouble dealing with an obnoxious owl clock and the concept of time. Even though his words are in caps, he is not yelling:

> DO YOU MIND IF I STOP THE CLOCK?
>   She clanked up at the boggle-eyed owl.
>   "What? Oh. Why?"
>   I AM AFRAID IT GETS ON MY NERVES.
>   "It's not very loud, is it?"
>   Bill Door wanted to say that every tick was like the hammering of iron clubs on bronze pillars.

No matter what method you choose for your dialogue mechanics and punctuation, make it appropriate for your story and keep it consistent.

Everything about dialogue—even the mechanics and format—should be used to reveal character, move the story forward, or create tension.

SPEAKERS, PARAGRAPHS, AND TAGS

When characters speak, they get their own paragraphs. Here are the bird Darzee and the mongoose Rikki-tikki-tavi in Rudyard Kipling's "Rikki-tikki-tavi" as they talk about their enemies, some local snakes (Nag and Nagaina). We join them just as Rikki-tikki-tavi asks Darzee to quit singing:

> "For the great, the beautiful Rikki-tiki's sake I will stop," said Darzee. "What is it, O Killer of the terrible Nag!"
> "Where is Nagaina, for the third time?"
> "On the rubbish-heap by the stables, mourning for Nag. Great is Rikki-tikki with the white teeth."
> "Bother my white teeth! Have you ever heard where she keeps her eggs?"
> "In the melon-bed, on the end nearest the wall, where the sun strikes nearly all day. She had them there weeks ago."

Each character speaks in his own paragraph. Only rarely will two speakers appear in the same paragraph.

Notice, too, that "Rikki-tikki said" and "Darzee said" are not needed in each case because the rhythm of who is speaking and their word choices indicate who is speaking. When each character's voice is clear, you will need only occasional **speaker tags**.

The "he said" and "she said" of dialogue are called speaker tags. Writers today keep them very simple, usually with the word "said," even when someone asks a question. No more "he murmured," "he sputtered," or "she complained." Those are considered *telling*—and you want to *show*. "Said" is invisible and, therefore, preferred today.

One other thing you may want to watch is this: When a paragraph ends with the narrative action of one character, readers expect the next dialogue to belong to that character, as in this example from Rudyard Kipling's "The Undertakers." The Jackal is a jackal; the Adjutant is a crane; and the Mugger is a crocodile. They are talking about what sort of animal the train's engine might be:

The Jackal had watched it time and again from the aloe hedges by the side of the line, and the Adjutant had seen engines since the first locomotive ran in India. But the Mugger had only looked up at the thing from below, where the brass dome seemed rather like a bullock's hump.

"M–yes, a new kind of bullock," the Mugger repeated ponderously, to make himself quite sure in his own mind.

If you occasionally do not use this pattern of narrative action-to-dialogue when moving from one paragraph to the next, make sure readers know quickly who the subsequent speaker is.

As mentioned earlier in this chapter, **avoid adverbs** in your speaker tags (adverbs underlined below):

"I must leave," she said hurriedly.
"But you've only just arrived," he said worriedly.
"I know, Percival, but think of the danger," she said fearfully.
"Penelope, I can protect you," he said manfully.

Adverbs in speaker tags were common years ago, but writers and editors frown on them today.

If you want to show someone in a worried state, make him do something like wrinkle his eyebrows or pick at the invisible lint on his shirt or frown at a passing cat. Narrative actions such as these say much more than "worriedly" can. Figurative language may also help at this point: " . . . he said in a voice that sounded like knuckles cracking." Use the tools at your disposal to make the scene as real as possible—without the adverb.

INDIRECT DIALOGUE

Occasionally you need to sum up a character's dialogue instead of writing it out in a he said/she said fashion. Summing up dialogue is called **indirect dialogue**. This is not to be confused with *indirect answers*, in which one character will not give a direct answer to another.

Direct dialogue is enclosed in quotation marks and looks like this:

"You know I hate it when you gargle," she said.

Indirect dialogue has no quotation marks and looks like this:

She told him she hated it when he gargled.

Indirect dialogue is simply reporting what someone said, and it comes in handy when readers already know the information or when the information appeared earlier in direct dialogue. No need to go over the same ground twice.

6.7 All Writers and Discussion

Use the "raw dialogue" sentences below as the basis for a scene in which neither character is listening to the other. It is between a ten-year old and an adult. Add these items:

› character names,
› speaker tags, and
› narrative actions.

Remove any exposition from the dialogue and put it somewhere in the narrative (like maybe in the narrative actions) or in descriptions.

Discussion: Read your version aloud to the group and listen to other members' versions. The variety will be astounding and instructive.

The raw dialogue:

"I found this stray cat. See? She's black and white with long fur."
"I see."
"Look here. She has, like, a sore behind her ear and her ear is cut off. It's just gone. She was probably in a fight."
"It's a he."
"How much would it cost to have her put down? I mean, she keeps coming around and I feel sorry for her, but she's, like, hurt and she needs to be put down."

"Just let him go. He's a stray. He'll come and go. Maybe he'll go home."

"I, like, feed her every day. She needs food. She's a stray. And at night, I, like, put her in this cage."

"He'll never go home if you keep feeding him and putting him in that blue animal cage every night."

"Did you, like, just hear her? She likes me. She just meowed."

"You're holding him too tightly. He wants to get down."

"I don't mind, like, paying to get her put down. Do I have to pay extra if they bury her? I could just bring her back here and bury her in our yard."

> **End of today's lesson**

OPTIONAL WRITING FOR DIALOGUE:

1. Find one small passage of dialogue with narrative action in a novel or short story. Save all the dialogue but remove all the narrative action. Use the remaining dialogue as a skeleton and put new meat on its bones by adding different narrative action (beats). In this way, you will create a scene showing a new emotion or a new interaction between characters.

2. You find a toy that talks. What five sentences does it say?

3. Someone gives your character a stuffed dog that has an internal recorder. What will your character say into it to play back later? For whom will he/she play it?

4. Your lead has just been wrongly accused. Write the dialogue that follows this accusation.

5. When you find a passage of dialogue you really like, copy it out and be the detective. Find out why you like it and what makes it tick.

6. Turn the volume off when you watch a scene in a movie with which you are unfamiliar. Then write what you think the characters are saying.

Chapter 6: Dialogue

> ## What you studied in this chapter:
>
> - ✓ Dialogue to reveal character, advance plot, create tension
> - ✓ Characters sounding like themselves
> - ✓ Narrative actions or beats
> - ✓ Subtext
> - ✓ What to avoid
> - ✓ Use of exposition in dialogue
> - ✓ Mechanics of dialogue and unusual formats
> - ✓ Speakers, paragraphs, and tags
> - ✓ Indirect dialogue

7: DESCRIPTION

Hansel and Gretel, two abandoned children, are wandering in the dark woods when they realize their trail of breadcrumbs, meant to lead them back to safety, has been eaten by the woodland creatures. They are alone. They are friendless. They are hungry.

And then, as if by magic, they see a cottage standing before them in a clearing. Studded with candy and other edibles, it looks appealing, and the children approach.

The old woman who lives there invites them in. Hansel and Gretel enter and are glad to have food and a safe home, but soon they realize their folly. The old woman is really a witch who imprisons Hansel and forces Gretel to feed the caged Hansel in order to fatten him up for the witch's dinner.

The day comes for Hansel to be cooked, so the witch orders Gretel to make ready the oven. But Gretel tricks the witch, pushes her into the oven, and rescues her brother. The brother and sister then rush from the little cottage that once looked so inviting.

"Great story," you say. "A little gruesome, but interesting. Now what?"

Here's the point: It is the writer's job to describe the cottage to readers as Hansel and Gretel first see it in all its delicious glory. Then it is the writer's job to describe how it looks in all its horror to those two escaping siblings who have been terrorized for weeks behind its doors. Same cottage. Same clearing. Same brother and sister. But are they really the same? No. Their experience has changed them. They see the cottage for what it is, and they know its dark secrets. The things they will notice about the cottage, both going in and coming out, will not be the same.

Writers create a **dominant impression** with their descriptions. The cottage's dominant impression at the beginning of the Hansel and Gretel tale is that of safety, perhaps even safety mixed with a subtle hint of danger, something that Hansel and Gretel ignore in their extreme hunger. The second glimpse of the cottage might give readers a sense of horror or shock as Hansel and Gretel have narrowly missed being eaten.

By creating a dominant impression, you not only keep your descriptions from being boring but also give readers an idea of a mood, feeling, or even a sense of **foreboding** (a feeling that things will not go well).

In *The Scarlet Letter*, Nathaniel Hawthorne uses a dark patch of woods to give a sense of foreboding—in this case, an idea that things may not go well for those who meet there. He describes the forest as "primeval" and "black and dense" with a "gleam of flickering sunshine" that

> might now and then be seen at its solitary play along the path. This flitting cheerfulness was always at the further extremity of some long vista through the forest.

In other words, happiness will always be just out of their reach. We expect trouble.

Brother Odd by Dean R. Koontz gives an example of how to weave foreboding and jeopardy into a scene by picking out one important detail. First the viewpoint character reports this as he feels threatened by the characters in the room:

> On the mahogany floor lay a Persian-style carpet. In the figured world of wool between my feet, a dragon twisted, glaring.

After some dialogue with those characters, he refers to the dragon in the carpet again:

> I didn't like the arrogant expression of the dragon in the woven wool, or the way bright threads lent violence to its eyes. I shifted my left foot to cover its face.

More dialogue, and then this:

> I half believed I could feel the carpet dragon squirming under my foot.

The menacing dragon is, quite literally, woven into the rug *and* the scene.

Dominant impressions do not have to be foreboding. Paul Fleischman uses his tools to paint a negative picture of Christianity in his book *Whirligig*. Each time Christianity is brought up in this interesting book, it is coupled with a negative connotation: (1) The victim's mother speaks negatively about an Old Testament law, (2) a sidewalk preacher shouts a negative verse at young Brent, the protagonist, (3) when Brent leaves a personal note for the maid, another maid writes back, "No one's alone with Jesus," by which Brent feels slapped rather than comforted, and (4) two churches are reported as "glaring" at each other. Any of these items alone might not make an impact, but all of them combine to build a negative dominant impression. While you are learning to be a skilled writer, also become a discerning reader.

So far, we've looked at foreboding, threatening, and negative dominant impressions. While "dark" is easier to write about than "happy," you have a wide variety of dominant impressions for which to aim. How about a hardware store being described in terms of a jungle—without ever using the word "jungle"? Here's H. G. Wells in "La Belle Dame Sans Merci," writing humorously about a piano piece being played badly next door. Watch as he creates the image of a storm at sea:

> The noises that come through the wall now, quicker, thicker, louder, are full of a tale of weltering confusion, marine disaster, a ship in sore labor; there is a steady beating like the sound of pumps, and a trickle of treble notes. There are black silences, like thunderclouds, that burst into flashes of music. Now the poor melody swings up into the air—

then comes down into the abyss. A crash, an ineffectual beating, a spasmodic rush. I seem to hear the pumps again, distant, remote, ineffectual. But that is not so; the struggle is over. Chopin's Study has been battered to pieces; only disarticulated fragments toss amid the froth.

All of his verbs, nouns, figurative language, and images revolve around this unfortunate storm. Choose the details your story needs, and begin painting.

As you choose what to include in your descriptions, think of William H. Strunk's advice: "The greatest writers are effective largely because they deal in particulars and report the details that matter."

Flannery O'Connor adds this: "Detail has to be controlled by some overall purpose, and every detail has to be put to work for you. Art is selective."

What is the overall purpose of any description you write? Select each detail with care. Be intentional.

7.1 All Writers and Discussion

Create a list of things to include in a description of the first glimpse Hansel and Gretel have of the witch's cottage. Because of their great hunger and need, make it seem inviting to them but include a hint of danger, as did Nathaniel Hawthorne in *The Scarlet Letter*.

Then create a list of things to include in a description of the cottage as Hansel and Gretel turn back to look at it one more time before they run for their lives. You may want to do this assignment in teams and then compare your lists.

End of today's lesson

Discussion: Discuss your lists with others in your group. Do you agree with their ideas?

DESCRIPTION HAS A JOB TO DO

Writers used to be able to go on and on in rapturous descriptive delight about a landscape or person, but today's readers and editors do not appreciate this. Long, effusive descriptions tend to bore the reader and stop the forward movement of the story. They are unwanted pit stops that many readers—including you?—skip.

Descriptions today are more focused on certain goals. Use them to

> › **Create a mood or a sense of foreboding** (as you practiced in the "Hansel and Gretel" assignment)
> › **Foreshadow events** (giving clues about what will happen later in the story)
> › **Characterize** (as you practiced in the chapter on characters and characterization)
> › **Reveal setting** (as you will practice later in this chapter)

In fact, make your descriptions do double duty. Make them do two things at once. For instance, you may want to describe a setting to readers to show where the characters are while immersing readers in a certain mood.

C. S. Lewis shows how to make a description do two things at once. In *That Hideous Strength*, he describes the changed town and promotes a feeling of peril for the lead Mark, who is looking for his wife. The N.I.C.E. soldiers are working for Lord Feverstone, someone who is anything but "nice":

> The whole town wore a new expression. One house out of three was empty. About half the shops had their windows boarded up. As he gained height and came into the region of large villas with gardens, he noticed that many of these had been requisitioned and bore white placards with the N.I.C.E. symbol—a muscular male nude grasping a thunderbolt. At every corner, and often in between, lounged or sauntered the N.I.C.E. police, helmeted, swinging their clubs, with revolvers in holsters on their black shiny belts. Their round, white faces with open mouths slowly revolving as they chewed gum remained long in his memory. There were also notices everywhere which he did not stop to read: they were headed *Emergency Regulations* and bore the signature, Feverstone.

Lewis describes the men and their effect on Mark.

Don't worry about your descriptions doing double duty when you write your first draft. Just get down what you want to get down without any mind-bending contortions. Then go back later and add specific items and details that will give subtle nuances to your description.

DESCRIPTION TOOLS

You have a wide variety of tools to use when writing the description of a person, place, or thing. This section of the course is longish not because you will use long descriptions but because there are so many little bits and pieces to it. Below is a list, which will be explored in detail after the list:

1. Sensory details
2. Figurative language
3. Organic imagery
4. Precise and vivid verbs
5. Direction
6. Weather
7. Time
8. Animals/nature
9. Show, don't tell
10. Specificity
11. Character reaction
12. Synesthesia
13. What to avoid

All right. Let's get started on that list.

1. SENSORY DETAILS

You experience life through your senses. How does the kitchen smell when someone is baking? What does the car's metal feel like when you run your hand over the hood? What does a gym shoe sound like during a basketball game, and how do you react when you hear it?

We turn to Flannery O'Connor again for some good advice:

Fiction operates through the senses . . . . The first and most obvious characteristic of fiction is that it deals with reality through what can be seen, heard, smelt, tasted, and touched.

Our senses affect us greatly—and we learn through them: Eat the cinnamon roll, walk around the dead skunk.

Using sensory imagery in your writing will put your reader in the scene. She'll be there with the character, sensing what he's sensing. What kind of senses are we talking about?

> **Tactile imagery**—Touch/Feel. How does it feel when you touch it or when it touches you?
> **Auditory imagery**—Sound. What does it sound like?
> **Olfactory imagery**—Smell. What does it smell like?
> **Visual imagery**—Sight. What does it look like?
> **Gustatory imagery**—Taste. What does it taste like?
> **Thermal imagery**—Hot and cold. What is its temperature?
> **Kinetic imagery**—Movement. What is its movement like?
> **Kinesthetic imagery**—Body sensations. How does your stomach feel when you are shooting down a roller coaster?

✳ **Tactile** imagery example from Sue Monk Kidd's *The Secret Life of Bees*, in which we find young Lily kneeling on dry, uncooked instant grits as a punishment:

> I'd been kneeling on grits since I was six, but still I never got used to that powdered-glass feeling beneath my skin.

✳ **Auditory** imagery examples:

> The moon is high in the sky, full and bright, and if it could make a sound, it would sound like moths in a lantern trying to get out. (Margaret McMullan's *When I Crossed No-Bob*)

> [The goose] was so low to the ground that we heard the whistle of its wings over the sound of the engine. And before we were even through jumping in our seats, the air around us exploded with honking geese, so close and flying so fast that they seemed in danger of crashing into the truck. Their rising shouts and the rushing sound of their wings, coming on us so suddenly, were as loud and frightening as unexpected gunshots, and as strange to our ears as ancient tongues. (Tony Earley's "Aliceville" in *Here We Are in Paradise*)

✱ **Olfactory** (and **thermal**) imagery example from *Out of the Dust,* written in blank verse by Karen Hesse:

> On Sunday,
> winds came,
> bringing a red dust
> like prairie fire,
> hot and peppery,
> searing the inside of my nose,
> the whites of my eyes.

✱ **Visual** imagery example from *Lost Horizon* by James Hilton:

> Then the whole range, much nearer now, paled into fresh splendor; a full moon rose, touching each peak in succession like some celestial lamp-lighter, until the long horizon glittered against a blue-black sky.

Visual imagery can include **colors**, which add to the mood of any description. Cormac McCarthy's *The Road* includes only dull, lifeless colors like "gray," "metallic," or "ashy." This preponderance of non-colors is part of the book's mood.

✱ Two **gustatory** imagery examples from Sung J. Woo's *Everything Asian*:

> Seawater rushed into my mouth and I spit out the salty contents, only to have more if it funnel back in.

> His teeth felt tingly and tight, and no matter how much coffee he drank, he couldn't get rid of the metallic taste in his mouth, as if he'd been sucking on a roll of nickels.

In these examples, you have the gustatory imagery of the "salty contents" and the "metallic taste," and you also get the kinesthetic imagery of his "tingly and tight" teeth. A two-for-one special.

✱ **Thermal** imagery example from *Lost in Rooville* by Ray Blackston, where the narrator is on the verge of popping the question:

I climbed out from the passenger seat of our orange Land Cruiser, only to be scolded by the Aussie sun as I stretched my back. Out here, in a matter of minutes a person could feel crispy like a French fry or dry roasted like a peanut, although in my ring-obsessed state of mind I could not be sure, just that you'd be some sort of snack food and very hot.

✷ **Kinetic** imagery example from F. Scott Fitzgerald's *The Great Gatsby*:

> Their house was even more elaborate than I expected, a cheerful red-and-white Georgian Colonial mansion, overlooking the bay. The lawn started at the beach and ran toward the front door for a quarter of a mile, jumping over sun-dials and brick walks and burning gardens—finally when it reached the house drifting up the side in bright vines as though from the momentum of its run.

Watch the verbs. What is moving in this passage?

✷ **Kinesthetic** imagery example:

> My stomach is churning like an old washing machine. (Joyce McDonald's *Devil on My Heels*)

Again, don't worry about putting all these images into your first draft. When you go back and see what you have written, add sensory details that make your scenes come alive. Make them as physical as possible, and try layering two or three senses into a scene.

7.2 All Writers

Write a bland paragraph or two about a zoo (real or imagined). Use only 100-200 words.

When you have finished, think about the dominant impression you want to create and then add at least two sensory images to support that impression.

Keep your zoo paragraph handy because you will be using it for many of the next assignments.

End of today's lesson

2. FIGURATIVE LANGUAGE

Description Tools
1. Sensory details
2. Figurative language
3. Organic imagery
4. Precise and vivid verbs
5. Direction
6. Weather
7. Time
8. Animals/nature
9. Show, don't tell
10. Specificity
11. Character reaction
12. Synesthesia
13. What to avoid

Figurative language is a rich mine in which you can dig for hidden treasures. It removes the literal and substitutes an image in its place, sometimes through the use of similes, metaphors, hyperbole, and personification. The following are some examples.

➤ **Simile:** [SIM a lee] using "like" or "as" to compare one thing to another

Molly's own face closed like a castle against him, trundling out the guns and slings and caldrons of boiling lead. (*The Last Unicorn* by Peter S. Beagle)

> A simile must be as precise as a slide rule and as natural as the smell of dill.
> —Isaak Babel

Captain Scratch ripped open the buttons of his greatcoat and squeezed the rain out of his flaming beard as if he were wringing a chicken's neck. (*The Ghost in the Noonday Sun* by Sid Fleischman)

➤ **Metaphor:** [MET a fore] comparing one thing to another but without the "like" or "as"

The unicorn made the soft sound again, and the castle of Molly's face lowered the drawbridge and threw wide even its deepest keep. (*The Last Unicorn* by Peter S. Beagle)

➤ **Hyperbole:** [hi PER bo lee] exaggeration. The fellow in this passage has just been shot:

The dark guy took a week to fall down. He stumbled, caught himself, waved one arm, stumbled again. His hat fell off, and then he hit the floor with his face. After he hit it he might have been poured concrete for all the fuss he made. ("Red Wind" by Raymond Chandler)

➤ **Personification:** [per Sahn if a CAY shun] giving human attributes to something not human

> Like the ugly ghosts of trees that had died, the Joshuas writhed in agony, casting deformed, appealing arms aloft. (*The Chinese Parrot* by Earl Derr Biggers)
>
> She looked down at her shoes—her green shoes with the sky-blue linings. And the shoes looked back up at her. *You've done it, Boss*, said the shoes. *Don't expect us to carry you all around town looking for another man. You had one and now you don't. Bad luck, Boss. Bad luck.* (*Blue Shoes and Happiness* by Alexander McCall Smith)

No matter what figurative device you use, paint word pictures for your readers, as Ray Blackston does in the Christian novel *Flabbergasted*:

> Life without cable, VCRs, and paved roads required adjustment, but the pace invigorated the soul. I had always pictured myself living on the face of a huge clock, running just ahead of the second hand that would slam me in the butt every time I tried to slow down. But in Ecuador I felt like I was being pulled along by the minute hand, slow and steady, with enough leisure to enjoy circumference, the arc of the day.

And later:

> Now, finally, I understood the difference between tick and tock. Tick flips from the end of the tongue like something fast and hurried, as something instant, surfacy, and shallow. Tock comes from a deeper place; it's a bass note, or at least a tenor. Tocks move more slowly. If there were a tocking time bomb, I would not run out of the building, but rather stroll through the lobby, order a café mocha, check the sports page for standings in the American League East, then hold the door open as a good Southerner should.

7.3 All Writers

End of today's lesson

Retrieve your zoo description and add a simile, metaphor, hyperbole, personification, or other figurative language to support the dominant impression you are trying to create.

3. ORGANIC IMAGERY

Description Tools
1. Sensory details
2. Figurative language
3. Organic imagery
4. Precise and vivid verbs
5. Direction
6. Weather
7. Time
8. Animals/nature
9. Show, don't tell
10. Specificity
11. Character reaction
12. Synesthesia
13. What to avoid

When you add sensory images and figurative language to your story, devise imagery that is **organic.** Organic imagery is imagery that grows naturally from your story.

First, the <u>wrong</u> way to do it: A story that takes place on an 1800s Canadian prairie describes stars twinkling like neon lights. Not only are neon lights anachronistic (not in the right time period) but they also do not flow out of the 1800s or the prairie.

Now, the <u>right</u>: Joanne Harris's *Five Quarters of the Orange* deals with a woman who loves to cook. Notice the natural organic imagery (and the many kinds of figurative language) that comes out of this love:

Simile	I noticed that age had shrunk him; had softly sunk him into himself, like a failed soufflé.
Metaphor	Everything swallowed up into a great hungry throat of darkness.
Kinesthetic imagery	A bright comet's tail of sensation, prickling at my armpits and flipping my stomach like a pancake.
Visual imagery	I remember her eyes were almost gold, the color of boiling sugar syrup as it begins to turn.
Analogy	In those days, I thought of Tomas like a starving man thinks of food.

Before you create your images, think deeply about how your character would describe something. Include imagery and figurative language that are appropriate to your story and that flow naturally from it.

7.4 All Writers

End of today's lesson

Check your zoo's figurative language to make sure it is organic, that is, that it makes sense coming from a zoo setting and supports your dominant impression.

4. PRECISE AND VIVID VERBS

F. Scott Fitzgerald has this to say about verbs: "All fine prose is based on the verbs carrying the sentence." And he's right. Take a look at the verbs in this passage from H. G. Wells' *The War of the Worlds*:

> There were sad, haggard women tramping by, well dressed, with children that cried and stumbled, their dainty clothes smothered in dust, their weary faces smeared with tears. With many of these came men, sometimes helpful, sometimes lowering and savage. Fighting side by side with them pushed some weary street outcast in faded black rags, wide-eyed, loud-voiced, and foul-mouthed. There were sturdy workmen thrusting their way along, wretched, unkempt men, clothed like clerks or shop-men, struggling spasmodically; a wounded soldier my brother noticed, men dressed in the clothes of railway porters, one wretched creature in a night-shirt with a coat thrown over it.

Description Tools
1. Sensory details
2. Figurative language
3. Organic imagery
4. Precise and vivid verbs
5. Direction
6. Weather
7. Time
8. Animals/nature
9. Show, don't tell
10. Specificity
11. Character reaction
12. Synesthesia
13. What to avoid

The fact that Wells is cataloging the evacuees is overcome by his use of strong verbs: tramping, smothered, fighting, pushed, thrusting, and so on.

Another example of vivid verbs comes from Charles Dickens' *A Tale of Two Cities*:

> So, he pushed open the door with a weak rattle in its throat, stumbled down the two steps, got past the two ancient cashiers, and shouldered himself into the musty back closet where Mr. Lorry sat at great books ruled for figures.

The name of this man who is pushing, stumbling, and shouldering is Stryver. These verbs are appropriate to his name and to his character (he's a "striver").

Choose just the right verbs for your descriptions, using your character or story as a guide. For instance, instead of writing the bland "He came through the gate and asked for a refund," think of what your character would do:

> He crashed through the gate and demanded a refund.

He slipped through the gate and wheedled a refund from the ticket-taker.

Be specific.

And keep your verb choices in **proportion** to the importance of the noun or character you are describing. If a minor character enters a room, he can walk in (instead of stride or saunter or skip). This does not draw attention to him or give him a greater meaning or proportion than he has in the story.

H. G. Wells reveals a solid writing strategy in *Experiment in Autobiography* when describing a boat that has little significance to the story:

> . . . in nineteen cases out of twenty I would just let the boat be there in the commonest phrases possible. Unless I wanted the boat to be important I would not give it an outstanding phrase and if I wanted to make it important then the phrase to use would depend on the angle at which the boat became significant.

Proportion also refers to the *amount* of words you spend on describing a character, setting, or anything else. The amount of words should be in direct proportion to its importance.

If you use many words describing a character or place, readers assume it is important. They will expect the character to do something special in the story. They will expect the setting to be significant in direct ratio to the amount of words you spend on it. It's that simple. So even if you have a super-great paragraph of description that could earn you a solid place in literary history, take it out or pare it down to match its significance in the story.

7.5 All writers

End of today's lesson

By now you know the drill. Remove any verbs that do not enhance your zoo's dominant impression; insert vivid and specific verbs that do.

5. DIRECTION

Reading a description can be confusing, but you can make yours easy to read by using a direction: top to bottom, left to right, etc. This is called a **spatial description**. An example of this is taken from Jessamyn West's "The Battle of Finney's Ford" from *The Friendly Persuasion*. What spatial direction is used as these characters prepare for an invasion? Notice, too, the vivid verbs and movement (kinetic imagery) in this passage:

<u>Description Tools</u>
1. Sensory details
2. Figurative language
3. Organic imagery
4. Precise and vivid verbs
5. Direction
6. Weather
7. Time
8. Animals/nature
9. Show, don't tell
10. Specificity
11. Character reaction
12. Synesthesia
13. What to avoid

> There were men throwing shovelfuls of earth out of deep holes, preparing to bury silver, money, keepsakes; whatever they and their wives cherished and thought a raider might fancy. There were boys barricading doors, boarding up windows, reinforcing bolts. There was a man who had turned his house into a store and was now busy ripping down his sign and trying to make his store look like a house again. There was an old fellow atop a gable of his house, peering off to the south through a long spy-glass.

What direction is the camera moving in this passage? (The answer is on the next page.)

Using a direction organizes all the material you include in your description and makes it easier for your reader to follow along.

You can use an outside-to-inside direction, too, when describing a character. You do this by starting with her looks or attire and then moving to her inner self by showing her doing something. Or how about a near-to-far direction as you describe a room?

7.6 All Writers

Organize something in your zoo description by choosing a direction in which to describe it.

End of today's lesson

6. WEATHER

Description Tools
1. Sensory details
2. Figurative language
3. Organic imagery
4. Precise and vivid verbs
5. Direction
6. Weather
7. Time
8. Animals/nature
9. Show, don't tell
10. Specificity
11. Character reaction
12. Synesthesia
13. What to avoid

Weather in fiction is often an indicator of future events (foreshadowing) and can be used to create a mood. "A dark and stormy night" bodes no good for the hero. This is the stormy beginning of Michael Crichton's *Jurassic Park*:

> The tropical rain fell in drenching sheets, hammering the corrugated roof of the clinic building, roaring down the metal gutters, splashing on the ground in a torrent. Roberta Carter sighed, and stared out the window. From the clinic, she could hardly see the beach or the ocean beyond, cloaked in low fog.

Roberta Carter has a small part in the book, but she is about to be thrown into a "storm" of mythic proportions.

Take another peek at the passage and enjoy the vivid verbs and the direction of the description.

Also notice that Roberta is reacting to her environment. Character reaction is one of your description tools (number 11 in this list).

> What direction does West choose for her description? First are the men in deep holes, then boys at doors and a man ripping down his sign. Last, someone is on top of his house: bottom to top (or low to high).

Here's the opening of Raymond Chandler's "Red Wind." In two sentences Chandler includes weather, a reaction to it, and kinetic/kinesthetic imagery created by verbs:

> There was a desert wind blowing that night. It was one of those hot dry Santa Anas that come down through the mountain passes and curl your hair and make your nerves jump and your skin itch.

7.7 All Writers

What bit of weather can you add to your description to make the scene more vivid to your readers and support your dominant impression? Add it now.

End of today's lesson

7. TIME

Time of day, day of the week, season of the year. All of these can be ingredients in your descriptions, and all of them can add to the mood or meaning of the story. This passage is from Ray Bradbury's "The Black Ferris." Notice how much weather Bradbury includes in addition to time elements:

> **Description Tools**
> 1. Sensory details
> 2. Figurative language
> 3. Organic imagery
> 4. Precise and vivid verbs
> 5. Direction
> 6. Weather
> 7. **Time**
> 8. Animals/nature
> 9. Show, don't tell
> 10. Specificity
> 11. Character reaction
> 12. Synesthesia
> 13. What to avoid

> The carnival had come to town like an October wind, like a dark bat flying over the cold lake, bones rattling in the night, mourning, sighing, whispering up the tents in the dark rain. It stayed on for a month by the gray, restless lake of October, in the black weather and increasing storms and leaden skies.
>
> During the third week, at twilight on a Thursday, the two small boys walked along the lake shore in the cold wind.
>
> "Aw, I don't believe you," said Peter.
>
> "Come on, and I'll show you," said Hank.
>
> They left wads of spit behind them all along the moist brown sand of the crashing shore. They ran to the lonely carnival grounds. It had been raining.

If a carnival comes to your town at twilight on a Thursday in the third week of October, do not go to it. All of those times—twilight, Thursday, late in the month, a month late in the year—indicate things winding down or dying. Plus, "it had been raining," and there was a "cold wind." Excitement is foreshadowed for Peter and Hank.

7.8 All Writers

End of today's lesson

What time elements will add to the dominant impression of the zoo? Incorporate them now.

8. ANIMALS/NATURE

Will this list never end?

> **Description Tools**
> 1. Sensory details
> 2. Figurative language
> 3. Organic imagery
> 4. Precise and vivid verbs
> 5. Direction
> 6. Weather
> 7. Time
> 8. Animals/nature
> 9. Show, don't tell
> 10. Specificity
> 11. Character reaction
> 12. Synesthesia
> 13. What to avoid

Try using animals or nature to support your dominant impression. Read how Edgar Allan Poe creates a dominant impression of gloom in "The Fall of the House of Usher":

During the whole of a dull, dark, and soundless day in the autumn of the year, when the clouds hung oppressively low in the heavens, I had been passing alone, on horseback, through a singularly dreary tract of country, and at length found myself, as the shades of the evening drew on, within view of the melancholy House of Usher. I know not how it was—but, with the first glimpse of the building, a sense of insufferable gloom pervaded my spirit . . .. I looked upon the scene before me—upon the mere house, and the simple landscape features of the domain—upon the bleak walls—upon the vacant eyelike windows—upon a few rank sedges—and upon a few white trunks of decayed trees—with an utter depression of soul which I can compare to no earthly sensation more properly than to the afterdream of the reveler upon opium—the bitter lapse into everyday life—the hideous dropping off of the veil.

This is one sorry place. You've got words like "oppressively," "insufferable," "bleak," and "hideous." The windows are personified with "vacant" and "eyelike." The weather is low clouds. The time elements indicate death: autumn, near twilight. The only color mentioned is white, and that refers to the "trunks of decayed trees." Poe's choice of nature includes the dead trees and the "rank sedges," grasses that grow only in marshy areas, which is seconded by the "mere house," meaning the house is by a lake. He definitely packs a lot of meaning into his description.

> A short story must have a single mood and every sentence must build towards it.
> —Edgar Allan Poe

Is anything moving in his description? Yes, the narrator moves through the scene on his horse, and this breaks up the litany of dying things and makes the description less tedious.

Animals and nature can be used anywhere. If a bird is singing on a city street, it can add to the setting's light mood. If a character gets caught in a swarm of mosquitoes and a thicket of thorny bushes, readers can get a sense of frustration or danger. Michael Crichton even uses an animal to warn about a character in *Airframe*: "He looked like a cobra about to strike."

7.9 All Writers

End of today's lesson

By now your zoo description is as overcrowded as a rabbit hutch in spring, but don't worry about it. You won't really add all these tools to any description you write; we're just having fun. We are having fun, aren't we? Add a bit of nature to your description to build your dominant impression.

9. SHOW, DON'T TELL

You've tackled "show, don't tell" in former chapters, and now you get to do it again, this time as it pertains to description.

Instead of *telling* readers something important, try *showing* it. For instance, do **not** write this:

> She knew she would never see him again.

But write this:

> From the pier, Angela watched Trevor turn his back to her and face the ocean as a leprous fog, white and spotted, rolled in from the water and swallowed him up.

Description Tools
1. Sensory details
2. Figurative language
3. Organic imagery
4. Precise and vivid verbs
5. Direction
6. Weather
7. Time
8. Animals/nature
9. Show, don't tell
10. Specificity
11. Character reaction
12. Synesthesia
13. What to avoid

In this way, you are not conveying a fact but an impression. It is much more effective this way and will make a greater impact on your reader.

How do you show that a character feels trapped? You describe something in his surroundings to indicate entrapment and let the reader take it from there. Here's how Len Deighton does it in his spy novel *Faith*:

> I went to the bathroom window, an old-fashioned double-glazed contraption, the brass handles tightly closed and tarnished with green mottle as if it had not been opened in decades. Along the bottom ledge, between the dusty sheets of glass, lay dozens of dead moths and shriveled flies of all shapes and sizes. How did they get inside, if they

couldn't get out alive? Maybe there was a message there for me if only I could work it out.

And again:

> He unlatched the gate and we went inside without pressing either bell. In the air there was the smell of burned garden rubbish. "We're only half an hour late," said the kid. "He'll wait." It was very quiet in Magdeburg. There was not even the sound of traffic, just the hum of a distant plane droning steadily like a trapped wasp. In the silence every movement seemed to cause unnaturally loud noises, our footsteps crunching in the gravel like a company of soldiers marching through a bowl of cornflakes.

Notice the simile "like a trapped wasp." It mirrors the narrator's sense of entrapment, and it adds an element of jeopardy. Notice, too, the senses in this last passage: smell, and then sound. These make the passage more dimensional, more grounded in reality.

> If you want to be a successful writer, you *must* be able to describe it, and in a way that will cause your reader to prickle with recognition.
> –Stephen King

Russian writer Anton Chekov gives this advice about descriptions:

> Don't tell me the moon is shining; show me the glint of light on broken glass.

There it is again: Don't tell. Show.

Avoid writing "It was a perfect day" unless you have plans to describe it. What is perfect to you may not be perfect to your reader.

The words "beautiful" and "heavenly" have the same problem as the word "perfect": they are too abstract.

C. S. Lewis has some words of wisdom on this subject:

> Don't say it was "delightful"; make us say "delightful" when we've read the description. You see, all those words (horrifying, wonderful, hideous, exquisite) are only like saying to your readers, "Please will you do my job for me?"

It is not necessary for you to use all these senses and tools in your first draft. You will add them later when you reread your draft and want to create a dominant impression. Create first; pound into shape later.

7.10 All Writers and Group Activity

Take a break from the zoo. In one short paragraph of about 100-200 words, describe the perfect day. The tone can be light, serious, ironic (in which everything goes wrong), or anything else you choose. Your topic sentence ("It was a perfect day"—something like that) can appear at the beginning of your paragraph or the end. Your choice. Prove to the reader that the day is perfect by *showing*.

End of today's lesson

Read your perfect day to others in your group. You may be surprised how different these perfect days are from each other.

10. SPECIFICITY

Be specific about your nouns and verbs. Don't write that an animal ran in front of the character's car; write that a deer bounded or a raccoon scuffled or a kangaroo hopped across the road.

Sung J. Woo is very specific about a young boy's fishing pole in *Everything Asian*:

> "Here we are," Father said, handing me a fishing pole. The one he gave me was new, the yellow enamel polished, the rubberized grip almost sticky, while the one he held looked like it might not make it to the end of the day.

Description Tools
1. Sensory details
2. Figurative language
3. Organic imagery
4. Precise and vivid verbs
5. Direction
6. Weather
7. Time
8. Animals/nature
9. Show, don't tell
10. **Specificity**
11. Character reaction
12. Synesthesia
13. What to avoid

And Woo writes of the worm:

It felt like a cold, wet noodle between my fingers.

How perfect!

7.11 All Writers

End of today's lesson

Back to the zoo description. Check it for specificity. For example, do you mention a tree? What kind of tree is it? Live oak with Spanish moss hanging from it? A fan-leaved ginkgo? A queen palm with lights wound around its trunk? Be specific.

11. CHARACTER REACTION

Description Tools
1. Sensory details
2. Figurative language
3. Organic imagery
4. Precise and vivid verbs
5. Direction
6. Weather
7. Time
8. Animals/nature
9. Show, don't tell
10. Specificity
11. Character reaction
12. Synesthesia
13. What to avoid

A description is fairly dead without a character in it. Who cares if it's raining or if the sun is too hot? Put the character in the frame and watch her react to her surroundings. Will she unfurl her umbrella or pull her coat tighter against the rain? Will she begin to sweat—excuse me, perspire—or shield her eyes from the sun? If your character does not react to her environment, that environment will be almost meaningless to your reader.

In God We Trust, All Others Pay Cash, from which the movie *A Christmas Story* is taken, gives readers an idea of the cold winters the author Jean Shepherd and his town endured. Notice that the setting comes alive and achieves its humor when we see how the children react to the cold:

> Early December saw the first of the great blizzards of that year. The wind howling down out of the Canadian wilds a few hundred miles to the north had screamed over frozen Lake Michigan and hit Hohman, laying on the town great drifts of snow and long, story-high icicles, and sub-zero temperatures where the air cracked and sang. Streetcar wires creaked under caked ice and kids plodded to school through forty-five-mile-an-hour gales, tilting forward like tiny furred radiator ornaments, moving stiffly over the barren, clattering ground.

The cold wind becomes important only when we see kids trying to move through it. Did you notice the great auditory imagery?

Here is Tara of Helium, in Edgar Rice Burroughs' *The Chessmen of Mars*, physically reacting to manacled headless men being herded together:

> Tara of Helium shuddered as she turned away. What manner of creatures were these?

When Marlow, in Joseph Conrad's *Heart of Darkness*, views the western coast of Africa from his ship, he describes the "formless coast bordered by dangerous surf," the rotting banks, and the "contorted mangroves that seemed to writhe at us in the extremity of an impotent despair." His reaction to it? He feels an "oppressive wonder" that seems "like a weary pilgrimage" and a nightmare. The features Conrad chooses to include, the specific verbs, and the character's reaction all create a dominant impression of gloom.

7.12 All Writers

End of today's lesson

In your zoo description, make an animal or a character react to something in his or her environment.

12. SYNESTHESIA

Synesthesia means using one sense to describe another. For instance, did you know that Kellogg's Corn Pops cereal not only tastes *sweet* but also tastes *yellow*? The company declares this on the front of their cereal box:

BIG YELLOW TASTE
SWEET PUFFED CRUNCH!

"Yellow taste" is synesthesia: visual sensory information aligned with a taste.

Description Tools
1. Sensory details
2. Figurative language
3. Organic imagery
4. Precise and vivid verbs
5. Direction
6. Weather
7. Time
8. Animals/nature
9. Show, don't tell
10. Specificity
11. Character reaction
12. Synesthesia
13. What to avoid

Notice, too, the gustatory imagery ("sweet") and the kinesthetic imagery ("crunch"). All that in six words.

Children often use one sense to describe another. I once heard a child describe an opera singer's voice as this: "Her voice is curly." Here's another example of synesthesia that I totally, without even thinking, just made up on the spot:

> The blue jay's caw was as rough as a splintered board.

That's the sense of sound being described by the sense of touch.

When Bean in *The Last Book in the Universe* describes the look and feel of the blue sky, she says it is "apple-flavored." It may be a revelation to you that blue sky tastes like apples, but it's a fun way of describing the peaceful feeling of eating apples under a cloudless sky.

Terry Pratchett uses synesthesia when he describes a horrific smell in terms of sounds in *The Amazing Maurice and his Educated Rodents*:

> If the smells in that room had been sounds, they would have been shouts and screams, thousands of them. They filled the long room with a strange kind of pressure. Even Maurice could feel it, as soon as Keith opened the door. It was like a headache outside your head, trying to get in. It banged on the ears.

End of today's lesson

7.13 All Writers

Try your hand at synesthesia and add it to something in your zoo description.

13. WHAT TO AVOID

Description Tools
1. Sensory details
2. Figurative language
3. Organic imagery
4. Precise and vivid verbs
5. Direction
6. Weather
7. Time
8. Animals/nature
9. Show, don't tell
10. Specificity
11. Character reaction
12. Synesthesia
13. What to avoid

Yes, you are at the end of a rather lengthy list, and you are almost through with that zoo description you've been working on. Here's the last item: Avoid **adverbs**—you know, those pesky "-ly" words. You've already learned not to use them in speaker tags. Now, take it a step further. Here are some examples of what **not** to write (adverbs underlined):

> He strode <u>vehemently</u> into the room.
> The rooster crowed <u>heartily</u>.

> The rain storm stopped <u>abruptly</u>, and the sun shone <u>brightly</u> through the trees.

Let your reader understand from the context of the scene exactly how the man strides. Other actions, events, and character reactions should *show* how these verbs are being accomplished without reverting to *telling* the reader with adverbs.

Can't you ever use them? Yes, but keep them to a minimum.

Avoid **clichés**—those worn-out, overused phrases and situations. You may be tempted to describe dew as "sparkling like a diamond," but that's been done a zillion times already. Write it in your first draft. That's okay. But then go back later and write the second or third thing that comes to mind. Dig into your characters and story and come up with something that is natural to them and that is new and interesting.

Avoid telling readers to **imagine** something or that something is "beyond description," or that you "have no words to describe" something. This is no longer acceptable in today's publishing world. After all, you are the writer, the wordmeister. It is your job to come up with the words to describe something.

7.14 All Writers

End of today's lesson

Comb through your zoo paragraphs for adverbs or clichés. Replace them.

SETTINGS

The list is finished. Now you can put some of that new knowledge to work in the topic of settings. Your story happens in a specific place and time, so clue readers in to this place and time early.

Some writers use actual dates, as in "The year was 1193, and England was at war with itself again" or as in headings on a letter. *O Pioneers!* by Willa Cather begins this way:

> One January day, thirty years ago, the little town of Hanover, anchored on a windy Nebraska tableland, was trying not to be blown away.

Wow. Time, place, weather, *and* reaction. Readers understand that "thirty years ago" refers to the writer's timetable.

Other writers refer to a historical event, have a song playing on the radio, or show their character using a piece of equipment that dates the story. "Wee Willie Winkie" by Rudyard Kipling begins like this:

> His full name was Percival William Williams, but he picked up the other name in a nursery-book, and that was the end of the christened titles. His mother's ayah called him Willie-Baba, but as he never paid the faintest attention to anything that the ayah said, her wisdom did not help matters.

The word *ayah* hints that this story is taking place in India during the British occupation. If we are in doubt about this, all is put to rest when we read the word *India* in Kipling's next paragraph.

Elizabeth Peters refers to a real person and cultural attitudes to anchor her story in history in the cozy mystery *The Deeds of the Disturber*:

> In a great many respects I count myself among the most fortunate of women. To be sure, a cynic might point out that this was no great distinction in the nineteenth century of the Christian era, when women were deprived of most of the "inalienable rights" claimed by men. This period of history is often known by the name of the sovereign; and although no one respects the Crown more than Amelia Peabody Emerson, honesty compels me to note that her gracious Majesty's ignorant remarks about the sex she adorned did nothing to raise it from the low esteem in which it was held.

Amelia Emerson refers to Queen Victoria by mentioning the time period and "her gracious Majesty." Mrs. Emerson is a British subject enjoying her frustration with that era's gender inequalities.

The following is an example of how to turn what could have been a boring description of a setting into angst-ridden action. Instead of telling readers that the city walls were thick and the steps were stone, Susanne Dunlap layers action with description and shows the city as the fifteen-year-old lead Theresa moves around in *The Musician's Daughter*. This scene occurs the day Theresa's murdered father is buried:

> I turned and continued tromping back toward the center of the city, which meant crossing the cold, sluggish Danube by the city bridge and passing through one of the gates that pierced the Bastei, the thick wall that ringed the city . . . . Instead of entering the crowded streets, once the sentry had let us pass through the gate I mounted the stone steps to reach the top of the Bastei. It was cold and gray, so no one promenaded around it to take the air and enjoy the view over the city and the countryside. That suited me. I could stride as fast as I wanted to and not bump into a soul. I think we circled the city about five times. Only then did I calm down enough to realize that nothing would be accomplished by storming around in anger at our dead papa.

Notice how much the reader learns about the city incidentally as Theresa stomps and storms around in it.

Willa Cather uses the **zoom-in effect** when introducing the town to readers in *O Pioneers!* In the phrases below, notice how she begins large and works her way down to a specific location and character:

- Nebraska tableland
- low drab buildings
- dwelling-houses on the tough prairie sod
- the main street
- on either side of this road
- the board sidewalks
- And finally: "On the sidewalk in front of one of the stores sat a little Swede boy, crying bitterly."

By zooming in, Cather moves her **vantage point** from broad (Nebraska) to narrow (a little boy). Frank Peretti does a similar thing in the Christian novel *This Present Darkness*. Readers

> **vantage point:** the place from which readers view the story's action, almost as though they are following the movement of a movie camera

follow "two figures" from a point "just outside the small college town of Ashton" to a vacant lot in the middle of town being used as a carnival, and then through the crowds and, finally, to a specific booth at the carnival

Your whole story will have a setting, but it will also be sprinkled with smaller settings for each scene. Any time the lead moves from one setting to another, describe the new setting for readers, even if you use only a few words or sentences. Put readers in the scene with the characters. Make them see the apartment building, the barn, the bedroom. You will use the same tools with these smaller settings as you use with any description: senses, organic imagery, weather, specificity, and so on.

7.15 All Writers and Discussion

How soon into *The Last Book in the Universe* do you know that this story happens in the future in a broken-down city? What are the clues Philbrick throws in? Make a list.

Every time Spaz moves from one location to another, he has to describe it so readers can be there with him. Find one description of a new setting and write it out.

Discussion: Discuss with the group what tools Philbrick uses in his description to put you in the scene.

> End of today's lesson

MOVING FROM ONE LOCATION TO THE NEXT

Just as you need **transitions** in reports and essays, you need them in stories to move your character and reader from one location to the next. Notice the simplicity of these time and place transitions (underlines added) from Raymond Carver's "A Small, Good Thing":

> › <u>On Monday morning</u>, the birthday boy was walking <u>to school</u> with another boy.
> › The child was <u>in the hospital</u> with a mild concussion and suffering from shock.
> › Howard drove <u>home</u> from the hospital.
> › He arrived back <u>at the hospital</u> <u>a little after midnight</u>.

Even TV shows and movies alert viewers to a change in setting by showing a few seconds of the outside of a building before switching to the inside shots. It may be an apartment building at night or a hospital during a downpour, but this lets viewers know where the action of the story is taking place. Do the same for your readers. Watch how three consecutive chapters begin in John Grisham's *Theodore Boone: Kid Lawyer*, showing the necessary changes in time and place:

> Chapter 18
> For the first time in several nights, Theo slept well.
>
> Chapter 19
> After golf, Theo and his father stopped by the Highland Street Shelter to check on Julio and his younger brother and sister.
>
> Chapter 20
> Theo was in the den watching a movie on cable when his cell phone vibrated in his pocket. It was eight thirty-five, Saturday night, and the call was coming from the shelter.

When your characters move through time and space, keep the reader in the loop by showing "where" and "when" they are.

7.16 All Writers

The account of Jonah takes place in many settings: his hometown, a port city, a ship, a fish's belly, a shore, an enemy city, a king's palace, and a dry hilltop. Read the book of Jonah from the Bible, and then write one paragraph of setting for each of the following situations, using your new tools to foreshadow an event in that setting, create a dominant impression, or mirror Jonah's mood:

> › Jonah's hometown just before he gets the message from God
> › The ship just before the storm arrives
> › The belly of the big fish
> › The enemy city of Nineveh just as Jonah enters it

End of today's lesson

> The next lesson →

7.17 All Writers and Discussion

Read the following sentence and imagine a scene for this character:

> She came into the room, removed her mask, and looked for a place to hide the letter.

Who is the character? How did she come into the room (vivid verb needed here)? What kind of mask does she have? Why does she have one? Why is she looking for a place to hide a letter? What is the letter? Is there anyone else in the room? You have a wide range of possibilities, everything from silly to serious.

After you have written about 200 words, go back and do some polishing. Think about the dominant impression you want to create. Then, **one at a time**,

> › Add sensory information.
> › Add some movement.
> › Use any two of the other tools you learned about in this chapter to describe the scene, create a mood, or characterize.
> › Insert words, phrases, or sentences to show how she is feeling and to show her reactions to events or her environment.

Do this piecemeal, one step at a time.

Use the checklist on page 160 to see how you are doing.

Discussion: Read your paragraphs aloud to the group and listen to other members' paragraphs. What dominant impressions were they trying to create?

7.18 Manuscript Track

Check your short story or one chapter of your novel against what you have learned in this chapter. Use the checklist on the next page. Rewrite and make any needed adjustments to your manuscript. Share your edited version with your group.

DESCRIPTION CHECKLIST FOR ALL WRITERS

Use this handy guide for checking your descriptive work. You need not use all these tools. Choose the ones that best suit your purposes.

Does the description/setting include . . .

- ❑ Sensory details

tactile ____ auditory ____ olfactory ____ visual ____ gustatory ____ thermal ____ kinetic ____ kinesthetic ____

- ❑ Figurative language
- ❑ Organic imagery
- ❑ Precise and vivid verbs
- ❑ Spatial orientation
- ❑ Weather
- ❑ Time
- ❑ Animals/nature
- ❑ Showing instead of telling
- ❑ Specificity
- ❑ Character reaction
- ❑ Synesthesia

Does the description avoid . . .

- ❑ Clichés
- ❑ Most adjectives
- ❑ Adverbs
- ❑ Telling (instead of showing)
- ❑ Words like "imagine" or "beyond description"

Does it hold the reader's interest?

Does your setting clearly . . .

- ❑ Show the character's location?
- ❑ Show the time of day?
- ❑ Show the time of year (if necessary)?
- ❑ Show the time period (if necessary)?
- ❑ Indicate the mood of the coming scene?
- ❑ Appear near the front of each new scene?

OPTIONAL DESCRIPTION WRITING

1. Read the following description from *The Last Book in the Universe* (page 192) that describes something common to us but unknown to the characters. Then describe something common to you as though you (or your characters) are experiencing it for the first time. Another such passage can be found at the bottom of page 193. It's about a brook.

   > Meanwhile me and Bean and Ryter spend a lot of our time outside. We discovered that the coolest thing in the world is to walk on grass with our bare feet. Grasswalking. It feels sort of tickly and smooth and alive somehow, even though it's just this green stuff that grows out of the ground.

2. Write a few paragraphs describing an amusement park that is dark or scary. Then write about one that is exciting or fun. Use specific words and phrases and the tools you learned in this chapter. For more fun, choose two teams, one for each kind of theme park. Then brainstorm and write for 20 minutes. Read to the group what you wrote.

3. Find a description you like in a story and write it out by hand. Then take out all the important words. Now you have a pre-made skeleton—complete with a built-in syntax and rhythm—upon which to build a new description. Fill in your own words to create a new dominant impression.

4. Write two descriptions of one thing (a car, house, park, refrigerator, etc.)—one when the viewpoint character is happy and one when he is sad, angry, hurt, full of regret, and so forth. This will show how a viewpoint character's frame of mind can color what he sees or how he sees it.

What you studied in this chapter:

- ✓ Descriptions are active and have jobs to do.
- ✓ Creating a dominant impression
- ✓ Writing for mood or foreshadowing
- ✓ Describing to characterize
- ✓ A variety of description tools
- ✓ Settings, including the zoom-in effect and vantage point
- ✓ Transitions

8: WORDS, WORDS, WORDS

You've been speaking and writing words for years. Now it's time to discover how those words you've been using can have a greater impact on your readers.

> The writer only does half the job. It takes two to make a book.
> —Ursula K. LeGuin

Audience and Word Choice

It is tempting to use your expansive vocabulary in your fiction writing, but most authors advise new writers to stick to the simple words. George Orwell, writer of the futuristic novel *1984*, says it this way:

Never use a long word where a short one will do.

Mark Twain puts in his seven cents on the topic:

> I never write *metropolis* for seven cents because I can get the same price for *city*. I never write *policeman* because I can get the same money for *cop*.

If you use a word you think might be a stretch for your audience, make sure they can guess the word from the context. Lois Lowry explains age groups in the futuristic young adult (YA) novel *The Giver* by using context:

> All of the Elevens were excited about the event that would be coming so soon.

And later:

> "You go, Lily," he said, seeing his sister, who was much younger—only a Seven—wiggling with impatience in her chair.

By this, readers understand that Elevens and Sevens are children grouped by their ages.

The same care is needed for jargon. Make it easy for your audience to guess the meaning of the word from the context or explain it soon afterward, as Rodman Philbrick does in *The Last Book in the Universe* when he uses the word "proov" and then adds that "a proov is a genetically improved human being."

C. S. Lewis, author of the Narnia series, has this to say about word usage:

> Don't use words too big for the subject. Don't say "infinitely" when you mean "very"; otherwise you'll have no word left when you want to talk about something *really* infinite.

Some published authors tell new writers to forget all about their audience, to be more loyal to the story than they are to the audience. Others advise them to pay attention to and respect the readers; after all, those are the ones who will be buying your book. Who's right? Who knows? This is one of those choices you will make as a writer, most likely based on your personality, your editor, and the dictates of your genre.

For this course, however, choose words that are appropriate for your narrator, your story, and your audience.

Chapter 8: Words, Words, Words   165

8.1 All Writers

Below is a paragraph from the famous "Rip Van Winkle" by Washington Irving. The story was written in the early 1800s, about 200 years ago, and its language and word choice were perfect for the day.

Rewrite the passage to make it ready for today's readers. Choose the **age** of your audience and choose the **gender**. Your choices for the age and gender will influence your word choices. Write the age and gender choices at the top of your paper so your teacher will know what you are aiming for. Because of Irving's vocabulary, you may have to keep a dictionary or thesaurus handy. [Note: A "curtain lecture" is one spouse lecturing the other behind the curtains on their bed at night.] Ready?

Excerpt from "Rip Van Winkle":

I have observed that he was a simple good-natured man; he was, moreover, a kind neighbor, and an obedient hen-pecked husband. Indeed, to the latter circumstance might be owing that meekness of spirit which gained him such universal popularity; for those men are most apt to be obsequious and conciliating abroad, who are under the discipline of shrews at home. Their tempers, doubtless, are rendered pliant and malleable in the fiery furnace of domestic tribulation, and a curtain lecture is worth all the sermons in the world for teaching the virtues of patience and long-suffering. A termagant wife may, therefore, in some respects, be considered a tolerable blessing; and if so, Rip Van Winkle was thrice blessed.

> End of today's lesson

CONNOTATION

The words you use have a **denotation** and a **connotation**. The denotation is the dictionary definition; the connotation is the feeling or implied meaning of the word. For instance, a wart may be defined as a blemish, but a "wart" sounds worse than a "blemish."

Earlier in this course you saw the difference between the harsh-sounding last name of Straik and the soft sound of the name Dimble. The *sound* of a word can influence readers. If a character *pushes* his chair back from the table, the action will be softer than if he *scrapes* his chair back. Think of what the word may sound like to your readers.

Be careful of words that *look* similar to each other. If a butcher shows up in your story with a maculate apron, readers may be tempted to think of the word *immaculate,* which means *clean*. However, *maculate* means spotted or dirty—the opposite of immaculate.

Words with long vowels or with consonants like *k, t,* or *z* will sound harsher than words with short vowels and consonants like *b, p,* and *s*. Would you rather be struck with a rock or bumped with a pebble?

Choose words as much for the sound and implied meaning as for their definition.

Choose them, too, for how people view them today. "Loony" or "crazy" may be objectionable, but stating the exact condition ("bipolar" or "phobic," for instance) may help readers understand the real problem. It all depends on what you are trying to achieve. An irksome character may use the word "crazy" while an empathetic one may use "bipolar."

CONTRACTIONS

If you want to emphasis the negativity of the word "not," don't make a contraction. Or, rather, do not make a contraction. Which sentence below has the stronger negative message?

> › It isn't fair.
> › It's not fair.
> › It is not fair.

Most likely, you chose the last sentence. Depending on what you are writing and how you want it to come across to your readers, you may want to un-contract some of your contractions for the most effect.

8.2 All Writers and Discussion

Check your version of the "Rip Van Winkle" passage for connotations and contractions. Make the necessary changes.

Discussion: Share the changes with your writing group. Listen to their changes. Do you agree with their editing changes? Do they agree with yours?

End of today's lesson

VERB TENSE

Most stories are told in the **past tense**: "We seemed to be alone, but I kept getting this creepy feeling that something was watching us."

Occasionally an author will employ the **present tense**, as with Erich Maria Remarque's *All Quiet on the Western Front*:

> I nod. We stick out our chests, shave in the open, shove our hands in our pockets, inspect the recruits and feel ourselves to be stone-age veterans.

What tense is *The Last Book in the Universe* written in?

Some writers believe that using the present tense makes the story seem more immediate, as though it were happening *now*. Your narrator's style or voice may determine which tense to use.

As a writing device, some authors change tenses during a scene. Sir James Barrie does this in *Peter Pan* when he introduces the island inhabitants. Barrie puts the reader behind some bushes and makes the lost boys, Hook, and the pirates file past the reader one by one. As they are filing by, Barrie changes the tense from past to present.

F. Scott Fitzgerald changes tenses in chapter three of *The Great Gatsby* when readers get their first view of one of Gatsby's parties. On the next page is a list of partial sentences showing the change in tenses.

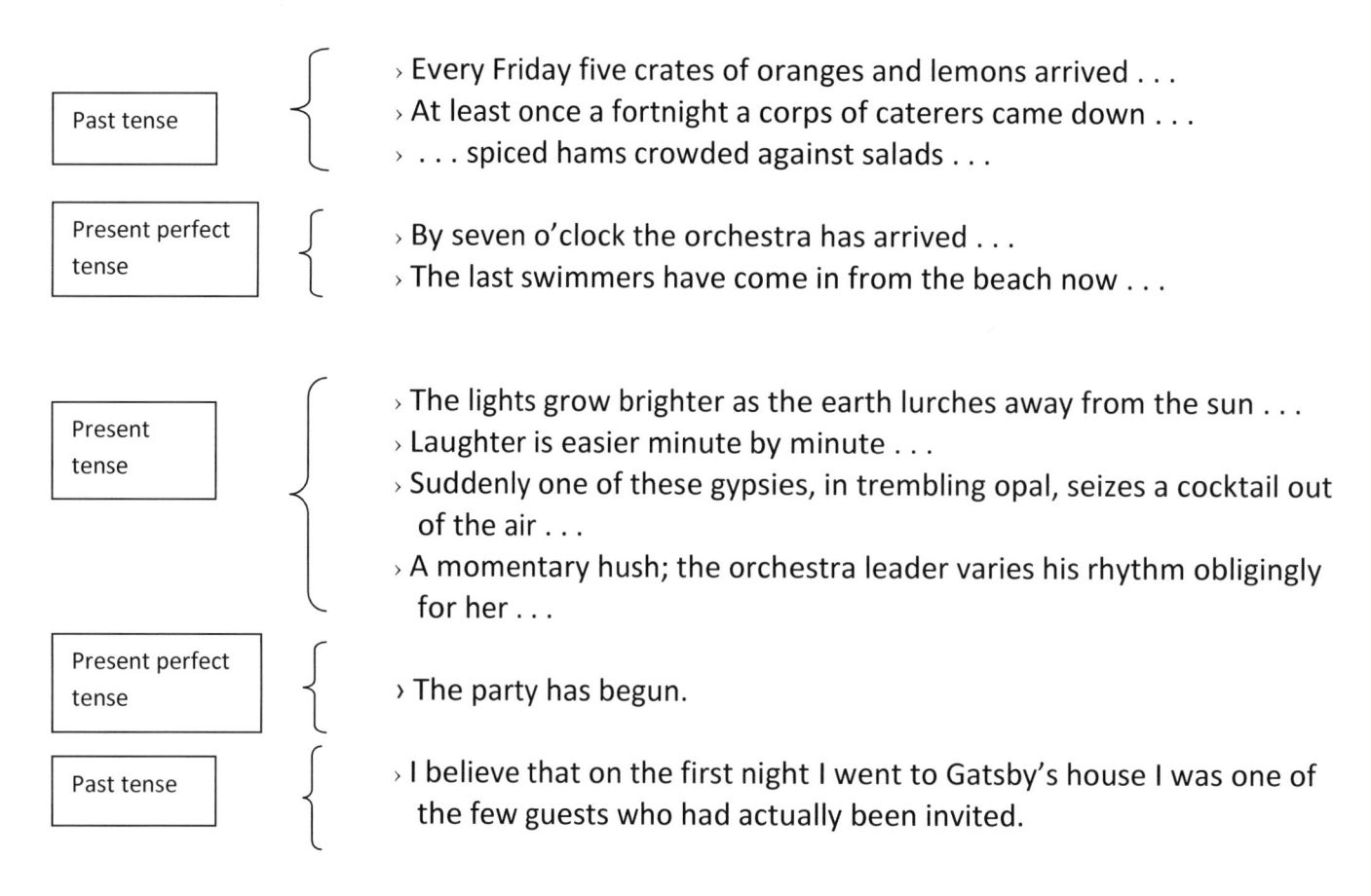

Past tense	› Every Friday five crates of oranges and lemons arrived . . . › At least once a fortnight a corps of caterers came down . . . › . . . spiced hams crowded against salads . . .
Present perfect tense	› By seven o'clock the orchestra has arrived . . . › The last swimmers have come in from the beach now . . .
Present tense	› The lights grow brighter as the earth lurches away from the sun . . . › Laughter is easier minute by minute . . . › Suddenly one of these gypsies, in trembling opal, seizes a cocktail out of the air . . . › A momentary hush; the orchestra leader varies his rhythm obligingly for her . . .
Present perfect tense	› The party has begun.
Past tense	› I believe that on the first night I went to Gatsby's house I was one of the few guests who had actually been invited.

This tense change, coupled with Fitzgerald's use of vivid verbs, has the effect of a headlong rush of activity until the party officially begins.

Other changes in tense are available to you. The conditional tense ("would have") has an interesting effect. It carries with it a sense of possibility or longing or wishing something could be different. Watch how Tim O'Brien uses the conditional tense as the main character Norman, a Vietnam veteran just home from the conflict, wrestles with his combat memories of a troubling incident on the Song Tra Bong River in "Speaking of Courage" from *The Things They Carried*. Norman, driving around his hometown lake, is wishing he could talk with his father:

> And then he would have talked about the medal he did not win and why he did not win it.
> "I almost won the Silver Star," he would have said.
> "How's that?"
> "Just a story."
> "So tell me," his father would have said.

Slowly then, circling the lake, Norman Bowker would have started by describing the Song Tra Bong.

The conditional tense can be powerful if used at the right time in your story.

8.3 All Writers and Discussion

Rewrite a passage in *The Last Book in the Universe* by changing the tense from present to past. How does it affect the story? Which do you like best for that passage?

Discussion: Discuss the changes in *The Last Book in the Universe* and discuss which version you like best.

8.4 Manuscript Track

Think about your story. Is there a passage or scene where a change of tense could be used to good effect? If so, rewrite that passage or scene and share the results with your critique group.

Or try your hand at using the conditional tense in a passage where a character longs for something that will not happen. Then share your results with the group.

[End of today's lesson]

SENTENCE IMPACT

When speaking of impact, sentences come in two varieties: loose and periodic. A **loose sentence** puts the important information in the beginning, like this sentence from Alan Paton's *Cry, the Beloved Country*:

Shocked and hurt, Jarvis put down the papers.

This is the first sentence of a paragraph, and the words "shocked and hurt" catch the readers' eyes immediately.

A **periodic sentence** puts the important information at the end of the sentence, near the period (thus, "periodic"). This example of two periodic sentences is from Ernest Hemingway's "The Short Happy Life of Francis Macomber." We join Macomber just after others have shot a wounded lion that charged the group:

> That was the story of the lion. Macomber did not know how the lion had felt before he started his rush, nor during it when the unbelievable smash of the .505 with a muzzle velocity of two tons had hit him in the mouth, nor what kept him coming after that, when the second ripping crash had smashed his hind quarters and he had come crawling on toward the crashing, blasting thing that had destroyed him.

The power of the first sentence is in the last word "lion." Hemingway could have written "That was the lion's story," but it would have put the emphasis on the "story," not on the lion whose death is emphasized by the powerful last words of the second sentence—"destroyed him." Notice, too, that the longer sentence is filled with motion and vivid verbs. This keeps it interesting and propels the reader through the action.

This next example, taken from *In God We Trust, All Others Pay Cash* by Jean Shepherd, also uses the periodic sentence structure as the character dreams of Christmas presents. Each section of the sentence builds upon the previous one, ending in a combination of words that is surprising and, therefore, effective:

> Through my brain nightly danced visions of six-guns snapped from the hip and shattering bottles—and a gnawing nameless frenzy of impending ecstasy.

In addition to the relentless push of that sentence as the tension mounts, Shepherd has combined "impending" with "ecstasy," an unexpected duo because "impending" is usually paired with a word that has negative connotations, such as "doom." His use of action verbs, alliteration, and the fun combo at the end make this sentence a keeper. Try imitating its form by using his sentence structure and substituting your own words.

Suspense writers and writers who are trying to create a suspenseful passage often employ periodic sentences. "Last words" are considered to be in a power position: the last words in a paragraph, scene, or chapter. They pack a punch. Readers, even subconsciously, feel the impact. Be careful of what your "last words" are. Or, to use a periodic sentence, choose your "last words" with care.

8.5 All Writers

By now you have a large portfolio of your fiction work. Examine a passage of about 200-300 words from something you have written for this course.

> - Have you used loose sentences where appropriate?
> - Have you used periodic sentences for the most impact?
> - Is the important word in each sentence where you want it to be?

Make the necessary editing changes. Hand in the old version and the new version.

End of today's lesson

ACTIVE/PASSIVE

If the subject of the sentence is doing the action, the sentence is in the **active voice**, like this:

> King Kong dragged Ann Darrow to the top of the Empire State Building.

King Kong is dragging. He is doing the action.

If the subject of the sentence is *receiving* the action, the sentence is in the **passive tense**, like this:

> Ann Darrow was dragged to the top of the Empire State Building by King Kong.

Ann Darrow is not doing the dragging; she is being dragged.

Your story will move along more swiftly and be easier to read if you use the active voice. In passages of tension and suspense, use the active.

Prefer the active voice unless you have a good reason to use the passive.

Use the passive voice occasionally if you want to convey a slower pace or if your style demands it.

8.6 All Writers

Use the same passage you used in exercise 8.5 and edit it again, this time looking for how you used the active voice or the passive voice. Be aware of your choice and why you chose the active or passive. Make necessary edits.

Hand in the original version and the new version.

End of today's lesson

PARALLELISM

Parallelism or **parallel structure** means using the same sentence structure or syntax in a repetitive manner. The following examples use parallel adjectives and prepositional phrases, sentences, and infinitive phrases.

George MacDonald's *Lilith* uses parallel adjectives and prepositional phrases to describe a horse:

> . . . huge of bone, tight of skin, hard of muscle . . .

MacDonald repeats the adjective and prepositional phrase structure to give a rhythm to the horse:

huge	of	bone
tight	of	skin
hard	of	muscle

The next example, using parallel sentence structure, is too good to miss. It is not from fiction but from the memoir *North to the Orient* by Anne Morrow Lindbergh. In it she chronicles her journeys with her famous aviator husband Charles Lindbergh (parallel structure underlined):

> We had flown to the limits of the flood and were now out in wilder land, above a circle of hills. And there it was. <u>In this circle there was a lake</u>. <u>And on this lake there was an island</u>; <u>and on this island there was a pagoda</u>. There it was, just like the fairy tale.

Lindbergh's description has the feel of a fairy tale by the way she uses parallel structure. Her structure also uses the power of three (circle, lake, island). And it uses the zoom-in effect. All that for one low price.

Mark Twain uses parallel sentence structure in this compound sentence from *The Prince and the Pauper*. The parallelism emphasizes the contrast between the young Prince of Wales and a little street urchin who have just switched clothing with each other:

> A few minutes later the little Prince of Wales was garlanded with Tom's fluttering odds and ends, and the little Prince of Pauperdom was tricked out in the gaudy plumage of royalty.

In *Great Expectations*, Charles Dickens uses a parallel structure to highlight the fear in little Pip as he encounters an escaped convict in a graveyard (parallel structure underlined):

> After darkly looking at his leg and at me several times, he came closer to my tombstone, took me by both arms, and tilted me back as far as he could hold me; so that <u>his eyes looked most powerfully down into mine</u>, and <u>mine looked most helplessly up into his</u>.

And let's not forget perhaps the most famous example of parallel infinitive phrases ever. This version is taken from *Star Trek II: The Wrath of Khan*:

> Space . . . the Final Frontier. These are the continuing voyages of the starship *Enterprise*. Her ongoing mission: to explore strange new worlds, to seek out new life forms and new civilizations, to boldly go where no man has gone before.

To explore, to seek out, to boldly go. Each infinitive phrase builds upon the previous one, increasing in momentum and the feeling of adventure.

And that's the point of parallel structure: make it *do* something. In all these examples, parallel structure is not just hanging around and looking like a cool device. It is performing a task—creating a rhythm, zooming in, giving the feel of a fairy tale, contrasting characters, contrasting a sense of power with a sense of helplessness, or increasing momentum. Of course, your parallel structure is not limited to these particular tasks. Use it to achieve the effect you need.

8.7 All Writers and Discussion

Use your edited version of the "Rip Van Winkle" passage for this exercise and create one parallel construction of any length in that paragraph.

Discussion: Read your parallel construction to the group. What task is yours performing? What tasks are the group's parallel constructions performing? Are they effective?

End of today's lesson

THE POETRY OF PROSE

Our English language can be quite descriptive and elegant, especially when you use writers' devices such as similes, metaphors, analogies, alliteration, and assonance. You've already studied figurative language in chapter 7, so just sit back and enjoy the beauty of these examples taken from Dylan Thomas's memoir "A Child's Christmas in Wales."

> . . . Mrs. Prothero was announcing ruin like a town crier in Pompeii.

> And [the bells] rang their tidings over the bandaged town, over the frozen foam of the powder and ice-cream hills, over the crackling sea.

> And then, at tea the recovered uncles would be jolly; and the ice cake loomed in the center of the table like a marble grave.

> The wind through the trees made noises as of old and unpleasant and maybe webfooted men wheezing in caves.

If you get the chance to read "A Child's Christmas in Wales," by all means, read it. It is a magical memoir crammed with fun language and powerful imagery (http://classiclit.about.com/od/christmasstoriesholiday/a/aa_childswales.htm).

Alliteration (a consonant sound that begins successive words) and **assonance** (an internal vowel sound repeated in successive words) can add elegance and rhythm to your work. Look for alliteration and assonance in this paragraph from Peter S. Beagle's *The Last Unicorn* as the magician Schmendrick tries using his magic to rescue the unicorn from her cage:

> A scratching of flinty phrases this time, and Schmendrick's bloody hands flickering across the sky. Something gray and grinning, something like a bear, but bigger than a bear, something that chuckled muddily, came limping from somewhere, eager to crack the cage like a nut and pick out bits of the unicorn's flesh with its claws. Schmendrick ordered it back into the night, but it wouldn't go.

You already know from the chapter on description that painting word pictures such as these draws readers into the story and can even be cause for delight. Or creepiness, as in this simile about the character Pollution from Neil Gaiman and Terry Pratchett's *Good Omens*:

> . . . his voice as insidious as something leaking out of a corroded drum into a water table.

Keep a notebook of word images you like. Write them out by hand, and then study them to discover the secret of their power. Soon you will find your own way of writing with that power.

> The world always seems brighter when you've just made something that wasn't there before.
> —Neil Gaiman, a prolific writer

End of today's lesson

8.8 All Writers

Find three word images that appeal to you in a short story or novel. Copy them out and bring them to class to read aloud.

EXCLAMATION POINTS AND CAPITALS

Avoid exclamation points in fiction!!! They clutter up the text and are telling instead of showing!!!! And you know what *that* means!!!

Exclamation points are acceptable in some chick lit (novels for young women) or YA (young adult) novels, but for the most part, they are the mark of an amateur. Don't be one!!!!!

Avoid using CAPITALS in your fiction writing too. Again, capitals are acceptable in some genres when used intentionally; most often, however, they are FROWNED UPON in *SERIOUS works!!!!*

STYLE

A writer's **style** consists of many choices: sentence length and structure, word usage, figurative language, the rhythm or flow of the sentences and paragraphs, and so forth. Style, incidentally, is the word choices you make and how you build sentences and paragraphs.

If you have been writing for any length of time, you already have a style. Your writing style is as innate as your personality. Sure, you can work on it some and even tweak it, but it will flow from you quite naturally. Everybody's does.

Let's look at the style of two famous writers. Ray Bradbury's style is effusive; Ernest Hemingway's is spare. This paragraph of description comes from Bradbury's "The Veldt" in which a father has just stepped into his children's futuristic room that makes settings seem real:

> And here were the lions now, fifteen feet away, so real, so feverishly and startlingly real that you could feel the prickling fur on your hand, and your mouth was stuffed with the dusty upholstery smell of their heated pelts, and the yellow of them was in your eyes like the yellow of an exquisite French tapestry, the yellows of lions and summer grass, and the sound of matted lion lungs exhaling on the silent noontide, and the smell of meat from the panting, dripping mouths.

This paragraph is from Hemingway's *The Old Man and the Sea*, in which is described a fish jumping out of the water:

> The line rose slowly and steadily and then the surface of the ocean bulged ahead of the boat and the fish came out. He came out

unendingly and water poured from his sides. He was bright in the sun and his head and back were dark purple and in the sun the stripes on his sides showed wide and a light lavender. His sword was as long as a baseball bat and tapered like a rapier and he rose his full length from the water and then re-entered it, smoothly, like a diver and the old man saw the great scythe-blade of his tail go under and the line commenced to race out.

Quite a difference between the two styles. Bradbury uses one long sentence punctuated by commas and stuffed with sensory details. Hemingway uses no commas where one would expect them; sticks to visual details; and uses short, easy words. Where he could have written "emerged," he wrote "came out." When he could have used "submerged," he used "re-entered." These are stylistic choices he made.

No one taught these writers their style; it flowed out of them as water from a fire hydrant. They practiced. They developed their strengths and skills. But their styles are uniquely their own.

Yours will be too.

It is tempting to imitate an author's style, especially if you like that author. As you learn to write, imitating may be beneficial to you. It allows you to better understand how successful writers make their magic. But as you grow in your writing abilities, work on developing your own emerging style and creating stories of your own that are not derived from someone else's work.

> Always be a first-rate version of yourself instead of a second-rate version of somebody else.
> –Judy Garland, actress

8.9 All Writers and Discussion

Find a passage—any passage of about 300 words—from a short story or novel. Write it out or type it out. Then rewrite it using your own innate style. Make choices about words and word usage, verbs, sensory details, sentence length and structure, figurative language, punctuation, paragraph construction and length, and so forth.

End of today's lesson

A Word of Caution

All this stuff about parallelism, metaphors, and style is great, but don't let the reader catch you at it. Drawing attention to one's superb story-writing skills is frowned upon by editors and readers alike. You want the reader to be conscious of the *story*, not of your *writing*. If your super-fantastic writing skills pull the reader out of the story, you may lose him or her.

When you write something stupendous and know it doesn't flow with your story, simply print it off and slip it in your "Too Good to Throw Away" file in your desk. It is deleted from your story, but now you can read it in the dead of night by the light of the gibbous moon and marvel at how tremendously good it is.

What you studied in this chapter:

- Audience and word choice
- Connotations
- Contractions
- Verb tenses
- Loose and periodic sentence structures
- Active/passive voice
- Parallelism
- The poetry of prose
- Exclamation points and capitals
- Style

9: THEME

In a literature class, you may feel as though you are interrogating a story under harsh lights, forcing it to surrender all its hidden secrets and juicy meanings. Or maybe you feel as if *you* are the one being interrogated!

But this is not a literature class. This is a fiction-writing course. There will be no interrogating, no wrestling with incomprehensible classics or unintelligible books you only half read.

Discussing theme from the fiction-writer's perspective can be much more enjoyable. Instead of standing on the outside of a story and looking in, you will be on the inside, looking out. You will know what the story is about because you wrote it. You assembled all the pieces and arranged them to have the desired effect.

The writer's aim is not to torment students and confuse the masses but to enrich, enlighten, and entertain. Paying special attention to how you treat your theme will help you do just that.

A **theme** is the unifying idea or meaning that pulls the whole story together and gives it depth. In one sense, it is like the unifying idea of an essay: It guides your writing and affects all of your choices. That's still pretty vague, so let's clear it up with some examples.

Themes generally come in two categories: (1) a "message" or (2) an exploration of a topic. Here's an example of a **message** some say they read in Herman Melville's *Moby-Dick*:

> Forget about looking for happiness. Even if you find it, it will only destroy you.

Those sentences never actually appear in the story, but everything that happens in the story seems to point in that direction.

Here are two examples of an **exploration of a topic**:

> › Nathaniel Hawthorne contemplates the nature of faith and disillusionment in "Young Goodman Brown."
> › F. Scott Fitzgerald examines ways in which the American dream has become corrupted in his novel *The Great Gatsby*.

Neither of those two stories seems to have a message or moral, as such; the authors simply contemplated their topics and examined the ramifications of them, and this became their theme.

Short stories generally contain only one theme because they are too short and concentrated to hold more than one. Novels or movies may contain more than one theme; they have more room to explore the world and the characters' lives.

Incidentally, a theme may be stated outright, like this one from Dr. Seuss's *Horton Hears a Who*: "A person's a person, no matter how small." Or the theme may be more subtle, woven into **thematic elements** such as events, characters, conflicts, descriptions, and endings, as when readers see Horton's efforts to save the tiny speck and subconsciously begin to believe that it might be heroic to buck the crowd in order to save someone who needs to be defended. (FYI: Both of these themes are of the "message" variety.)

thematic elements or devices: any story elements employed to add to or open up the meaning of your story, to support the theme.

In the next lessons, you will learn common problems writers can encounter with theme (along with the solutions, of course), and you will learn some tools at your disposal as you ponder your own theme, but for now, read and think about this quote from *Brave New World* by Aldous Huxley:

> And, of course, stability isn't nearly so spectacular as instability. And being contented has none of the glamour of a good fight against misfortune, none of the picturesqueness of a struggle with temptation, or a fatal overthrow by passion or doubt. Happiness is never grand.

9.1 All Writers and Discussion

Using Aldous Huxley's quotation as a jumping-off point, discuss why it is easier to write about misery and trouble than to write about happiness.

9.2 All Writers and Discussion

View the Disney/Pixar movie *WALL•E* and discuss what you see as possible themes in it, whether in the form of messages from the screenwriters (Andrew Stanton, Pete Docter, and Jim Reardon) or in the form of topics to be examined. Give examples from the story to support your idea of the movie's themes. (Note: There may be more than one theme.)

End of today's lesson

THREE PROBLEMS WITH THEME—AND HOW TO FIX THEM

You may encounter one of the following common problems when writing your stories. These problems belong on a continuum because you can find yourself anywhere along the line:

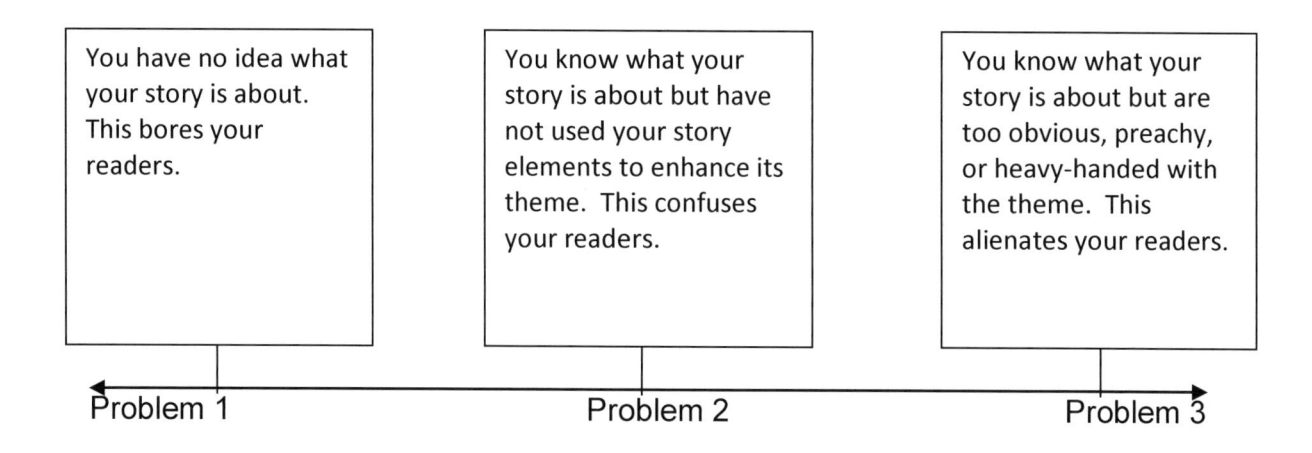

Problem 1	Problem 2	Problem 3
You have no idea what your story is about. This bores your readers.	You know what your story is about but have not used your story elements to enhance its theme. This confuses your readers.	You know what your story is about but are too obvious, preachy, or heavy-handed with the theme. This alienates your readers.

PROBLEM 1

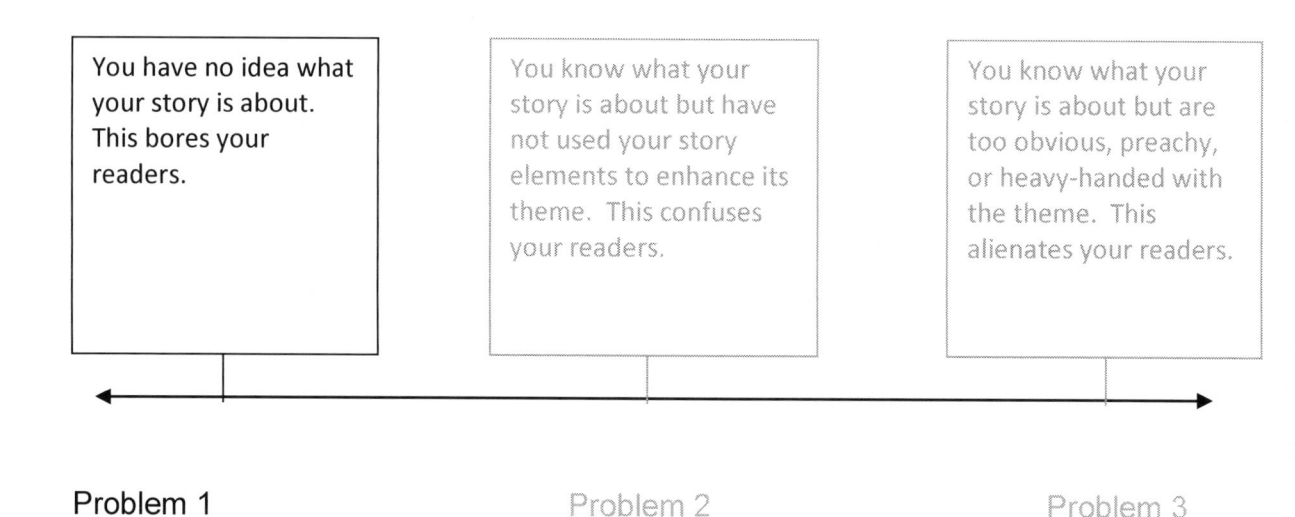

Problem 1	Problem 2	Problem 3
You have no idea what your story is about. This bores your readers.	You know what your story is about but have not used your story elements to enhance its theme. This confuses your readers.	You know what your story is about but are too obvious, preachy, or heavy-handed with the theme. This alienates your readers.

You've written an awesome story filled with sparkling characters and thrilling events and have given it to a trusted friend to read. He comes back with, "I don't get it. What's it about?"

That's a problem. Most likely, you didn't build meaning into the events you squeezed your characters through. You didn't imply anything about life or focus on one aspect of life long enough for your friend to make sense of your story. Or your friend is just dense.

> Charlotte was a story of a friendship, life, death, salvation.
> —E. B. White, on *Charlotte's Web*

You've learned some things about life, and you've experienced some interesting things. Now it is your turn to say something meaningful.

A story is much more than a series of events. It is a communication between you and your readers. What do you want to communicate to them?

When William Saroyan, writer of *The Daring Young Man on the Flying Trapeze and Other Stories*, was a young writer, he asked himself an important question as he began writing "The Broken Wheel": "What's going on? Why are you writing about the old English walnut tree in the backyard of the rickety frame house at 2226 San Benito Avenue in Fresno?" He answers by remembering his mother's younger brother, the "kid brother":

> A writer writes, and if he begins by remembering a tree in the backyard, that is solely to permit him gradually to reach the piano in the parlor upon which rests the photograph of the kid brother killed in the war. And the writer, nine or ten years old at the time, can notice that his mother is crying at the loss of the kid brother, who, if the truth is told, was nothing much more than any kid brother, a brat, a kind of continuous nuisance, and yet death had made him the darling of the family heart.

How to fix Problem 1: Reread your story. Inside this brilliant and highly imaginative story, what kernel of meaning keeps coming to your mind? What topic does it revolve around?

The best stories do not simply entertain; they also confront something solid and meaningful about life. Entertainment *and* meaning—the double whammy.

If you are in the planning phases of a story, ask yourself these questions:

› What have I noticed about life that I find interesting?
› What have I learned about life that I might want to convey to others?
› What interests me (friendship, betrayal, hope against all odds, etc.)?

From the answers to these questions, you may be able to construct a story and a meaningful theme.

> A man's work is nothing but a slow trek to rediscover, through the detours of art, those two or three great and simple images in whose presence his heart first opened.
> –Albert Camus

Good news: You do not have to have a theme in mind before you begin your story. In fact, some writers fear that focusing on a theme while they write will leave their work stilted, stiff, and "preachy." Published authors sometimes caution beginners to write their stories without any idea of a theme. Simply write a story you are interested in telling. Then, as you review your story and begin to see patterns, you will discover that you have subconsciously written a theme into your story. As you make this discovery, use your thematic elements to support and enhance your theme. (More on this in the section on Problem 2.)

On the other hand, Eudora Welty, author of *The Optimist's Daughter* and many short stories, reports in *Conversations with Eudora Welty* that her story ideas often came from a theme: "Sometimes I go around for a long time with a theme or point in my mind. And then, suddenly, I hear something or see something, and I know in an instant that I have a bottle for the theme I've been thinking about." The idea for her "Why I Live at the P.O." came to her when she saw an ironing board in the back of a small-town post office, but before that,

> . . . it was a lifelong listening to talk on my own block where I grew up as a child, and that was in my head to write out of all the time. The sight of the lady ironing was the striking of the match that set it off, but I wouldn't have written a story just about seeing somebody with an ironing board in the post office.

Your story becomes a vehicle, or "bottle," for your theme.

9.3 All Writers

Write a letter to your younger self. Choose a time in your young life when you could have used some help or wisdom, a time when you were making an important decision, or a time when you were confused. Then write to that younger self and give the help, encouragement, advice, or wisdom you now can offer.

End of today's lesson After you have written your letter, examine the themes you discover there—the messages or topics that emerge. How can you incorporate these into your next story?

PROBLEM 2

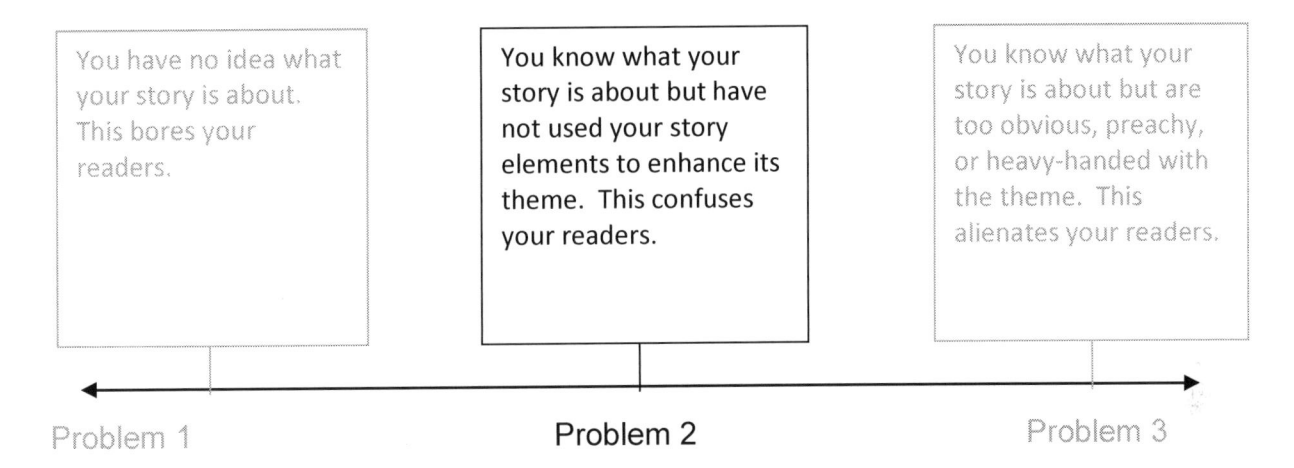

| You have no idea what your story is about. This bores your readers. | You know what your story is about but have not used your story elements to enhance its theme. This confuses your readers. | You know what your story is about but are too obvious, preachy, or heavy-handed with the theme. This alienates your readers. |

Problem 1 — Problem 2 — Problem 3

Let's say you are writing a story about being free. Good so far. You develop your protagonist, write a bang-up metaphor using a hamburger, add some imagery about cats, and use an eclipse as a symbol. Now you're in trouble.

Why? Even though the writing may be creative and fun to read, it is not centered on your theme of being free. You have done nothing to subtly build a solid foundation for your great theme. The metaphor comparing something to a hamburger may be well written, but why not try one using a caged lion in a zoo or a heron slicing through the sky? Either of those images can bring to mind freedom—the first one because it is an opposite and the second because it exemplifies it. And instead of cats and eclipses, try using some imagery and symbols that actually have something to do with being free.

How to fix Problem 2: Use your story elements as **thematic elements**. When you use story elements to support your theme, they are called thematic elements. Some story elements are as follows: the title, character names, characterization, motivation, description, dialogue, plot points (story events), figurative language (simile, metaphor, analogy, symbol, personification, etc.), imagery, setting, and so forth. Basically, everything is at your disposal when enhancing your theme.

Using recurring or opposing imagery can be particularly powerful and add depth to your theme. See how the writers in the next examples use birds, cars, weather, colors, a rented house, and even baseball to enhance their themes.

★ Willa Cather uses birds to underline one of her themes in *O Pioneers!* Migrating ducks, in a short discussion between old Ivar and young Emil, come to symbolize how hard the first wave of pioneers had to work: "Yes. The point of the wedge gets the worst of it; they cut the wind." The "point of the wedge" also puts into readers' minds the shape of old plows that broke up the rough sod for planting. In another bird image, Cather uses a seagull to represent people who come to the prairie but who clearly don't belong there or are never at home there. Old Ivar recounts a story of a seagull that happened to get lost in the middle of the land-locked prairie: "She was more mournful than our birds here; she cried in the night." Stories, images, and thoughts of birds occur enough times in the book to enhance Cather's themes. If the reader catches on, she may be delighted; if she doesn't get it, she still can enjoy the story and may even absorb the imagery subconsciously.

★ Flannery O'Connor acknowledges this subconscious osmosis in *Mystery and Manners* as she reveals two of her symbols:

> The truer the symbol, the deeper it leads you, the more meaning it opens up. To take an example from my own book, *Wise Blood*, the hero's rat-colored automobile is his pulpit and his coffin as well as something he thinks of as a means of escape. He is mistaken in thinking that it is a means of escape, of course, and does not really escape his predicament until the car is destroyed by the patrolman. The car is a kind of death-in-life symbol, as his blindness is a life-in-death symbol. The fact that these meanings are there makes the book significant. The reader may not see them but they have their effect on him nonetheless. This is the way the modern novelist sinks, or hides, his theme.

★ Another thematic device—weather—emerges in Tim O'Brien's *In the Lake of the Woods*. It contains the story of a successful but confused Vietnam vet who cannot fully remember his past even as it comes back to trouble him and involve him in a possible murder. How better to emphasize mental confusion than with a thick fog completely swallowing the deep woods in which he is recuperating?

Edith Wharton uses color to support her theme in *Ethan Frome*. When the married Ethan first sees Mattie, she is wearing a red scarf. At this point in the story, this bright splash of red is the only color in a drab town and life. Ethan imagines happiness for himself and for Mattie. When you read Mattie's last name, however, you know that Ethan will not find happiness in this affair. How do you know this? Mattie's last name is Silver—another drab and lifeless color.

Jane Austen, in *Persuasion,* provides readers with an insightful image that underlines her theme. Anne Elliot, the protagonist, is persuaded by her family friend Lady Russell not to marry Captain Wentworth. Lady Russell has so much influence over Anne that Anne quickly breaks off the engagement, even though she loves Wentworth. Years later, an admiral leases Anne's ancestral home from her family, and this rental arrangement becomes a metaphor for Anne's life. Her physical house is occupied by someone other than her family, which can be compared to Anne as she "leases" her mind and heart to the influential Lady Russell and many others who tell her how to think and what to do.

And one last example: When Ernest Hemingway wrote *The Old Man and the Sea*, he wove baseball throughout the fabric of the story, specifically the Yankees' race to win the American League pennant in 1950. How did he do this?

According to C. Harold Hurley, editor of *Hemingway's Debt to Baseball in* The Old Man and the Sea, "the actual historical events of the American League pennant race correspond to Hemingway's fictional account of the aged fisherman." Conversations about the Yankees often come up between old Santiago and young Manolin, and the Yankees' and Joe DiMaggio's endurance inspires Santiago to persevere under horrendous conditions for days on the ocean alone. From *The Old Man and the Sea*, here is the old man thinking to himself during his ordeal with a large fish:

> This is the second day now that I do not know the result of the *juegos* [games], he thought. But I must have confidence and I must be worthy of the great DiMaggio who does all things perfectly even with the pain of the bone spur in his heel.

And this:

> Do you believe the great DiMaggio would stay with a fish as long as I will stay with this one? he thought.

Hurley explains it this way:

> Running parallel to the internal action of the novel, the games of baseball's "September Stretch" serve not only to heighten and intensify Santiago's heroic encounter with the great marlin and the sharks, but also to place that encounter against the heroes of a sport that in the mythic sense is emblematic of humanity's struggle to endure and prevail. For Santiago it is the constant measuring of self against the yardstick of the incomparable DiMaggio that sustains him in the agony of his ordeal, and his thoughts of the game itself that console and divert him when that agony becomes too great.

The battle to win the ball games mirrors the battle the old man has with the powerful marlin.

Birds, cars, fog, colors, a rented house, baseball. All of these and more can be used in your own epic struggle to bring your story under the one umbrella that is its personal theme.

9.4 All Writers and Discussion

Choose a one-word theme that interests you, something like rejection, strength, conformity, endurance, pain, or hope. Then write a passage or scene of a story (about 500-700 words) and focus on weaving an image, simile, metaphor, symbol, color, weather, nature, description, or anything else into the scene to underline your theme. For this exercise, keep the actual word that is your theme out of the scene.

Discussion: When you meet with your group, read aloud your passage or hand out copies of it to your group, and then have them guess what your theme is. Each member of your group will present his or her work, too, so you can guess each theme.

End of today's lesson

> **The next lesson →**

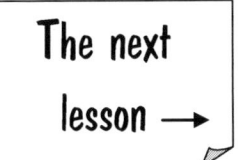

9.5 All Writers and Discussion

After you watched *WALL•E*, you discussed some of its themes. Now identify and discuss the thematic elements that support those themes. For instance, when you discuss themes of, say, personal responsibility or choosing life-affirming actions over life-damaging actions, look for character names, place names, events, symbolic images, character choices and their results, and so forth, that support those themes.

PROBLEM 3

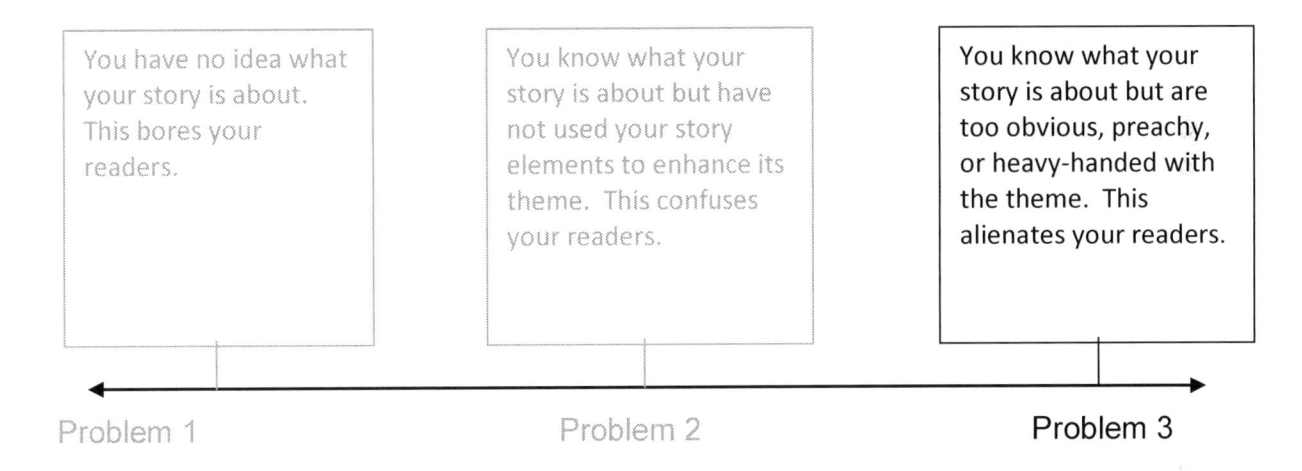

| You have no idea what your story is about. This bores your readers. | You know what your story is about but have not used your story elements to enhance its theme. This confuses your readers. | You know what your story is about but are too obvious, preachy, or heavy-handed with the theme. This alienates your readers. |

Problem 1 — Problem 2 — Problem 3

    Almost nothing stops a reader from reading a work of fiction faster than finding a heavy-handed lecture where a story should be. And if a writer wants to irritate his reader, all he has to do is be super obvious about his theme in an effort to make it very clear to his supposedly thick-headed, clueless readers.

    H. G. Wells reveals in *Experiment in Autobiography* that he was surprised anyone liked his books because he considered himself "grimly and desperately educational," more of a teacher than a storyteller and his stories as merely teaching vehicles. If you have read any of his work, you know what he means by this and may have yawned during his lectures on life and society. Somewhere along the way, though, he must have paid some attention to his storytelling or he would have completely lost his readers through boredom.

> The whole theme ... [was] meant to come over the reader by stealth.
> —C. S. Lewis, on his disappointment that the jacket blurb gave his theme away

How to fix Problem 3: In Problem 2, you examined how thematic elements highlight your theme. Cleverly using thematic elements is one time-honored method to fix the problem of shouting your theme to readers.

Here are two more methods in the art of subtlety:

(1) If you choose to write your theme as a sentence in your story, insert it at a point of tension or great meaning for the protagonist. The example below from *A Wrinkle in Time* shows one way to do this.

(2) If you anchor your theme to actions, events, or characters, you may never have to state outright what your theme is. The quote below from C. S. Lewis shows what this means.

As an example of the **first method**, we'll look at Madeleine L'Engle's *A Wrinkle in Time,* which deals with a theme of conformity versus individuality. It contains Meg, a teenager who perceives herself as a misfit and who finds herself on the planet Camazotz where everyone is forced to act exactly alike. It should be a conformist's heaven, but she finds that the planet's people are living in fear.

> You can't clobber any reader while he's looking. You divert his attention, then you clobber him and he never knows what hit him.
> –Flannery O'Connor

We join Meg as she fights to keep her mind from being taken over by the planet's controller. She is also fighting to free her younger brother from the controller and her father from imprisonment. The following epiphany happens when Meg stands in front of the powerful controller that is trying to take over her mind. Meg, trying to resist, quotes the only thing she can remember at the moment—the Declaration of Independence ("We hold these truths to be self-evident, that all men are created equal . . .")—as a way to combat the mind control. The first sentence is the controller's reply to Meg's quote:

> "But that's exactly what we have on Camazotz. Complete equality. Everybody exactly alike."
> For a moment her brain reeled with confusion. Then came a moment of blazing truth. "No!" she cried triumphantly. "*Like* and *equal* are not the same thing at all!"
> "Good girl, Meg!" her father shouted at her.
> But [the controller] continued as though there had been no interruption. "In Camazotz all are equal. In Camazotz everybody is the same as everybody else," but he gave her no argument, provided no answer, and she held on to her moment of revelation.

> Like and equal are two entirely different things.

With her new knowledge that she doesn't have to be just like everyone else in order to be as important as they are, Meg sets out to free those who are under the controller's power.

L'Engle states her theme as a line of dialogue and then as a line of character thought. She hits it briefly twice and then lets the remaining story events carry out the theme.

And she chooses a moment of great tension for Meg, a moment when Meg's failure would have dire consequences for all concerned. In reality, the truth of her stated theme has already been established in the lives of Meg and two other "misfits" as readers watch them struggle through their story with courage, insight, and resourcefulness. At this point in the story, they have already proven themselves worthy by their actions, but they are the only ones who still don't understand the truth about themselves. Other story characters and readers do, however. This event in the plot is a good place to state the theme because L'Engle already laid the groundwork for this turning point.

> Don't write about Man. Write about a man.
> –E. B. White

The **second method** involves letting your characters live the theme through the story's events. Let the story events *be* the theme. To use an example from the Bible, how better could God teach that a godly heart is more valuable than physical strength than to recount the lopsided fight between David and Goliath? The theme and the event become one entity.

Here's what C. S. Lewis has to say about the unity of theme and story action:

> On the imaginative level I think the deepest truths enter the mind much better as arbitrary marvels than as universal theorems. Cinderella has to be back at midnight—Psyche must not see Cupid's face—Adam and Eve must not eat the fruit: how much better these statements are than any philosophical generalities about obedience.

Donald Glover, in *C. S. Lewis: The Art of Enchantment*, says of Lewis that he favored this indirect approach because then the theme "would slide past the reader's inhibitions and prejudices and catch him unaware."

Readers understand story meanings on a deeper level when those meanings come in the form of story actions rather than lectures disguised as dialogue, narrative, or exposition. Let your *story* talk.

9.6 Manuscript Track

Reread one of your short stories or a chapter from a novel manuscript and decide what your theme is. Then check to see if your figurative language, symbolism (if any), dialogue, character choices, story events, repetition of imagery, etc., support your theme. In other words, make sure you are using some story elements as thematic elements.

If you have trouble identifying your theme, make your main character write an essay or journal entry about the meaning of her story, about what is going on and how she feels about her life in this story. This is for your benefit only and will not be repeated in its entirety in your story though you may want to lift a sentence or two from it and insert it in your story.

OPTIONAL WRITING FOR THEME

1. Take apart the movie *The Island* (with Ewan McGregor and Scarlett Johansson, rated PG-13) to find its thematic elements. How do the screenwriters (Caspian Tredwell-Owen, Alex Kurtzman, and Roberto Orci) support their themes? Choose one theme you find there and follow it through to the end of the movie, marking down which elements support the theme. (Hint: Dialogue, symbolism, character motivation, images, and even subtleties such as color enhance this movie's strongest themes.)

2. View the movie *Cast Away* (with Tom Hanks, rated PG-13) to find its thematic elements. How does the screenwriter William Broyles Jr. underscore the themes? Choose one theme you find there and follow it through to the end of the movie, marking down which elements support the theme (dialogue, symbolism, character motivation, images, events, and so on).

3. Choose a book or short story with which you are familiar and write down its theme (whether a one-word theme or a statement). Next, study a section or passage and find how the author used his thematic devices to

support the theme. When you find something you like, practice it by imitating it. Later you can incorporate that device into your own story in an original way.

> **What you studied in this chapter:**
>
> A "message" theme
> An "exploration of a topic" theme
> How to fix these problems:
> - ✓ You have no idea what your story is about.
> - ✓ You did not use your story elements to enhance your theme.
> - ✓ You were too obvious or heavy-handed with your theme.

10: PLOT

In *The Amazing Maurice and his Educated Rodents* by Terry Pratchett, a young protagonist Malicia (a human) argues with Maurice (a cat):

> "Look, cat, there's two types of people in the world. There are those who have got the plot, and those who haven't."
>
> "The world hasn't got a plot," said Maurice. "Things just . . . happen, one after another."
>
> "Only if you think of it like that," said Malicia, far too smugly in Maurice's opinion. "There's always a plot. You just have to know where to look."

You can write a story without a plot. Many literary writers have done so because the literary genre can be more experimental than other genres published today. John Cheever, for instance, wrote the ironic short story "A

Miscellany of Characters that Will not Appear," in which he lists characters and situations he will not write about—while he writes short vignettes about them in his short story and explains why he will not write about them.

But what about the rest of us? Do our stories really need a plot?
The simple answer: Most readers prefer a plot.
Another simple answer: Editors of today's fiction know that most readers prefer a plot.

So what is a plot?

In your literature classes, a plot can be a one-sentence summation of the story's action. *Frankenstein*'s plot can be stated this way: "A scientist animates a sewn-together corpse that frightens the town." When you write your story, get into the habit of summing it up in one sentence, like the television guides do.

For the purposes of writing fiction, however, plot has a larger definition. *Plot is . . .*

> (1) the story's **events**, the things that happen in the story (the answer to "What happened next?"), and
> (2) the **arrangement of events,** the **sequence** you use to organize your story's events.

The rest of this lesson will explain more about the story's events and their arrangement.

1. Plot is a **series of events**, one event building upon another. They are *causal*, not arbitrary or coincidental. When you think of causal, think "cause and effect"; one event happens *because* another event occurred earlier. Later events are built upon former ones and upon the choices characters make. [Note: Not all plots use cause and effect: allegory or character sketch, for example, do not.]

> Grab 'em by the throat and never let 'em go.
> —Billy Wilder, screenwriter, director, and producer

Choose events that will squeeze your lead to best show off or develop his inner character. In *The Princess Bride*, Westley is challenged by three men (the swordfighter, the giant, and the brains) so we can learn that Westley is wily, strong, and smart. Later he endures torture, and by this we understand the depth of his true love.

Choose events, also, as they relate to your story's *value*. A story's value can be stated in one word and is the sieve through which all story events must pass. Some writers may call the value a theme. One story value in *The Last Book in the Universe* is "belonging" or "belonging vs. isolation." Spaz is torn from his family unit and is a misfit with the violent gangs because of his epilepsy; he doesn't belong to the Urb, to any of the gang territories he passes through, or to Eden; when he finally feels he belongs with Ryter, who has become a father-figure to him, he watches as Ryter is violently ripped out of his life; and last, when he meets the one person to whom he biologically belongs, he rejects that relationship. Notice the escalating nature of the "belonging" value.

The account of Moses in Exodus can be evaluated in light of the story value of obedience. Below are some of the events in Moses' life, in no particular order:

› The pharaoh disobeys God.
› The pharaoh breaks his promise (disobeys his own word).
› Moses' mother and the midwife disobey the pharaoh's edict to kill all newborn males.
› Moses obeys God by tossing a piece of wood into unsafe water, making it potable.
› Moses argues with God at the burning bush.
› Moses obeys God by going back to Egypt and confronting the pharaoh.
› The Israelites rebel against God and complain about the water supply.
› The Israelites rebel against God and complain about the manna.
› Moses disobeys God and strikes the rock twice, not once, for which he is prohibited from entering the Promised Land even after all his years of leadership.
› Miriam obeys her mother to the letter and watches the pharaoh's daughter pick baby Moses out of the river.
› A band of Israelites and Egyptians rebel against Moses' authority.
› Moses' brother and sister challenge his leadership.
› Moses has to wander the desert with the Israelites because *they* rebelled against God.

> A novel, for example, can be cleaned up, altered, trimmed, improved. Life, on the other hand, is one big messy rough draft.
>
> –Harlan Coben, best-selling mystery and suspense writer

It seems as though events are included based on God's rating system of obedience/disobedience. Notice that Moses experiences all kinds of obedience/disobedience in varying degrees, both his own and others'.

This should be true of your story events, too. Include them only if they pressurize the character and belong to the story value. Be sure to explore the whole spectrum of your value, from the positive to the negative (obedience/disobedience; truth/lies; life/death; justice/injustice; safety/danger; and so forth).

2. Writers arrange their series of events (often called plot points) into a **sequence** that enhances the story, plays havoc with the leads, and gives the reader enough tension to keep him reading. A story event or plot point, incidentally, isn't a character simply moving into a new house—unless that character is one of three pigs and the house is made of straw. Plot points affect the story and the character; they have consequences

If you were to arrange Moses' life according to the value of obedience, you would probably put the striking-the-rock-twice event near the end of the narrative. Why? Because this is the event that has the most at stake for him; it is the one that has the largest consequences for him. After forty years of wandering due to no fault of his own, after all the reversals, after being called a friend of God and the most humble man on earth, after being attacked by foes and family, after all the times Moses obeyed God in the face of great fear and opposition, now he will not achieve his goal of leading God's people into the Promised Land. (The amazing thing is that he does make it into the Promised Land during the Transfiguration with Jesus—an ironic ending.)

Make sure your story events escalate in meaning to your protagonist.

The shape or pattern of your plot may reflect your theme. In Paul Fleischman's *Whirligig*, Brent, a high school junior, kills a promising young woman in a DUI accident. After the trial, the young woman's mother asks Brent to make and set whirligigs in the four corners of the United States as a sign of respect for the dead girl. The odd chapters follow Brent chronologically through the accident, the trial, and his counter-clockwise journey from Chicago to Washington to California to Florida and to Maine. The even chapters follow people upon whom his homemade whirligigs have an effect, and they are in this order: Maine, Florida, Washington, and California. This is not the order in which Brent visited them, and, in fact, the occurrence in Maine is years in the future (a flash forward). What gives? Why the confusion and disorderliness of the even chapters?

Brent's chronological story feels like a steady arm moving in a circular motion from beginning to end. It represents the orderly movement of one arm of a whirligig. The alternate chapters are whirling in disarray and represent the happy confusion one might see on a spinning whirligig. The shape of the plot mirrors the shape and motion of the atonement items Brent is asked to make.

Most story events, however, have a much simpler sequence as they grow in importance to the lead. Try writing your events on index cards or sticky notes so you can move them around to find the greatest effect on your story and your lead.

10.1 All Writers and Brainstorming

Enough of theory! It's time to write.

Pretend you are writing a story and then determine your story's value—freedom, for example. (Louis Sachar's book and movie *Holes* deals with this story value.) Now think of your lead's desire as it pertains to freedom (freedom from the grief of losing a sister; freedom to be herself and not what someone expects of her; freedom from a particular school or job; freedom from a family curse, as in *Holes*; and so forth). Your lead will experience many events on the freedom/enslavement spectrum, even to the point of experiencing something that feels like freedom but is really enslavement (or entrapment).

Brainstorm 10 events or plot points that are related to your story value and that can happen to your lead based on his or her specific goal. Remember, "freedom" and "enslavement" do not necessarily have to be physical but can also be mental, spiritual, emotional, and so forth.

End of today's lesson

THE HERO'S JOURNEY

Some people say there are only 26 different plots in the world and we simply keep using them to create new stories. Others say there are only two plots: (1) a stranger comes to town, and (2) someone goes on a journey.

Examples of a stranger-coming-to-town plot are the movies *High Noon*, *The Music Man*, *Mary Poppins* (she is known to "pop in"—get it?), and *K-PAX*, and the novel *The Great Gatsby*.

But in this lesson, we're going to study the second option: Someone is going on a journey, also known as the hero's journey.

The hero's journey plot is so powerful that it has become the underlying structure in many books and movies. You can find it in movies such as *The Wizard of Oz*, *Star Wars: Episode IV—A New Hope* (1977), *Iron Man*, *The Island*, *The African Queen*, *Matchstick Men*, *Galaxy Quest*, *The Interpreter*, *I Am Legend*, and Disney/Pixar's *Up* and *Tangled*; in short stories like Richard Connell's "The Most Dangerous Game"; and in the books *A Christmas Carol*, *Don Quixote*, *A Wrinkle in Time*, *The Hobbit* and—surprise!—*The Last Book in the Universe*. This is only the tip of the iceberg when it comes to writers using the hero's journey plot.

Even though this particular plot structure is called a *hero's* journey, the lead can be male or female. The feminine of *hero* is *heroine*. Because of that word's unfortunate similarity to the illegal drug heroin, Maya Angelou, author of *I Know Why the Caged Bird Sings*, suggests that instead of the word *heroine* we use the word *shero* or *she-ro* (pronounced SHEE-rō to rhyme with *hero*). What do you think?

Also, let's use the term *hero* loosely. Some leads aren't heroes in the adventurous/knight/mythic sense. Some are anti-heroes or so wounded that there is little heroic about them. And some are thieves as in capers like *Ocean's Eleven*, *The Italian Job*, and Michael Crichton's *The Great Train Robbery*. So, whether the lead is a true hero or not, the term still applies.

Below is the basic structure for the hero's journey. Explanations of each appear after the list, with examples from *The Last Book in the Universe* and many other sources:

> - The Hero's Ordinary World
> - The Call to Adventure
> - Crossing the Threshold
> - Into the Journey's World
> - Into the Heart of the World
> - Crossing the Threshold to Return to the Ordinary World
> - The New Ordinary World

The Hero's Ordinary World Readers learn of the lead's normal world, what it's like there; what he's like, what he does, and what he longs for; and some of the backstory. The MDQ is established and so are the protagonist's goals. It is here that readers learn of Spaz's deep wound (evicted from his family due to epilepsy) and deep need (the need to belong). They also learn of his goals: to see Bean before she dies (his conscious goal) and to find his true story (his subconscious goal). Of course, the "ordinary" of the ordinary world does not mean "boring." Spaz's ordinary world is far from boring as he navigates the tricky world of the Bully Bangers and their latch. Readers see the lead in action; Spaz robs the gummy, meets Little Face, interacts with a proov, and has an altercation with Billy Bizmo. He's a busy fellow.

> **The Hero's Journey Plot**
>
> The Hero's Ordinary World
> The Call to Adventure
> Crossing the Threshold
> Into the Journey's World
> Into the Heart of the World
> Crossing the Threshold to Return
>   to the Ordinary World
> The New Ordinary World

The Call to Adventure The call to adventure begins with an event that entices, pushes, or pulls the lead out of his ordinary world. Many terms exist for this event: the **inciting incident**, motivating incident, catalyst, disturbance, and so forth. Why are there so many terms for the same event? Who knows? The main thing is that it occurs. For Spaz, it is the arrival of a runner who tells him that his sister is dying.

> **The Hero's Journey Plot**
>
> The Hero's Ordinary World
> The Call to Adventure
> Crossing the Threshold
> Into the Journey's World
> Into the Heart of the World
> Crossing the Threshold to Return
>   to the Ordinary World
> The New Ordinary World

Now Spaz is in motion: He goes to Billy Bizmo. The rest is history.

One major component of the call to adventure is the **refusal**. Most leads simply refuse to go. *The Hobbit*'s Bilbo Baggins refuses to leave the Shire because he is comfortable and regards adventures as nasty things; Dorothy in *The Wizard of Oz* feels the tug of loyalty to her aunt and uncle and turns back, despite having gotten as far as Professor Marvel's carnival trailer. Spaz's refusal is not for himself but for Ryter. Spaz tells Ryter not to come, which Ryter ignores.

During this phase of the story, the hero picks up a **mentor**. In Scrooge's case, it's his three ghostly visitors. With Bilbo, it's the wizard, the one who called him to the adventure. In Spaz's case, it is Ryter.

The hero also acquires **traveling companions**. Dorothy meets the Tin Man, the Scarecrow, and the Cowardly Lion. *Star Wars*' Luke Skywalker acquires the droids R2-D2, C-3PO, and eventually Han Solo. Spaz's companions are Little Face and his mentor Ryter.

The hero may also be given **gifts** (Lucy's healing potion in *The Lion, the Witch, and the Wardrobe*), **warnings** (Aslan's warnings and signs to Jill Pole in

The Silver Chair), or **powers** (today it's usually in the form of high-tech gadgetry, as in Tony Stark's palladium core in the *Iron Man* movies, but it could be authority conferred upon him, as when former marshal Kane picks up his badge again in *High Noon*).

The hero's journey plot has some flexibility to it. For example, Dorothy Gale's gift of the ruby slippers, with its accompanying power to summon Glinda, isn't conferred until Dorothy arrives in her new world. And, other than Toto, she does not meet her traveling companions in her call-to-adventure phase but in her journey's new world. The originality with which you use these phases can delight readers.

Crossing the Threshold Moving from the ordinary world into the world of the adventure is such an auspicious and dangerous moment that it deserves its own plot section. Think of the four Pevensie children and their move from the wardrobe to Narnia. Think of Dorothy whirling into the land of Oz. Think of Spaz and Ryter in the Pipe.

> The Hero's Journey Plot
>
> The Hero's Ordinary World
> The Call to Adventure
> Crossing the Threshold
> Into the Journey's World
> Into the Heart of the World
> Crossing the Threshold to Return
>   to the Ordinary World
> The New Ordinary World

Each of these scenarios has something in common— **threshold guardians**, characters who guard this new world. The Narnian world has Mr. Tumnus and Mr. and Mrs. Beaver. Oz has the Munchkins and the man in the door to Oz. In westerns, it's often the men in the saloon. The movie *Secondhand Lions* has an amusing take on the threshold guardians: hand-painted signs along the old uncles' driveway warning of rabid dogs and nuclear radiation, and, later, a pack of dogs, a pig, and the sound of gunfire. Soon after this, young Walter is sitting on the uncles' doorstep hearing his mother and the uncles argue about him, the literal threshold just behind him, when he is accosted by the pig. This world is not welcoming him.

Sometimes the threshold guardians are working for the antagonist. The hero has to make allies of these guardians, defeat them, or trick them in order to get any further in his journey. In Spaz's case, the threshold guardians are the Monkey Boys, working for Mongo the Magnificent. How does he get past them?

Into the Journey's World   Some writers call this phase the "woods" or the "cave" because both of those are time-honored motifs denoting darkness and testing. Whatever you call it, the protagonist is squarely in the new world, where he has to **learn its rules**, go through **testing**, **acquire enemies**, and **acquire allies**. Walter's uncles in *Secondhand Lions*, though originally part of the threshold guardian array, eventually become his allies and mentors. Spaz and Ryter prove themselves to Gorm and create an ally in the Great Gorm; save Lanaya; navigate a minefield; tussle with Lotti Getts and receive a task from her; pretend to be traders for the forbidden mindprobes; learn valuable information from Vida Bleek; are beset by Furies; find a dying Bean; and so forth.

> **The Hero's Journey Plot**
>
> The Hero's Ordinary World
> The Call to Adventure
> Crossing the Threshold
> Into the Journey's World
> Into the Heart of the World
> Crossing the Threshold to Return
>   to the Ordinary World
> The New Ordinary World

If the hero has an encounter with the antagonist early in this phase, it will go badly for the hero.

Into the Heart of the Journey's World   Sometimes called "inmost cave," this phase of the journey takes place on the antagonist's home ground and/or on his terms. It may happen in an office, on a ship, in a courtroom, on a battlefield, in the innermost sanctum of a wizard (*The Wizard of Oz*), or in a Death Star (*Star Wars*). Sometime just before or just after the hero enters the heart of the journey's world, he experiences a **death-and-rebirth event**. For Luke

> **The Hero's Journey Plot**
>
> The Hero's Ordinary World
> The Call to Adventure
> Crossing the Threshold
> Into the Journey's World
> Into the Heart of the World
> Crossing the Threshold to Return
>   to the Ordinary World
> The New Ordinary World

Skywalker in *Star Wars*, it is watching his mentor die at the hands of Darth Vader. At this point, the heroic "spirit" passes to Luke. In *The Princess Bride*, Westley dies at the hands of his torturer and is reborn by Miracle Max's pill. Before this, Westley thought the way to win his woman was to leave her and become worthy and strong; now he rises from death (barely) to battle for her in his weakness.

In *Secondhand Lions*, Walter experiences death and rebirth when he talks one of his uncles out of doing "something crazy," that is, building, flying, and possibly killing himself on a homemade airplane. Walter wants his uncle to live long enough to give him the "what a boy needs to know to become a man" speech. Convincing his uncle to live gives Walter the hope he needs, the bonding he craves, and the strength to endure his next event—the supreme test.

Spaz experiences a death-and-rebirth event through Bean, who is dying but who wakes from the coma after the gene-therapy treatment. One of his deep wounds has been healed; he is ready for the next—and toughest—phase of the hero's journey.

The effect of the death and rebirth is to motivate and ready the hero for confrontation. He is now a changed man and it is a good thing, for he will soon have to undergo the **supreme test** or **ordeal**—the confrontation with the antagonist. Dorothy's imprisonment, in *The Wizard of Oz*, gives her the courage and strength to come to the Scarecrow's aid when he is threatened by the witch in the witch's castle. Sometimes the hero's supreme test does not deal with the antagonist but the antagonist's representatives or underlings, as in *Secondhand Lions*. Walter undergoes his supreme test against the antagonist's representative, his mother's boyfriend, who gets Walter alone and beats him up.

Philbrick allows Spaz to be passive during the trial in Eden as Spaz listens to the clash of ideas between prejudice and reality. Readers experience the test through Lanaya as she struggles to gain justice for Spaz, Bean, Ryter, and all the normals.

If the hero lives through this ordeal, he gains a **reward** or **boon**, which he may take back to his original world with him. It could be justice, inner knowledge, wisdom, gold, a Jedi sword, medicine to heal someone back home, a fact to catch a murderer, self-respect, freedom, a new confidence, a spirit of generosity resulting in gifts bestowed on Tiny Tim and his family, setting free the Wicked Witch of the West's soldiers, or insights such as "There's no place like home." The boon aids the lead *and* his community. Stanley Yelnats, in Louis Sachar's book and movie *Holes*, brings back a concrete boon (the buried treasure, which he shares with Zero) and an abstract boon (freeing his family from a generational curse). Boons are as varied as the stories.

Spaz's boons are knowledge and justice. He and Ryter, through Lanaya at the trial, alert the proovs that someone in Eden is manufacturing and distributing the illegal mindprobes, thus setting the stage for the latches to be cleaned up and less violent. And although he doesn't know it yet, he has absorbed enough of Ryter's philosophy to become the next Ryter.

Crossing the Threshold to Return to the Hero's Original World The hero returns to his original world, usually wiser and with the prize, but the crossing is fraught with danger. Often, this is where the chase scenes are in movies. The antagonist or the antagonist's representatives chase the hero in a last-ditch effort to grab the prize or kill the hero. Crossing the threshold looks like a piece of cake for Dorothy. All she has to do is get in the balloon and sail back to Kansas. This is not to be, however, and her return is thwarted. Walter, in

---

The Hero's Journey Plot

The Hero's Ordinary World
The Call to Adventure
Crossing the Threshold
Into the Journey's World
Into the Heart of the World
Crossing the Threshold to Return to the Ordinary World
The New Ordinary World

Secondhand Lions, does not leave on his own; he is dragged back to his original world by his mother, where there is much tension. Spaz, separated from his sister, is shuttled back to his original world in a takvee.

While crossing the threshold to return home, or after the hero is home, he may encounter the antagonist again. In fact, this can often be the climax of the story. Think of Jack in "Jack and the Beanstalk" as the giant pursues the little thief... just when Jack thinks he is safe. Walter crosses the threshold back to his ordinary world when his mother comes back for him and takes him away from his uncles. In the car, Walter realizes that his mother is not going to get rid of the man who attacked him; in fact, she plans to marry him. As soon as Walter realizes this, he jumps out of the car and has a confrontation with his mother, who has a history of not taking care of him. Walter chooses to be a man; he chooses to live with his uncles, with whom he has bonded.

In the Peter Pan movie *Hook*, the hero Peter Banning wins his swordfight with Captain Hook, who pleads for mercy. Peter grants him mercy and does not kill his old foe. When Peter gathers his children (one of his rewards) and prepares to reenter his original world, the wily captain attacks while Peter's back is turned. Now they have to finish it, and they do in a most appropriate way. Peter, played by Robin Williams, sums up crossing the threshold with this statement: "I've done what I came to do, and now I have to go back."

Much variety exists in how writers choose to express these phases. For instance, in the movie *The Island*, the leads cross over into their new world but return to their old world so they can free the clones. In the movie *Enchanted*, one character moves into the lead's former world, but the lead chooses to stay in the world of the journey to bless it with her upbeat personality, outlook, and skills. Jason Taggart, the ego-centric lead in the movie *Galaxy Quest*, crosses the threshold from outer space back to Earth only to find his antagonist is right behind him.

The New Ordinary World   Here the hero bestows his boon to the community and lives his life in light of the new insights he has learned on his journey. In a literature class, you might call this the resolution. Celebrations may welcome the hero home, or he may be met with suspicion and animosity.

The mentor may have to explain the meaning of the journey to the hero, as Ryter does when Spaz is crouched against the wall of Ryter's old stackbox near the end of the story.

> The Hero's Journey Plot
>
> The Hero's Ordinary World
> The Call to Adventure
> Crossing the Threshold
> Into the Journey's World
> Into the Heart of the World
> Crossing the Threshold to Return
>   to the Ordinary World
> **The New Ordinary World**

What happens to Spaz and Ryter when they return to their original world? They are attacked by a mob on jetbikes, a mob made angry by the loss of the mindprobes. This is not the hero's parade. Spaz has one last battle—and it is his worst.

This is also where the loose ends are tied up. In *Holes*, Stanley Yelnats gives Zero a share of the treasure, arranges for Zero to meet his lost mother, buys a new house for his parents, and makes friends with the sport hero who accused him of the theft that sent him to Green Lake.

You learned in chapter 4 about character arcs, that is, the changes the lead goes through from the beginning of his story to the ending. Character arc is related to the phases of the hero's journey because your character learns, grows, makes mistakes, matures, and battles inner and outer demons. All of this changes him, transforming him into a better man (or her into a better woman). In fact, from a writer's perspective, that's the point of the journey.

The hero's journey is a classic plot structure many have used through the ages because it is satisfying and powerful. If you want to delve more deeply into the topic of the hero's journey, read Christopher Vogler's *The Writer's Journey* (Michael Wiese Productions, 1992) or James N. Frey's *The Key* (St. Martin's Press, 2000).

10.2 All Writers and Discussion

Watch the Disney/Pixar movie *Up* or *Tangled* and write down the phases of the hero's journey as they appear in the movie.

End of today's lesson

Discussion: Discuss with your group the phases of the hero's journey you find in *Up* or *Tangled*.

LA RONDE

This next plot structure is fun and looks like a circle.

In 1900, Arthur Schnitzler, an Austrian playwright, wrote a play titled *La Ronde*. Its first scene is between a prostitute and a soldier, and the prostitute ends up giving something to the soldier. The next scene is between the soldier and a maid, with the soldier passing that something to the maid, and on it goes, a series of two-character scenes in which one character passes something to the next character. The last scene is between a count and the original prostitute. The story has come full circle, which is what the title implies. The "something" they've been passing to each other is syphilis, a sexually transmitted disease.

Alan Alda (Hawkeye Pierce on TV's *M*A*S*H*) reveals in *Never Have Your Dog Stuffed* that he used *La Ronde*'s structure when he wrote the *M*A*S*H* episode "The Long John Flap." The setting of *M*A*S*H*, which stands for Mobile Army Surgical Hospital, is South Korea during the Korean War in the 1950s, and the long johns arrive during a bitterly cold winter; everyone wants them and will do almost anything to get them. So the long johns make the rounds through "scenes of love, bartering, extortion, and losing at poker."

News Flash: It's not about the long johns. It's about the relationships and how far people will go to get what they want. The long johns are simply the vehicle used to tell the story.

Alda used the round structure again when writing the *M*A*S*H* episode "The Rooster Crowed at Midnight." In this episode, a soldier receives a murder mystery in the mail, and that book is passed around (or stolen or bartered) until the end of the episode, at which point someone discovers that the ending has been ripped out of the book. No one knows the book's "whodunit," and all the readers are upset.

But the episode isn't about the book. It's about life's uncertainty, like what's going to happen next or how things will end.

Ann Brashares uses a form of this structure in *The Sisterhood of the Traveling Pants*. Four life-long, teen friends must part during the summer and maybe forever. When they find a pair of jeans that fits them all, they decide to send it around to each other during the summer. This is a way for the girls to stay in touch with each other. Before departing, they make rules for how the jeans should be treated and what can be done while wearing them.

The book, you may have guessed, is not about the jeans. It's about the girls and their varied lives and problems.

There are *so many* other plot structures we could talk about—maturation, rescue, pursuit, revenge, and so forth—if we only had the time! Two books you may find helpful on this topic are *20 Master Plots and How to Build Them* by Ronald B. Tobias (Writer's Digest Books, 1993) and *Story Structure Architect* by Victoria Lynn Schmidt, Ph. D. (Writer's Digest Books, 2005).

10.3 All Writers

Write a short story with the structure of *La Ronde*.
As you plan and write, ask yourself these questions:

> What will be passed around?
> Who will pass it?
> How will it be passed from character to character?
> What is the story **really** about?

End of today's lesson

10.4 Manuscript Track

Concentrate on your story's inciting incident and your character's reaction to it by answering these questions:

- ☑ What propels your character into his/her story?
- ☑ How does your character refuse the call?
- ☑ Why does your character change his/her mind and decide to go on a journey or decide to get involved?

After you have answered these questions about your manuscript, make any needed changes and bring copies of your new version to the group for their critique.

As you consider the structure of the hero's journey, are there any other changes you want to make to your own story?

What you studied in this chapter:

- ✓ Plot as a series of events
- ✓ Story value
- ✓ Plot as a structure or pattern
- ✓ The hero's journey
- ✓ La Ronde

11: SCENES

You may have heard an exasperated mother scold her young drama queen by saying, "Don't make a scene!"

Well, guess what. Make a scene!

That's right. Stories are constructed by artfully adding one scene to another. But scenes are more than building blocks at a construction site. They are your story's heartbeats.

THIS IS NOT A SCENE

Before we define a scene, let's take a look at what a scene is not. The following is from *The Last Book in the Universe*. I took a perfectly good scene and compressed it into simple narrative:

> I have to rip off this old gummy named Ryter, so I go out to the Edge next to the Pipe. I find the old geez who, get this, is sitting there like he's waiting for me. He's got all his stuff piled up by his door. He tells me to take it but really can you trust a gummy who hands over his

stuff? It makes me think he's hiding something, so I look around and find these papers hidden in a crate with small marks on them like the footprints of bugs. He talks about the backtimes and the future and about how I have a story, but I don't believe him. I'm thinking he wants to cut my red.

The above paragraph is **narrative summary** (or summation). It is not a scene. You will need narrative summary occasionally (we'll cover that later in this chapter), but here it only *tells* the action instead of *showing* it. This first meeting of the main characters in *The Last Book in the Universe* needs a full scene complete with action, narrative action, and dialogue.

Please take a few minutes to reread pages 12-20 in *The Last Book in the Universe* to see how Philbrick fully fleshes out this meeting by using a scene. It happens as though you are watching it and uses dialogue, narrative actions (beats), and action. (The paragraphs about Little Face are discussed in this chapter in the "Pat the Dog" lesson.)

THIS IS A SCENE

What is a **scene**? Something written as though it were being acted out on a stage. It happens in "real time" so readers can see it unfolding moment by moment. Each scene takes place generally in only one location, uses a certain amount of time that has a beginning and an ending, and is of significance to the plot and the characters.

A scene is like a story within a story. In the beginning of a scene, you hook your readers and plant a question in their minds; in the middle, you build up tension; and in the ending, you answer the question you hinted at in the beginning. A scene has the same rhythm and pattern as a full-blown story.

Take a look again at pages 12-20 of *The Last Book in the Universe*. The scene includes these portions:

A beginning, including a scene question ("Will Spaz be successful in robbing the gummy?") and a particular point of view (first person). The bulk of the scene happens in one place—Ryter's stackbox—and it takes only a few minutes to complete.

A middle, where Spaz and readers learn information and where tension is increased by complications. One complication is that the gummy is expecting Spaz and even has gathered his possessions together for easy stealing. This makes Spaz suspicious. Another complication is that the gummy does not react with fear but talks to Spaz as an equal, as someone important who has a story. This confuses and unnerves Spaz. And a last complication is that Ryter, while seeming to be honest and open about his belongings, is really hiding something.

An ending that includes a hint of further trouble and an answer to the scene question ("Yes, he robbed him, but...").

The major impetus driving any scene is the character's goal. What does the character want to do? What does he want to happen? What plan is he putting into action? In the scene, the character's goal becomes the **scene goal**. Your character must have a goal and must be taking actions to achieve that goal, just like Spaz traveling to Ryter to rob him. Much of the time, the scene goal (some call it the *scene intention*) will be stated somehow in your story. For the scene we've been examining in *The Last Book in the Universe*, the scene goal is stated as this: "So the deal is, I'm here to steal. Stealing is my job."

The scene goal can be stated outright by the protagonist, as with the above example. It can also be stated in dialogue ("I'm here to rob you") or in narration ("Spaz was determined to rob the gummy"). Or it simply can be implied, as are many of the scene goals in *The Last Book in the Universe*; readers know that the characters have to get through the minefield safely in chapter 15, for example, even though the scene goal is not stated outright. If you do not state the scene goal clearly, make sure *you* know exactly what the scene goal is and have communicated it somehow to the reader.

The scene goal turns into the **scene question** in the reader's mind: "Will Spaz successfully rob the gummy?"

Every scene must have a scene goal and a scene question.

This keeps the reader engaged in your story and anxious about what happens to the characters. If the scene goal is to safely travel through the Pipe, as it is in chapter 9 in *The Last Book in the Universe*, then the scene question in readers' minds becomes, "Will Spaz and Ryter make it through the Pipe safely?"

A story's major dramatic question (MDQ) takes the whole story to answer, whereas the scene question is answered by the end of the scene. In a way, the

MDQ is like the thesis statement of an entire essay, and the scene question is like the topic sentence of a paragraph in that essay.

The scene question is specific and measurable. By the end of the scene, your readers should know whether your character achieved his or her goal, so avoid vague scene questions like "Are all princes charming?" or "Can you trust a Martian?"

The actual beginning of your scene can be written many ways. You may begin your scenes with any of the following techniques. For these examples, two characters are arguing at an amusement park, and the examples show varying ways you can begin the same argument scene:

> **Time/day:** The sun set while they were still arguing about which ride to go on next.

> **Weather:** Candy wrappers and empty paper cups scraped against the cement paths as the wind picked up. Travis shook the first splat of rain off his arm.

> **A short description:** The Ferris wheel was a bright circle in the sky, as was the aerial dog bone-shaped ride as it whipped around in its screaming arc. Beneath those sat squares of booths containing shooting and throwing games of skill for which grown men paid great sums of money to win sawdust-stuffed, iridescent teddy bears for their women who would donate the bears to a local charity in the morning. And nearby, under the clanging flagpole, stood Travis and Jeri, throwing sharp exclamation points at each other as they argued.

> **An attention-getting sentence or image:** The Black Cobra. Thor's Thunder. Two of the best heart-crashing roller coasters ever. "But you have to go on the Tunnel of Love?" Travis shouted, leaning into the wind.

> **A statement of the scene goal:** "I don't care how safe the Tunnel of Love is. I'm going on the Black Cobra," said Travis.

> **A beginning that is seemingly unrelated to the last scene:** Travis smelled disinfectant and rubbing alcohol before he opened his eyes and confirmed that, yes, he was lying in the hospital. He moved to sit up but cried out in pain. His right arm was in a cast. What was a cast

doing on his arm? Oh, right. The Tunnel of Love. [Soon after you begin this new scene, you will connect it up with the last one, as Philbrick does on pages 138-9 of *The Last Book in the Universe*.]

11.1 All Writers and Discussion

Read chapter 16 of *The Last Book in the Universe* and determine the scene's implied goal (which is also Spaz and Ryter's goal) and the scene question. Notice that Lotti's scene goal is not the same as Spaz's. What is Lotti's scene goal?

Lotti's scene goal is very different from Spaz's. That's where the conflict comes in. Make sure each character in your scene has his own scene goal, the most important scene goal being that of the protagonist or the particular scene's viewpoint character.

End of today's lesson

PAT THE DOG

One tried-and-true way writers gain reader empathy for the protagonist is to insert a pat-the-dog scene. In a literal sense, a pat-the-dog scene is one in which the protagonist is running for his life when he happens upon a dog that would be hurt if caught in the crossfire. So the protagonist, even in the extremity of his life-threatening circumstance, bends down, pats the dog, and vows to take care of the hapless animal because, on some level, the protagonist identifies with its vulnerability. Most likely, you have seen this or variations of it in many movies.

The pat-the-dog scene can be used in a figurative sense too. In the 1993 movie *The Fugitive,* Dr. Richard Kimble (played by Harrison Ford) must clear his name of a crime he did not commit. As characters from both sides of the law are coming against him, he sneaks into a hospital to search for some crucial medical records. The scene is tense. Viewers see the pursuers closing in. Dr. Kimble, too, knows he has little time. In the hall, Dr. Kimble comes across a young patient who he clearly sees has been misdiagnosed. What does he do? Instead of continuing his search for the crucial medical records and fleeing the hospital, Kimble tries to tell a medical professional the boy's problem. When this does not work, he takes the young boy in the elevator to the correct floor and explains the misdiagnosis to a doctor there while viewers watch the antagonists hot on his trail.

The essence of a pat-the-dog scene is that even as the protagonist is wrestling with some conflict, he stops to help someone smaller, younger, or more helpless than he.

Spaz does this in *The Last Book in the Universe* too. On his way to doing something he is being forced to do against his will (rob a gummy), he stops and gives some candy to a little orphan boy. Even though the action is not entirely altruistic (he turns Little Face into a guide), it shows readers that somewhere in that street-smart, epileptic, thieving boy, there is a heart.

If you use a pat-the-dog scene, consider allowing something from the scene to have consequences in a later scene. In Spaz's case, his interaction with Little Face has negative consequences in later scenes (the boy becomes an irritating tag-along).

Some writers believe a pat-the-dog scene is unnecessary, something employed by a lazy writer who did not earlier do the work of showing the internal workings of the character. However, when written creatively and when something in the scene has an effect later in the story, it can add to the story's characterization and tension.

YES? NO? MAYBE?

Let's look at how to end a scene.

In the scene that begins on page 21 in *The Last Book in the Universe*, the scene goal is implied: "I'd like to get back to my cube without being killed." The scene question is this: "Will Spaz make it back to his cube safely?" When the takvee shows up, readers become fearful for Spaz and his safety. The takvee and the proov are that scene's complications.

So, does Spaz make it back to his cube safely? Yes, but . . . he's been stunned with a stunstik and receives a bag of edibles, and the edibles become the setup for getting him into trouble with the Bully Bangers in the next scene.

Any scene question can be answered in one of four ways. This list is adapted from Jack M. Bickham's *Scene and Structure*:

1. Yes
2. No
3. Yes, but . . .
4. No, and furthermore . . .

These scene answers signal the end of the scene. After readers know the answer, it's time to move on. Let's set up a scene to see how these possible answers to the scene question could play out.

In this imaginary scene, Travis and Jeri are still arguing about which ride to ride at the amusement park. Travis's scene goal? To ride the Black Cobra roller coaster—with or without Jeri. Jeri's scene goal? To ride the Tunnel of Love with Travis. For this experiment, Travis will be the viewpoint character, even though both characters have clearly defined goals.

The middle of the scene will play out with lots of tension, but we'll get to scene middles in the next lesson. For now, let's see how Travis might do by the end of his scene. Here are the possibilities:

1. **Yes,** he rides the Black Cobra, and Jeri is happy to ride it with him. With this scene answer, readers relax on Travis's behalf. They may even close the book and stop reading. After all, the conflict now feels finished because Travis obtains what he wants.

2. **No**, he doesn't ride the Black Cobra. A number of things could happen now. He could pout through the Tunnel of Love ride with Jeri, leave the amusement park, choose another ride, argue so long with Jeri that the park closes, see Jeri's former boyfriend Grant and ride the Tunnel of Love with Jeri in a misguided effort to show off—anything that makes sense in your story. This answer may work best if you introduce a new piece of information during the scene to give a credible reason for the "no." Try something like this: During the argument, Jeri reveals that her older brother was killed on a roller coaster three years ago. Travis relents, but is Jeri telling the truth?

3. **Yes,** he rides the Black Cobra, **but . . . .** But what? He goes alone and loses Jeri's friendship and respect. Or he goes alone and watches from above as Jeri and Grant meet and walk away with each other. Or maybe Jeri rides it with him, despite her older brother's death, and vows to get even with the insensitive Travis. Notice that Travis's "yes" is Jeri's "no."

4. **No**, he does not ride the Black Cobra, **and furthermore . . . .** This scene answer twists the knife after it's been plunged into the heart, so to speak. Imagine Travis's surprise when he exits the Tunnel of Love with Jeri and is beaten up Grant. Or maybe Jeri is so upset after the argument that she decides to tell the whole school some personal or

secret information Travis has revealed to her. Or maybe Travis discovers on the ride that Jeri wanted to ride it only to make Grant jealous. Or perhaps the argument is so hot that security throws him out of the park in front Grant. Remember that dead brother? Maybe he really didn't die but Jeri made that up to gain sympathy for her cause—and Travis finds this out on the ride.

Whatever scene answer you choose for your poor, luckless protagonist, make sure that when he leaves the scene, he is in worse shape than when he entered it.

Also, make sure that the scene answer has something to do with the scene question. If the scene question is "Will Shawna ask Ryan on a date?" readers anticipate one of the "yes/no" possibilities listed on page 214, and they expect the answer to be about the date question, not about something like "Will Shawna overcome her fear of flying and board the plane?" Just as it is possible to go off track in the larger story and answer a MDQ that was not originally asked, it is also possible to go off track in your scene and answer a scene question that was not asked.

By the end of the scene, you protagonist must experience some sort of change in any of the following:

- His situation
- His motivation
- His loyalties
- His ideas about his scene goal
- An addition of new information for him or for the reader
- Consequences
- Character growth
- The negative or positive quality of the scene value

If nothing changes for your protagonist by the end of the scene, it is a wasted scene. Consider changing or deleting it.

A word about the **scene value**: You learned in chapter 10 (Plot) to write with a story value in mind. For instance, if your story value is freedom, your protagonist will experience or come into contact with freedom, then to some kind of enslavement, and then to some kind of enslavement that looks like freedom before you return him to freedom. Robert McKee explains this important pattern in his acclaimed book *Story*.

In addition to this *story* value, each *scene* will also have a value or a value continuum that is related to the story's major value. For instance, say Travis goes into his ride-the-Black-Cobra scene with a great deal of ego; then it might be a good idea to deflate his confidence by the end of the scene. If he goes in with self-doubt, allow him to encounter something further down the self-confidence/self-doubt continuum, something like a total lack of confidence in his abilities, a self-loathing, or contact with someone who thinks Travis will never amount to anything.

The scene value must slide on the continuum by the end of the scene. Travis cannot go into his scene happy and leave happy.

There is one exception to that rule. If you give the reader new information in that scene, information that Travis does not know or does not understand, the reader can be worried for Travis, who does not know what is about to hit him.

Aside from answering the scene question, scene endings should be enticing enough to keep the reader reading. Throw in a new complication at the end. Announce some new and surprising information. Paint a sense of foreboding with a short description or a narrative summary. Your scene's last lines should be provocative enough to heighten your reader's interest and worry factors.

Charles Dickens knew the value of an intriguing scene ending, especially as some of his books were first printed in serial form in his weekly magazine *All the Year Round*, two chapters at a time. He had to keep readers interested so they would buy the magazines. This is similar to today's TV series that continue plots from one week to the next and end each week's episode with a cliffhanger.

Here's a scene ending (which also ends the chapter) aimed at capturing readers, taken from Dickens' *A Tale of Two Cities*. It takes place in England during a trial for treason. The defendant is Charles Darnay, and, after readers get an explicit and gruesome description of being drawn and quartered, Darnay sees a young woman who obviously has pity for him and sees "nothing but the peril" ahead for him. But there's a problem. The crowd figures out who the young woman is and passes along the news:

> "Witness."
> "For which side?"
> "Against."
> "Against what side?"
> "The prisoner's."

> The Judge, whose eyes had gone in the general direction, recalled them, leaned back in his seat, and looked steadily at the man whose life was in his hand, as Mr. Attorney-General rose to spin the rope, grind the axe, and hammer the nails into the scaffold.

Things are not looking good for the young woman forced to be a witness against someone she pities. And they aren't looking too good for the handsome defendant, either. That's how page turners are created.

11.2 All Writers and Discussion

Read pages 194-196 in *The Last Book in the Universe*, beginning with the sentence "They come for us one day while Bean and me are climbing apple trees."

Answer these questions and discuss them:

› What are the differences between the beginning of the scene and the ending?
› What is the scene value while Spaz and Bean are in the apple trees? What is the value at the end of the scene?
› How is Spaz worse off by the end of the scene?
› Write out the last few sentences of five scenes in *The Last Book in the Universe* and determine how these "curtain lines" keep readers interested in the story. Share your results with the group.

End of today's lesson

11.3 Manuscript Track

Read a scene from your short story or novel and ask yourself these questions. Make the needed changes.

☑ Is the scene goal clear?
☑ Is it near the beginning of the scene?
☑ Is the scene's question clearly answered by the end of the scene?

THE SCENE'S GUTS

I confess, we've done this out of order. First we looked at the scene's beginning and then skipped to the scene's ending. This order helped when examining the relationship between the scene goal/question and the scene answer, but now it's time to move to the scene's guts—the middle.

The character's goal becomes the scene's goal, but why does the character hold that particular goal? The character's **motivation** affects the character's goal and colors the scene's middle.

If the lead is trapped in a cave, her goal will be to get out. But why? What is her motivation? Does she want to get out because she is fearful of the bats? Because she found the treasure and is driven to show it to the world? Because she's such a klutz that no one would believe she could actually save herself? Because her life is in danger from suffocation? Her motivation will affect her actions and the scene's tension.

What is motivating your protagonist to achieve her scene goal?

Remember Travis and his attempt to ride the Black Cobra? Suppose Travis's motivation is to show off. Most likely, no reader will really care because the motivation is selfish. But what if Travis's motivation is firmly rooted in the deep wound you developed for him earlier? Let's suppose that Travis wants to ride the death-defying roller coaster because his father helped develop it and Travis, normally afraid of heights, yearns to win his father's approval.

Now you have a meaningful motivation for the scene goal. In fact, now the **stakes are high**, and readers will worry more about Travis and his goal. It will matter more if he fails.

Make sure readers know what the scene stakes are for your protagonist, that if your protagonist fails, it will be a big deal.

Include new **information** in your scene. In *The Curious Incident of the Dog in the Night-Time* by Mark Haddon, the protagonist is Christopher, a 15-year-old boy who is a mathematically gifted but socially challenged autistic savant. While he is detecting the death of a neighbor's dog, he writes clues in a book. One day when he is looking for his book, he comes across something he's never seen before in his father's room:

> And that was when I saw the envelope.
>   It was an envelope addressed to me and it was lying under my book in the shirt box with some other envelopes. I picked it up. It had never been opened. It said

>Christopher Boone
>36 Randolph Street
>Swindon
>Wiltshire
>
>Then I noticed that there were lots of other envelopes and they were all addressed to me. And this was interesting and confusing.

He takes one of the letters and reads it later in his bedroom. It is from his mother, who has been dead for some time; the letter mentions her new job in London working for a steel manufacturer. Here's Christopher again:

>Then I was really confused because Mother had never worked as a secretary for a firm that made things out of steel. Mother had worked as a secretary for a big garage in the center of town. And Mother had never lived in London. Mother had always lived with us. And Mother had never written a letter to me before.

This information is important to Christopher's hunt for the dog's killer, but it is also important to readers understanding Christopher.

Any new information should lead to other **complications**, as in William Golding's *Lord of the Flies* when some of the little boys report they've seen a frightening "beastie," which eventually leads to a hunt for the monster.

And complications *must* arise in the scene. Again, in *Lord of the Flies*, Ralph, with the help of the corpulent Piggy, calls a meeting of the stranded boys by blowing a conch shell. During this scene on the shore of a deserted island, Ralph and Jack spar for leadership of the meeting and of the boys, and new information is given about a monster. The scene moves on to plans of hunting pigs and making a rescue fire. Here's where a complication arises for Ralph, who represents the voice of civilization, as the wilder Jack makes his move to usurp the leadership of the castaways. The first speaker is Ralph:

>"There's another thing. We can help them to find us. If a ship comes near the island they may not notice us. So we must make smoke on top of the mountain. We must make a fire."
>
>"A fire! Make a fire!"

> At once half the boys were on their feet. Jack clamored among them, the conch forgotten.
> "Come on! Follow me!"
> The space under the palm trees was full of noise and movement. Ralph was on his feet too, shouting for quiet, but no one heard him. All at once the crowd swayed toward the island and was gone—following Jack. Even the tiny children went and did their best among the leaves and broken branches. Ralph was left, holding the conch, with no one but Piggy.

Your lead's attempts to fix things or gain balance in his life will not work out as he had planned because you will have scene complications up your sleeve. Scene complications often become the action behind the next scene's goal. For instance, in *Lord of the Flies*, the next scene deals with Ralph and Jack tussling over how to build the fire and where to build it. And, of course, things only get worse from there.

The middle of your scene is where, through action and dialogue, you show lots of **conflict**, something you studied in chapter 5. If you don't have any conflict for your characters, you really don't have a scene. Characters need not be arguing or be at each other's throats all the time, but even characters who share the same goal should disagree about how to achieve it.

Conflict, as you know, can be external or internal. In a scene in *To Kill a Mockingbird* by Harper Lee, the young protagonist Jean Louise ("Scout") Finch tries to act like a lady during her aunt Alexandra's ladies' meeting at the house. That is her scene goal. Scout's internal conflict occurs as some of the white ladies speak negatively about black people and about Scout's father's defense of a young black man. While Scout fights with herself to "be a lady," readers get new information about hypocrisy and about the fate of the black man in question.

> For when we came into Macedonia, this body of ours had no rest, but we were harassed at every turn—conflicts on the outside, fears within.
> –Apostle Paul in II Corinthians 7:5 (NIV)

Motivation, what's at stake, new information, complications, conflict—these are effective techniques you can employ to make sure the middle of your scene is full of interest and tension.

11.4 All Writers and Discussion

Read chapter 22 (pages 148-52) in *The Last Book in the Universe*. The scene goal is really on the page before the chapter begins. It is the last sentence in chapter 21. What story value does the scene begin with? What story value does it end with?

Below is a list of the techniques Philbrick uses to keep the excitement going in the middle of this scene/chapter. Give examples of each of the techniques he uses in this scene.

> › Motivation to go to Eden
> › What's at stake
> › New information
> › Complications
> › Conflict

11.5 All Writers

Write a scene in which two characters are physically attached to each other by, say, duct tape, handcuffs, rope, dental braces, glue, or whatever you wish. Their scene goal is to get free, but neither character can agree with the other as to how to do it.

Keep your scene to about 500-750 words.

Check with your teacher to see if you should hand in the scene or make copies to share with your writing group.

11.6 Manuscript Track

Using the same scene you used in exercise 11.3, ask these questions of the scene and make the necessary changes:

> ☑ Is my character's motivation clear and believable?

- ☑ Are the stakes high enough?
- ☑ Have I included new information for the character or for the reader?
- ☑ Does the new information lead to complications?
- ☑ Does the scene contain the right amount of conflict?

NARRATIVE SUMMARY

Narrative summary, as you saw at the beginning of this chapter, is different from a scene. It does not give you moment-by-moment action but, rather, summarizes action or relates character reactions and ruminations after a scene.

You need narrative summary in your story—in the right places.

The following examples of narrative summary are taken from *Cape Fear* by John D. MacDonald and show summary's usefulness in compressing time; moving characters from one location to another or to a later time; or relating backstory, information (exposition), or description. Sam is the protagonist and is married to Carol; Nancy and Jamie are two of their children.

Compressing time:

> Nothing happened on Friday. On Saturday he drove down to Suffern, and on Sunday they visited Nancy and Jamie. He was back at his desk on Monday morning.

Moving characters through time or location (called *transitions*):

> They were home by four.

And:

> Sam was back at the hospital by quarter to five.

Backstory:

He had met Carol on a Friday noon in late April of 1942 at the Horn and Hardart Cafeteria near the campus of the University of Pennsylvania. He was in his final year of law school. She was in her senior year in the undergraduate school.

Exposition (explaining something):

The New Essex Yacht Club is four miles east of the city. It has an ample yacht basin, dock space, its own breakwater, a long club building, with terraces, bars and ballrooms. The motor-cruiser owners call the devout sailors the Magellan Set. The sailors call the cruiser owners the Stinkpot Group.

Description:

Dr. Lowney was a big placid man with white hair, bright-blue eyes and an easygoing manner.

NARRATIVE SUMMARY AND THE END OF A SCENE

A scene may end abruptly or with a summary of sorts. A summary is a passage that will not play well on a stage because the characters are in their heads, dealing with the physical and emotional results of the now-ending scene.

If a summary is employed to allow the character to react to the previous scene and to develop the next scene's goal, it can be called a **sequel**. In this case, *sequel* is not a movie sequel, as is *Toy Story 3*, a movie that follows up on *Toy Story* and *Toy Story 2*. It is simply the name of the passage that appears at the end of a scene and links it to the next one by ruminating on the past scene and developing the goal for the next one. Almost every scene will have its own sequel.

In the example below, Travis has just finished a scene. His scene goal was to ride the Black Cobra. Scene question: Will Travis ride the Black Cobra? Scene answer: No.

Now he ends his scene by reacting to his failure to ride his ride. In addition, he has to formulate a new goal and begin acting on it:

Chapter 11: Scenes 225

Ruminating about his possibilities — All right. He'd go on the stupid tunnel ride. But he wondered how he could face the rest of the football team Monday morning if Grant caught him in the Tunnel of Love with Jeri and that lunatic teddy bear. Yes, she and Grant had broken up last Tuesday, but you never knew.

Maybe Travis could hide his face. It was dark in there, after all. But even getting on the ride would be a problem. He couldn't hide his face while he was waiting in line. He couldn't hide that he was there with Jeri. There were so many ways he could go wrong, and he seemed to already have done most of them tonight. What did Jeri think of him?

Formulating a plan based on his motivation — He needed a plan, one that would not embarrass himself or alienate Jeri. He thought about the tunnel and the water. Then he reached into his pocket and pulled out what money he had left—six dollars and fifteen cents. Would that be enough to bribe the guy taking tickets?

The next scene's goal—getting onto the ride without being seen—and the first step in his new plan of action — Forget the bribe. He would get on that ride fast without Grant or any of the other guys on the team seeing him. Quick as lightning, he struck Jeri's elbow. The teddy bear went flying.

Occasionally, your scene will not need a sequel. The scene simply ends with a short narrative summary and then jumps into the next scene by moving through time clearly. To see how this works, read this excerpt from Richard Adams' *Watership Down*, whose characters are rabbits in the wild. The scene goal is to free some rabbits living in a hutch in a barn, but things go very awry, and Hazel, one of the male leaders, gets shot ("Yes, but . . ."). We join him just after he scrambles into a drainage pipe in a ditch to elude his human shooters:

The silence returned, but still Hazel lay motionless in the whispering chill of the tunnel. A cold lassitude came over him and he passed into a dreaming, inert stupor, full of cramp and pain. After a time, a thread of blood began to trickle over the lip of the drain into the trampled, deserted ditch. — *Narrative summary to end the scene*

* * * ← *Visual break*

Bigwig, crouched close to Blackberry in the straw of the cattle shed, leaped to flight at the sound of the shot two hundred yards up the lane. He checked himself and turned to the others. — *Beginning of new scene with a different set of characters and scene goals*

No sequel is needed because Adams cuts to another set of characters. Hazel finishes his scene in the pipe—after we know his scene answer—with some physical reactions ("stupor," "cramp and pain"), and we leave him as he bleeds into the ditch. After a visual pause on the page, the story follows another group of rabbits Hazel earlier had sent on their way.

As long as it makes sense in your story, there may be no need to fill in the lapsed time with narrative between the scenes.

Many scenes or breaks in the action are separated by a blank space on the page. In your manuscript, you will use asterisks when separating your scenes unless the scene break is at the end of the chapter.

Sometimes you simply need to *tell* by using narrative summary instead of *show* with a scene, but keep these times to a minimum so as not to give your readers a yawn.

11.7 All Writers and Discussion

Find examples of these jobs that narrative summary does in *The Last Book in the Universe*:

> › Compressing time
> › Moving characters from one location to another or to a later time
> › Telling backstory
> › Telling information (*exposition*)
> › Telling description
> › Physical and mental reactions to the scene that is just ending

11.8 All Writers

Pages 47-9 of *The Last Book in the Universe* contain narrative summary of part of Spaz's backstory with Bean. It is not a scene.

Write it as a scene, as though it were happening moment by moment with an audience watching the action and listening to the dialogue. What is Spaz's scene goal? What is the scene question? What is the answer to the scene question? How will you increase the tension and conflict in the middle as you show Bean, Charly, Kay, the healer, and Spaz interacting?

You may use as much of Philbrick's text as you want to, in addition to your own. Keep the scene to around 700 words.

Check with your teacher to see if you should hand in the scene or make copies to share with your writing group.

SOME COMMON SCENE MISTAKES

You've already learned one common scene mistake—not answering the scene question that you set up in the beginning of the scene.

And you've learned another common scene mistake, that of answering the scene question with something unrelated to the question and the story. Remember Travis and his attempt to ride the Black Cobra? It would be a mistake if you ended his scene question with a "no" due to an attack of ravenous locusts, forcing everyone to run for cover. Astute readers would find this hard to believe. The scene ending and answer have to grow logically out of the story, the characters, and the scene.

Now it's time to examine some additional mistakes.

The **first** is a mistake of logic. Readers expect things to happen in a certain order. Below is a paragraph with two logic mistakes in it. Can you find them?

> Antasia crept through the misty woods, the sword in her belt hitting limbs and thick roots. She must keep it quiet or the beast would hear her coming. Soon she stood at the edge of the woods. A meadow stretched out before her, but it was not empty. The beast stood in the clearing, the sun spangling its scales. Antasia watched him lift his head as he caught her scent and turned toward her. He pawed the ground. Fire shot from his nostrils and burned the leaves above Antasia's head. She dropped to the ground. A singed scent reached her nostrils, and she wondered how the feather in her hat had fared. Antasia rushed out of the woods and sliced off the beast's head with her sword.

What are the writer's mistakes? First, she doesn't tell readers that Antasia stood up (the writer left her on the ground), and second, she doesn't have Antasia draw her sword; the character's attack feels abrupt and out of place, and the action of slicing the beast's head off feels unreal to the reader.

Including something like this would have helped:

> Antasia jumped up and drew her sword. The beast must die. She rushed out of the woods and sliced off the beast's head.

Keep the actions logical. Show the steps.

Incidentally, Antasia does not decide to attack as a result of standing around and thinking about it. She attacks because she's been prodded to by the stimulus of the beast's fiery volley. Her stimulus to attack is physical; her response is physical too. This physical stimulus-response pattern is important in creating a logical, credible story.

And that leads to the **second** common scene mistake. Remember that law you learned in science class, the one that governs reactions? It goes something like this: "For every action, there is an equal and opposite reaction." Something similar is true in story writing.

If Chucky punches Roderick on the jaw, Roderick is not going to stand around and ponder what to do next or have an internal discussion on the ethics of hitting someone back and defending oneself or remember the advice his mother gave him just this morning on how to deal with bullies. No. He's going to have an "equal" reaction, that is, because the stimulus is physical, his reaction is going to be physical and then emotional. He may jump back, fall to the floor, feel the adrenalin course through his body, brace himself for another attack by raising his fists—something physical and emotional. Only *after* he has reacted physically and with emotion will he react mentally, that is, have thoughts and make decisions.

The next time someone punches you, notice that your *first* reaction is physical/emotional and your *second* reaction is mental. The same should be true for your characters.

Here's author Sid Fleischman remembering some of his early mistakes in this area, taken from his essay "The Ouch Factor":

> In my haste to keep a story moving, I was apt to leap from action to action, unwilling to pause for reactions. If one of my characters hit his thumb with a hammer, I didn't give him time to say ouch.

Silas Marner, the reclusive weaver in George Eliot's *Silas Marner*, shows us first a physical reaction (or "ouch") and then a mental reaction as he discovers someone has robbed him of all his life's savings (a physical action that readers watched in the previous chapter): "The sight of the empty hole made his heart leap violently." We then read that his hand trembles as he shines the candlelight into the gaping hole. Here's what happens next:

> At last he shook so violently that he let fall the candle, and lifted his hands to his head, trying to steady himself, that he might think. Had he put his gold somewhere else, by a sudden resolution last night, and then forgotten it?

Physical then mental reactions

In similar fashion, your whole scene will benefit from this action-reaction pattern. Let's say you write a fictional Allie onto an airplane and make the plane begin its fall from the sky. The scene is tense, lots of action, Allie crashing into the seat in front of her and then whiplashing into the back of her seat. She tries to get her seatbelt off. She scrambles for the flotation device under the seat. She grabs the oxygen mask and jams it on her face. All of this is physical, responding physically and emotionally to physical problems and stimuli (external stimuli, not thoughts). It is only *after* you record her physical and emotional reactions that you can take time to write the narrative summary that is Allie's mental reaction to the situation. Physical, emotional, and then mental.

During the scene's sequel in which she has a mental reaction to her horrific experience, maybe even taking inventory of her situation, Allie will most likely think about her options and develop a plan for what to do next. Her plan will become the goal for the next scene.

This pattern is important in the small actions throughout the scene and in the scene's rhythm of moving from the *action* of the scene to the *reaction* in narrative summary or sequel.

Jack M. Bickham, in *Scene and Structure*, calls this action-reaction pattern a stimulus-and-response pattern. It is so important that, according to Bickham, using the pattern makes a strong statement about life:

> Because this kind of presentation shows a world in which things *do* make sense—in which everything isn't just meaningless chaos and chance—the resulting story also has the effect of offering a little hope to the reader: a suggestion by implication that life doesn't have to be meaningless, and that bad things don't always have to happen to good people for no reason . . . a hint that maybe the reader can seize some

control of his own life after all, and that good effort may sometimes actually pay off—and our existence may indeed even have some kind of meaning.

Wow! Who knew that being logical in your writing could be so powerful?

A **third** and very common scene mistake is changing viewpoint characters within the scene. Here's how *not* to do it, using a passage from Rex Stout's *Immune to Murder*, a Nero Wolfe mystery. Here we watch Wolfe's private detective Archie Goodwin reporting to Wolfe, who was asked to cook his specialty—trout. Fritz is the head chef. I rewrote the passage using two viewpoint characters instead of the one from the book (the added bits are underlined):

Underlined portion from Wolfe's perspective →

"You're early," [Wolfe] grunted. "Satisfactory." <u>He wondered if Goodwin would do anything right this weekend.</u>

Underlined portion from Goodwin's perspective →

"Yes, sir. I've got four trout and one supertrout to take back to Fritz, as promised. How was the lunch?" <u>And thanks for saving me some, thought Goodwin. His stomach growled.</u>

Back to Wolfe →

"Passable. I cooked twenty trout and they were all eaten. I'm nearly packed, and we can go. Now." <u>Wolfe was tired of the cabin and all this camping out. He wanted to get back to New York and civilization.</u>

Goodwin's turn again →

"Yes, sir. First I have a report." <u>I was packed, too, and wanted to return home, but I guessed my report would keep him from his precious orchids a few more days.</u> "About three-quarters of a mile downstream I found Secretary Leeson against a boulder near the bank, his feet out of the water and the rest of him in. He had been there some time; his armpits were good and cold."

The scene feels too scattered, too confusing, because it is from two perspectives instead of one. Writing other characters' thoughts and feelings only clutters it up.

Generally, readers want to stick with one viewpoint character throughout the story or, at least, throughout the scene. Beginning writers should choose one viewpoint character for the scene and stick with that character. How do you know which viewpoint character to use? If you have more than one viewpoint character in your novel, choose the character that has the most to lose in that particular scene, the one with the highest stakes.

Chapter 11: Scenes 231

11.9 All Writers and Discussion

There is an action-reaction error on page 24 of *The Last Book in the Universe*. Identify it and fix it. Then share your result with your writing group.

11.10 All Writers and Discussion

Read the complete "A Good Man Is Hard to Find" by Flannery O'Connor (http://pegasus.cc.ucf.edu/~surette/goodman.html) and identify its three scenes. Then sum up each scene goal, question, and scene answer. Discuss your findings.

11.11 All Writers and Discussion

Below is the ending of a scene. It ends with a punch because it gives new and startling information.

Write a sequel to the scene. Begin with a physical response grounded in an emotional reaction, and then move to the mental response where the character begins to make a plan to put into operation. This narrative summary or sequel can be as short or long as you need it to be for your imaginary story.

Here's the scene ending:

> I pulled my phone out of my backpack to call Melanie and turned it back on. I really hate that I have to turn it off during class. There was a voice message waiting for me. How long had it been there?
> "Hey, Sweetie," said Mom's voice. I slowed my pace. She never calls me Sweetie unless there's trouble, unless she needs to soften me up for the blow. "Listen," her voice continued, "call me as soon as you get this. Your dad's been in a car accident, and it isn't looking very good. Love ya. Bye."

The rest of this chapter is for the **manuscript track.** If you are not in that track, feel free to peruse the information or skip it. Your choice.

If you are in the manuscript track, the next two lessons are for you. Get ready to dig a little deeper.

> What you studied in this chapter:
> - ✓ What a scene is not
> - ✓ What a scene is
> - ✓ Scene goal
> - ✓ Scene question
> - ✓ Scene answer
> - ✓ Scene value
> - ✓ Ramping up the tension in the scene's middle
> - ✓ Pat-the-dog scene
> - ✓ Narrative summary and sequel
> - ✓ Scene mistakes

FLASHBACKS

Flashbacks are real scenes showing something that happened before the present time in your story, something in a character's history. They are most useful to your story when they will have an emotional impact on the story, the reader, or the lead. A flashback scene should reveal something important from the lead's history. As J. Madison Davis puts it in *Novelist's Essential Guide to Creating Plot*:

> In the best flashbacks, the revelation of what happened becomes a way of commenting on what is happening in the story's "present." In pointless flashbacks, the material from the past only confirms what readers already know.

The passage on pages 33-4 in *The Last Book in the Universe* may look like a flashback but is not. Why? It is summary. It is not a scene. Please take a few minutes to read Spaz summing up his first meeting with his baby sister. Begin with Ryter saying, "Start at the beginning," and end with him saying, "So you were a foundling." I'll wait.

***

Spaz's recall of this information is important to the story because it shows how much he loves Bean, the kind of person he is at his core. But it does not flesh out, moment by moment, what happened at that first meeting. It does not happen as though it were on a stage. Although the summary is important, it's not a flashback scene.

So, what is a flashback scene?

A flashback is a real scene shown in real time as though on a stage, complete with action, narrative action, and dialogue, and it contains information of emotional import to the story or the protagonist. Its content occurred sometime before the present time of the story.

A flashback uses a trigger to "remind" the narrator of the past event. A trigger could be a scent, an event, a color—anything that links the present story to the flashback scene.

To move your present story into a flashback scene and back again,

› Use a trigger that puts the flashback into the narrator's mind. Then begin a new paragraph to start your flashback.
› Use time-related phrases like "I remember when…," "Last Christmas…," "Before her mother died…," and so forth, to show readers they are no longer in the present story.
› Use the word "had" in one or two of the first sentences of the flashback and then drop it so readers can get closer to the scene.
› Use clear markers to show when you leave the flashback and return to the story, usually a reference to the time, day, place, or action of the present story.

There is a small writers' controversy (that's a small controversy for writers, not a controversy for small writers) about the word "had." Some writers believe it to be unnecessary; others believe it helps the reader over that first flashback speed bump. For now, use it in your first flashback paragraph and then drop it for the remainder of the flashback.

Here are two examples of how to get into and out of flashback scenes. They are both from *The Remains of the Day* by Kazuo Ishiguro. The first one uses the traditional "had" for the first paragraph.

Going into the flashback with the stoic English butler Stevens:

Trigger with revelation of distress

> I have also, no doubt, been prompted to think along such lines by the small event that occurred an hour or so ago—which has, I admit, unsettled me somewhat.

"Had" in first paragraph; clear wording in first sentence to delineate a past event

> Having enjoyed a good morning's motoring in splendid weather, and having lunched well at a country inn, I had just crossed the border into Dorset. It was then I had become aware of a heated smell emanating from the car engine. The thought that I had done some damage to my employer's Ford was, of course, most alarming and I had quickly brought the vehicle to a halt.

Fully into the flashback; drops the "had"

> I found myself in a narrow lane, hemmed in on either side by foliage so that I could gain little idea of what was around me.

The rest of the flashback, which happens just an hour before the present part of the story, chronicles his rescue and a surprising revelation in dialogue, the thing that "unsettled" him.

Here is Stevens coming out of that flashback after being rescued by the batman mentioned in the paragraph (Note: a "batman" is a British officer's servant or orderly):

Clear time phrases like "a little over a half an hour ago" and "now" to show him rejoining the present time of the story

> The Ford seemed to be in fine form again, and since the pond in question was but a small detour off my route, I decided to take up the batman's suggestion . . . . [A]fter some searching, I found a signpost to 'Mortimer's Pond', and so it was that I arrived here at this spot a little over a half an hour ago.
>
> I now find myself much indebted to the batman, for quite aside from assisting with the Ford, he has allowed me to discover a most charming spot which it is most improbable I would ever have found otherwise.

The emotional importance of this flashback is that even when Stevens is identified as "one of them top-notch butlers" by the veteran, Stevens denies ever having worked for his former employer, a man to whom he gave years of faithful service. That information is worth a flashback. It makes us wonder why he would deny such a thing.

Just before *The Remains of the Day* slips into another flashback elsewhere in the book, Stevens says that his encounter with another employee "produced curious results" years ago. Then he begins the flashback this way:

> I recall a mist starting to set in as I crossed the lawn that afternoon.

And he comes out of it this way:

> Now that I have recalled this episode of the dismissing of the Jewish employees . . .

This information, along with how Stevens reacts to his part in the discriminatory lay-off, reveals Stevens' employer's prejudice and Steven's subconscious conflict about this.

The Remains of the Day is a helpful book to study if you want to learn more about flashbacks because so much of the book is in flashback scenes.

Anton Chekhov's "The Bet" begins with a flashback scene that recounts the bet and how it came about because in the present story the terms of the bet are almost at an end, a full fifteen years after it was made:

> It was a dark autumn night. The old banker was walking up and down his study and remembering how, fifteen years before, he had given a party one autumn evening. There had been many clever men there, and there had been interesting conversations. Among other things, they had talked of capital punishment. The majority of the guests, among whom were many journalists and intellectual men, disapproved of the death penalty. They considered that form of punishment out of date, immoral, and unsuitable for Christian states. In the opinion of some of them the death penalty ought to be replaced everywhere by imprisonment for life.
>
> "I don't agree with you," said their host the banker. "I have not tried either the death penalty or imprisonment for life, but if one may judge *a priori*, the death penalty is more moral and more humane than imprisonment for life."

- Trigger with revelation of distress
- Clear delineation of "now" and "then"
- "Had" in the first few sentences

Beginning of a moment-by-moment conversation in the flashback

The conversation continues for many paragraphs as guests of the banker debate both sides of the issue, which readers read in a moment-by-moment argument. A deal is struck, a bet is made in which a young lawyer volunteers to stay in solitary confinement for fifteen years—and tomorrow ends the fifteen-year confinement. After recounting the argument and the bet, Chekhov returns to the present story thus:

"Now" the banker is back in the present story.
> And now the banker, walking to and fro, remembered all this, and asked himself, "What was the object of that bet? What is the good of that man's losing fifteen years of his life and my throwing away two millions?"

Generally speaking, flashbacks slow or halt the forward movement of the story and can sometimes be distracting, so keep them short and use them sparingly, if at all.

11.12 Manuscript Track

Try your hand at creating a flashback scene. Follow the format that includes a trigger, clear wording to delineate a time shift, "had" in the first paragraph, and clear wording to indicate the transition to your present story.

Here are your choices:

- ☑ Choose a spot in your manuscript to insert the flashback scene. Is there a place where the backstory could be more fully fleshed out to add depth to the protagonist?
- ☑ Find a place in an existing novel and insert a flashback scene. Either completely fabricate the character's history and information or take some piece of backstory and turn it into a moment-by-moment flashback scene.

Write 750 words or fewer. Make enough copies of your flashback scene for your critique group.

End of today's lesson

MIRROR SCENES

Mirror scenes are two scenes that are alike in most of their elements; the differences exist to showcase an event or a change of some sort.

We'll examine four mirror scenes, one from a TV episode, one from a movie, and two from novels.

The pilot for USA Network's TV series *Monk*, "Mr. Monk and the Candidate," contains mirror scenes. In the first mirror scene, the "defective" detective Mr. Adrian Monk, who has many phobias, climbs a fire escape ladder to reach a fleeing miscreant, but Monk's fear of heights overcomes him and he clings to the ladder instead of grabbing the fellow, who blithely steps down the ladder and gets away. Because of Monk's failure, he loses the respect of the captain and is even further from obtaining his story goal of getting his police badge back.

Near the end of the episode, in the scene that mirrors the ladder scene, Mr. Monk descends a ladder into the sewer system to reach a fleeing miscreant, but this time the stakes are higher: the perpetrator has kidnapped Mr. Monk's nurse/assistant Sharona. Mr. Monk *must* overcome his fear of heights, germs, and enclosed spaces in order to save his assistant. He failed on the fire escape. Will he fail in the sewer?

That's the question viewers have in their minds when they view the second mirror scene.

The elements that are the same: the character Mr. Monk, a criminal, a ladder, Monk's phobias.

The elements that are different: going down into the sewer instead of climbing up a fire escape, dealing with multiple fears instead of only one, saving Sharona instead of simply catching a criminal (what is at stake).

In this case, the mirror scenes highlight the character's growth.

Another example of mirror scenes occurs in the 1995 movie version of Jane Austen's *Sense and Sensibility* written by Emma Thompson. Early in the movie, Marianne, one of the protagonists, gets caught in a rain storm and twists her ankle. The dashing but questionable John Willoughby happens by and carries her into her house. Thus begins Marianne's relationship with Willoughby while a more generous and kind man waits in the wings for her affections. Near the end of the movie, after Marianne's heart has been broken by Willoughby's deceit and selfishness, she wanders off at a friend's house, gets caught in another rain storm, and collapses in her weakened state. This time, the generous and kind Colonel Brandon rescues her and carries her into the house, thus beginning Marianne's relationship with him.

The elements that are the same: the character Marianne, a rain storm, a rescue by being carried.

The elements that are different: the sprain is quickly healed but the collapse in the second storm brings her to the point of death; the one rescuer brings her heartache, the other brings her happiness.

The effect of these mirror scenes is to show the change in Marianne's heart and outlook on life.

A set of effective mirror scenes can be found in C. S. Lewis's *The Magician's Nephew*. Near the end of "The Bell and the Hammer" chapter and into "The Deplorable World," readers see Digory strike a golden bell of which he and Polly had been warned, "Strike the bell and bide the danger." The bell's note begins as sweet but soon becomes unbearably loud and then "horrible," with the air "throbbing." Soon the two children hear a "disastrous noise" that sounds like a large tree crashing and "great weights falling" and then experience something like an earthquake in which part of the building falls in. All of this, of course, is the prelude to the Witch awakening and creating havoc in all the worlds she enters.

The scene that mirrors this one occurs in the later chapters "The Fight at the Lamp-post" and "The Founding of Narnia." Polly and Digory have fallen into a dark world where they hear a voice as it begins to sing, and Digory thinks it is "the most beautiful noise he had ever heard. It was so beautiful he could hardly bear it." "Tingling, silvery voices" soon join it, and a light begins to grow in the darkness, making it possible for the children to see the "fresh, hot and vivid" colors of the new world and the singer himself, a huge lion, who is singing a fresh Narnia into life.

The elements that are the same: the characters Digory and Polly, a musical sound that has the power to create.

The elements that are different: The sound of the bell has the power to create (or awaken) great evil; the song of the voice has the power to create great good.

The effect of these mirror scenes is to show the differences between and the effects of evil and good.

The last example is from Stephenie Meyer's book *Twilight*. In the first mirror scene, the protagonist Bella is walking alone in town on an empty street lined with "blank, doorless, windowless walls" when four men begin to surround her, intending to attack. As she contemplates techniques from her self-defense class, someone comes to her rescue. In the scene that mirrors this one, Bella follows the instructions of her mother's kidnapper and reports to a ballet studio to give herself up as a sacrifice so her mom can go free. There she admits, "I'd never been more alone in my entire life." And during the grueling attack, someone comes to her rescue.

The elements that are similar: the character Bella, her life-threatening situations, the feeling of aloneness, the fear she feels and the anxiety on her behalf that readers feel, her rescue.

The elements that are different: Bella happens into a nest of attackers in the first scene; she walks purposefully into the second. The street is lined with blank walls in the first scene; in the second the studio is lined with mirrors. The antagonists are strangers in the first scene; she knows the one in the second. Her rescuer removes her from the situation in the first scene; he arrives late and is more violent in the second.

The effect of these mirror scenes is to show that even though Bella sees herself as cowardly, the facts prove otherwise. Also, if a rescue of one sort is possible earlier in the story, a rescue of a similar nature is possible later in the story. In other words, the earlier rescue shows that the later rescue is not coincidental. More strongly than that, readers *expect* the rescue. They are waiting for it. The question is not "Will he rescue her?" but "How is he going to save her now?"

You will notice that mirror scenes depend on patterns and repetition. You set up the pattern in the first scene and repeat key parts of it in the second. For Mr. Monk, it is the ladder and his fears. For Bella, it is the walls/mirrors in the background and the fact that she is being attacked. You may want to repeat a bit of dialogue, imagery (hummingbirds in one, helicopters in the next, for instance), description, emotional content (fear, in Bella's case), or character reaction, or you may want to repeat the scene goal or value in each scene. Pairs of opposites will also connect the two scenes: one in daylight, one in the dark of night, say.

The point of mirror scenes is not to show off a cool technique but to highlight your theme, your character's changes, the contrasts in your story, and so forth. Make your mirror scenes accomplish some task, not just stand there looking pretty.

Here are some resources that may help you in your quest for exciting and credible scenes:

> *Scene and Structure* by Jack M. Bickham
> *Make a Scene* by Jordan E. Rosenfeld
> *Novelist's Essential Guide to Crafting Scenes* by Raymond Obstfeld

11.13 Manuscript Track

Write a mirror scene. Choose one of the following options:

- ☑ Identify a scene in your manuscript that might benefit from a mirror scene or just choose one in your manuscript to play around with. What will be the similarities between the two scenes and what will be the differences? Why did you choose those differences?
- ☑ Find a scene in an existing novel that could benefit from a mirror scene. (For example, the scene in which Willoughby carries Marianne in the rainstorm in the book version of *Sense and Sensibility* does not have a full mirror scene. The rainstorm is repeated but not the "carrying." Actress and screenwriter Emma Thompson created the scene of Colonel Brandon carrying Marianne as a mirror to the original scene.) What will you keep the same or repeat in the mirror you write? What will you change? What will the changes or repetitions accomplish for the story?

End of today's lesson

Write 750 words or fewer. Make enough copies of your flashback scene for your critique group.

OPTIONAL WRITING IN SCENES:

1. Watch *Inkheart* (2008). Then choose three scenes and identify these parts:

   › The viewpoint character's scene goal
   › The scene question
   › What's at stake (What will the character lose if he/she fails?)

- The lead's motivation
- Scene complications
- The new information (for viewers or characters)
- How the scene question is answered
- What went wrong at the end of the scene to make it end badly for the protagonists
- What changed in the viewpoint character (the situation, loyalty, motivation, information, etc.) by the end of the scene
- How a new scene begins
- Statement of the new scene goal

Are there any pat-the-dog, flashback, or mirror scenes in the movie?

[Note: This movie's plot is the hero's journey. For additional insight into this type of plot, identify the steps of the hero's journey as shown in chapter 10, "Plots."]

2. Choose a novel and evaluate three scenes to identify the parts mentioned in #1.

12: BEGINNINGS AND ENDINGS

You have already learned how to hook your reader by promising tension, excitement, intrigue, suspense, and thrills. But wait! There's more!

12.1 All Writers and Discussion

Think about this question: What does a reader expect to know—and what does a reader *have* to know—in the first few pages of a story? Make a list of the things a reader expects to know and has to know early in the story. If you have trouble answering this question, think of the things *you* expect to learn in the first few pages of a novel.

Discussion: Discuss your list with the group.

A Recipe for a Great Beginning

What is a "beginning"? The **beginning of a short story** is its first few paragraphs. The **beginning of a novel** typically is its first few pages.

You know about hooks, characters, voice, and so forth; this chapter pulls them all together and shows you how to use those and other elements for a stellar beginning.

Here is the "to do" list for your beginning:

> › Hook your reader.
> › Establish the genre, POV, rules of the story, setting, and tone.
> › Introduce your protagonist and the protagonist's voice.
> › Plunge your character into an interesting situation.
> › Promise future conflict.
> › Parcel out pieces of backstory as needed.

Word of wisdom: There's no need to be concerned about all of this when you write your first draft. In fact, having all this stuff in your head when you write is crazy-making.

Just write. Get the story down on paper.

Later you can go back and revise your drafts.

Have *The Last Book in the Universe* on hand; you will need it for many of the exercises in this chapter.

Hook Your Reader

Strong first sentences are essential to hooking your reader. In chapter 1, you already learned how to hook your reader with an attention-grabbing, intrigue-promising beginning, so this section will be a review for you.

- ☐ **Hook your reader.**
- ☐ Establish the genre, POV, rules of the story, setting, and tone.
- ☐ Introduce your protagonist and the protagonist's voice.
- ☐ Plunge your character into an interesting situation.
- ☐ Promise future conflict.
- ☐ Parcel out pieces of backstory as needed.

Try out these first words written by Joel C. Rosenberg in *Dead Heat*:

It was going to be bloody, but it could be done, if they moved fast.

The sentence begins the story with a bang, and, more important, the story delivers what is promised.

The Westing Game, a YA novel by Ellen Raskin, begins with the clue to solving the whole mystery:

> The sun sets in the west (just about everyone knows that), but Sunset Towers faced east. Strange!

H. G. Wells' *The War of the Worlds* begins with an ominous discovery. Hint: The ominous discovery is <u>not</u> the British spelling of *scrutinized*:

> No one would have believed in the last years of the nineteenth century that this world was being watched keenly and closely by intelligences greater than man's and yet as mortal as his own; that as men busied themselves about their various concerns they were scrutinised and studied, perhaps almost as narrowly as a man with a microscope might scrutinise the transient creatures that swarm and multiply in a drop of water.

Wells sets the mood with his first sentence and shows the Martians' opinions of Earthlings before we even meet a Martian. Incidentally, if you have read the book, you will recognize that the ending is in the beginning. Did you find it?

On the other end of the "heavy-light" spectrum of first sentences is O. Henry, here poking fun at storytelling as he begins the short story "Springtime à la Carte":

> It was a day in March.
>   Never, never begin a story this way when you write one. No opening could possibly be worse. It is unimaginative, flat, dry, and likely to consist of mere wind.

A little way into his story, he warns in parentheses about the dangers of backstory (which we'll study soon):

On the previous summer Sarah had gone into the country and loved a farmer.

(In writing your story never hark back thus. It is bad art, and cripples interest. Let it march, march.)

Sarah stayed two weeks at Sunnybrook Farm. There she learned to love old Farmer Franklin's son Walter.

A writer commenting on his own work is perfect for this story because the ending has much to do with a typist subconsciously commenting about her heart in a very amusing place.

12.2 All Writers and Discussion

Visit a library or book store and write down the first sentences of at least seven books.

Discussion: Share the sentences with your class or small group. How well did the authors hook you? What is it about the beginnings that draws the reader in? Do any of them contain hints about the ending, as *The Westing Game* and *The War of the Worlds* do?

End of today's lesson

GENRE, RULES OF THE STORY, SETTING, AND TONE

- ❏ Hook your reader.
- ❏ **Establish the genre, POV, rules of the story, setting, and tone.**
- ❏ Introduce your protagonist and the protagonist's voice.
- ❏ Plunge your character into an interesting situation.
- ❏ Promise future conflict.
- ❏ Parcel out pieces of backstory as needed.

Genre: Books fall into categories, better known as *genre*: mystery, thriller, romance, horror, western, suspense, science fiction, fantasy, historical fiction, young adult, literary, and so on. Even each genre has subheadings: The mystery genre, for instance, contains police procedurals, cozy mysteries, private detective, amateur sleuth, capers, and much more.

Readers feel tricked when they think they are reading one kind of book but it turns out to be in another genre. Maybe this has happened to you. You sit down to get involved in a suspense story but find that somewhere, somehow, it morphs into a sci-fi story with extra-terrestrials. Absurd, you say? I can think of at least two movies that do just that without first setting the stage.

The folks who write movie trailers or previews know all about this disappointment, and they work hard to *position the audience*; that is, let potential viewers know what kind of movie this is going to be so the preview will snag the right viewers.

The front and back covers of a book should reveal the genre to readers, but it doesn't always work that way, nor is the jacket always clear—or right. Ray Bradbury worked for years to get the science-fiction label off his books because, although some of his stories are in that genre, not all of them are.

Many authors today are *branded*, which sounds painful but isn't. It simply means they become known for a specific genre—a specific "brand" of story—and readers expect that kind of story from them. So-and-so writes political thrillers. So-and-so writes vampire stories. You get the idea. Readers depend on name/genre recognition. If a well-known author wants to write something outside her genre, she may use a pen name for it so readers won't be disappointed in this new type of story.

While *The Last Book in the Universe* may appear to be a sci-fi story, it really fits neatly into two other categories: young adult (YA) and futuristic.

Don't disappoint your reader. Know the conventions of your chosen genre and know what is expected. For instance, mystery readers expect, among other things, (1) a dead body somewhere in the first third of the book, (2) a protagonist who is not the killer, and (3) a killer who appears early as one of the suspects. Room for much creativity still exists in each genre's expectations, however, and you may delight readers by using the conventions in intriguing ways.

Point of View: What is your story's POV? Whichever POV strategy you use (for review, see chapter 2), stay focused on it and funnel the information through your viewpoint character(s). POV is a subtle yet strong rope that ties the reader to your story.

Rules of the Story: What is meant by "the rules of the story"?

Every story is different, and the author needs to say, in essence, "Look, here are some things you can expect." Helping readers know what to expect will allow them to suspend their disbelief early and enter the world of your book. This often extends beyond the first pages and uses the first few chapters to establish "the rules." The following paragraphs deal with some particulars that will help your reader relax and enjoy your new-made world.

If your story is being told by **more than one character**, let readers know that information early. Chapter one, for instance, can be from one character's perspective and chapter two can be from another's. Don't wait until the middle of your story to introduce a new point of view or perspective. It knocks your readers for a loop and feels like you cheated.

If your story uses a bit of **magic realism**—an animal can talk, a child has a super-power, a hobbit can disappear while wearing a ring—let the characters exhibit this quality early so readers will understand what is possible. If you wait until later on, the talking animal will seem far-fetched and the invisible hobbit will seem too coincidental to be believable.

If your story uses **time travel**, establish the rules of how it works, how to get from one time to the next, and so forth, by showing characters in action.

If you are going to tell a story in **two time periods** (the current story and the past), establish some ground rules. *The King's Fifth* by Scott O'Dell is a good example of this. The story is told by an almost-seventeen-year-old Estéban, who is a cartographer and member of a Spanish expedition in 1541 to what is now the American Southwest. His present story is told in first person from his tiny prison cell ("three strides one way, four strides the other"), using the present and present-perfect tense. His jailer has given him writing supplies with which Estéban is to draw a treasure map:

> I am now ready to begin. The night stretches before me. It is quiet in my cell except for the sound of water dripping somewhere and the lap of waves against the fortress walls. The candle sheds a good light. Some say that in the darkness one candle can shine like the sun.

The next chapter begins the story of the past, the reason he is in jail. It is told in the past tense, still from Estéban's perspective:

> It was eight bells of the morning watch, early in the month of June, that we entered the Sea of Cortés. On our port bow was the Island of California. To the east lay the coast of New Spain.
> I sat in my cabin setting down in ink a large island sighted at dawn, which did not show on the master chart. The day was already stifling hot, so I had left the door ajar. Suddenly the door closed and I turned to face Captain Mendoza.

The chapters switch between the present jail scenes and the past story for the whole book, but this early shifting of chapters from present to past establishes the rules of the story by the second chapter.

To keep readers in your story, let them know your story's rules.

Setting: Setting is nothing new to you; you studied it in chapter 7. You will remember that the words, images, and specific details you choose will help set the mood for the scene or even the whole book.

Charles Dickens begins *Great Expectations* in a graveyard in a marsh country near a prison. The protagonist, the boy Pip, is sitting among the tombstones, reading his mother's and father's inscriptions, on a "raw afternoon towards evening" and describes it as a "bleak place overgrown with nettles" adjacent to a "dark flat wilderness." Are you getting the picture?

Setting is useful for establishing time, place, and mood. It also can foreshadow future events. In Pip's case, the graveyard setting foreshadows his life with the dead-but-living Miss Havisham, the emotionally dead Estella, and events that will sorely test him as an adult in the ending.

Give readers enough information in your beginning to anchor your characters to a place and a time period. But give them only as much as they need at this point in your story. For instance, Philbrick does not need to explain in the first chapter of *The Last Book in the Universe* how things got so bad in the Urb. We learn in chapter one that the times are troubled and that the story is taking place in the future. But we don't yet know how things fell apart until chapter two when we learn about the Big Shake. Philbrick gives us enough of Spaz's setting to let us be where Spaz is.

Dole out your information as needed. This satisfies reader curiosity and intensifies story suspense.

Tone: Tone is how the story feels to the reader. When you read Mark Twain's *A Connecticut Yankee in King Arthur's Court*, you notice that the first part of the book is light-hearted and funny; Twain is rollicking through his story, and you are having fun with it and laughing at Hank's antics. By the second half, you notice that the fun tone is gone; instead, Twain is much more serious, even angry, about his story and the subject matter. You sense a darkness in the events. What happened between the first half and the second half? Twain began writing his story, let it rest for a few years, and then finished it later. His attitude about the Medieval Ages changed due to his reading on the subject. He was now angry and sickened about what he learned, which is reflected in his writing.

How will you treat your subject? Fifty authors writing about the topic of unrequited love will end up with fifty different tones: light and frothy, dark, irreverent, ironic, sad, world-weary, excitable, cynical, angry, tired, respectful, and so forth. (The tone of the text you are reading now is conversational.) It all depends on your personality, your views on the subject, your character's views on the topic, and the needs of your particular story.

Readers will pick up on how you are treating your story and your characters. Do they feel the irony? The slapstick comedy? The realism? They will feel the tone of the story, even if they are not consciously aware of it, if you work to make your beginning reflect a certain tone.

Philbrick takes a serious, realistic (but not dark or heavy) tone with *The Last Book in the Universe*.

12.3 All Writers and Discussion

With new eyes, reread the first chapter in *The Last Book in the Universe*, answer the following questions, and discuss them with your group:

› Make a list of the indications that this is a futuristic story.
› How early do you know the setting (time *and* place)? Make a list of the clues.
› What rules of the story do you learn in chapter one?

End of today's lesson

PROTAGONIST AND PROTAGONIST'S VOICE

- ❑ Hook your reader.
- ❑ Establish the genre, POV, rules of the story, setting, and tone.
- ❑ **Introduce your protagonist and the protagonist's voice.**
- ❑ Plunge your character into an interesting situation.
- ❑ Promise future conflict.
- ❑ Parcel out pieces of backstory as needed.

The opening scene belongs to your main character.
—Jordan E. Rosenfeld

Introduce the protagonist: This may seem too obvious to state, but readers need to know who the main character is. They need to be cheering for someone or be concerned for someone early in the story so they can care about what happens next. Believe it or not, it is possible to find books in which the protagonist is not clear until a few chapters into the story. Don't let this happen to you.

In *The Last Book in the Universe*, you know it is Spaz's story right away. He's the one narrating; he's the one in trouble, being asked to do something he doesn't want to do. You read about his future "sidekick" and mentor (Ryter) in chapter 1 and meet him in chapters 2-3. Even though you don't see Ryter again until chapter 6, you have a good idea that he will be a major player in Spaz's story because of their original interchange and the way Philbrick ends chapter 3.

Avoid confusing your reader. Establish your lead.

Readers should know your lead's major dramatic question by the time they finish the beginning.

Voice: When readers pick up a book, they want to spend time with an interesting character or set of characters. The character's voice (how he or she sounds on the page) is one way readers determine whether they want to spend time with this character. To review voice, turn to chapter four.

By Spaz's voice in *The Last Book in the Universe*, you know he is street-smart, world-weary, and straightforward. By chapter three you hear some cynicism and fear, and you get an idea that he is hiding some inner pain. Philbrick is planting the information a little at a time, just enough for us to absorb, just enough for us to understand the lead.

Let your readers get a sense, in the very beginning, of what kind of character your lead is.

AN INTERESTING SITUATION

Interesting situations abound in fictions' first pages. A wealthy man moves into the neighborhood, and strangers make plans to marry him off (Jane Austen's *Pride and Prejudice*). A young orphan is sent to the wrong house (L. M. Montgomery's *Anne of Green Gables*). A young English couple is shipwrecked (Edgar Rice Burroughs' *Tarzan of the Apes*). A plane is hijacked (James Hilton's *Lost Horizon*). And, of course, a teenage boy is ordered to rob someone (*The Last Book in the Universe*).

- ❏ Hook your reader.
- ❏ Establish the genre, POV, rules of the story, setting, and tone.
- ❏ Introduce your protagonist and the protagonist's voice.
- ❏ **Plunge your character into an interesting situation.**
- ❏ Promise future conflict.
- ❏ Parcel out pieces of backstory as needed.

Even though Spaz's situation does not directly plunge him into his quest, it shows him in action and allows him to have an initially combative relationship with his future mentor.

Through this old man, Spaz learns that everyone has a story. His first situation is related to his story-worthy problem, that of being without a family and feeling the lack of it deeply. Hence, he sets out on his quest to find his sister and eventually

> An actor coming through the door, you've got nothing. But if he enters through the window, you've got a situation.
>
> —Billy Wilder

becomes connected with his real story. Make sure your protagonist's initial situation is related to the story's major problem and the protagonist's inner goal.

You studied the inciting incident in the chapter on plot. To review, it is the event that plunges the character into the story and often appears near the end of the initial situation. In *The Remains of the Day* by Kazuo Ishiguro, Mr. Stevens is the butler of an old estate that has just been sold. His life is on the edge of big changes. An interesting situation. He does not know what will happen, and neither do we. But nothing has occurred to incite Mr. Stevens to take action. He's just hanging around, working and obsessing. Then his new boss advises him to hire some new people and to take a vacation while things settle down. Mr. Stevens has never taken a vacation and is not about to do so now—until he gets a letter from a former co-worker for whom he had feelings. She sounds lonely. Maybe he could visit her and rehire her. Ah, now he takes his vacation. Now he is fully in his story.

Ishiguro pushes his interesting situation to the edge so Mr. Stevens can take action.

> Beginning a book is unpleasant. I'm entirely uncertain about the character and the predicament, and a character in his predicament is what I have to begin with.
> —Philip Roth

12.4 All Writers

Characters have to meet each other, and in every boy-meets-girl story, writers work to find new and inventive ways for the two to meet because, after all, bumping into each other in the hall or in the grocery store is so common that it has become clichéd.

Write an inventive scene of about 500-700 words in which boy meets girl (or girl meets boy). Throw them together in some clever way, and allow the consequences or the chemistry to be negative. If you need to give your creative juices a squeeze, watch the beginnings of a few movies to get some ideas.

Read your scene to your small group.

End of today's lesson

THE PROMISE OF FUTURE CONFLICT

The promise of future conflict keeps readers reading, especially if they become so interested in the protagonist that they feel fear, anxiety, or some other strong emotion on his behalf.

Future conflict can be foreshadowed by your use of **description** and **imagery**. Take a look at how, on her first page, Geraldine McCaughrean promises conflict in *The Pirate's Son*. Nathan, asleep in a safe dorm room, is not yet aware that he will soon become involved in sea adventures with a questionable character:

> ☐ Hook your reader.
> ☐ Establish the genre, POV, rules of the story, setting, and tone.
> ☐ Introduce your protagonist and the protagonist's voice.
> ☐ Plunge your character into an interesting situation.
> ☑ **Promise future conflict.**
> ☐ Parcel out pieces of backstory as needed.

> Cold gnawed on him like a rat. Around him, the dun and grey blankets of the other beds rose and fell like the swell of a bleak, dirty sea. Nathan had no idea what had woken him—he was still exhausted—and yet some upheaval had washed him up above the waterline of sleep. He was afraid, without knowing why.

Using a simile ("like the swell of a bleak, dirty sea") and a metaphor ("some upheaval had washed him up above the waterline of sleep"), McCaughrean foreshadows Nathan's future. Readers want to see how it is going to play out.

Robert L. Fish uses **action** as he packs the first pages of *The Bridge that Went Nowhere* with plenty of question-invoking conflict. The story opens with two unnamed men sitting near a small plane in a clearing in a jungle. The younger man says to the older one, "I don't think there's any doubt. Your hunch was right." One paragraph later he tells the older man, "I've never seen anything like it. You know, you're a lucky man." We still don't know what they are talking about, but we're interested because it promises conflict between characters.

Then the older man reacts:

> He pulled himself heavily to his feet, tugging his gun belt to a more comfortable position, sighed, and then shook his head almost sadly.

When the younger man asks, "Why the long face?" the older man says, "Because not everyone is as lucky as I am.... You, for example."

Three short paragraphs later, the older man shoots the younger one and kills him. That's starting a story with a real bang. Did you notice the foreshadowing of the older man tugging on his gun belt?

In *The Last Book in the Universe*, Philbrick promises future conflict by mentioning the Bully Bangers and their aggression, Spaz's former family, and a passing reference to events that happen in Spaz's **future**. What future event does he mention?

Foreshadowing, with its promise of future conflict, can also be achieved by a **careful placement of props**. If you mention a box of old letters, you are hinting to the reader that by the end of the story those letters are going to be used in an interesting way.

> If in Act I you have a pistol hanging on the wall, then it must fire in the last act.
> —Anton Chekhov, playwright

It can also be achieved by giving characters **warnings**. In C. S. Lewis's *The Silver Chair*, Aslan gives Jill Pole signs to look for on the journey so she and the others will be safe. The signs point to potential trouble, first because they are necessary and, second, because they can be forgotten, which Jill does.

What's the warning five-year-old Charles Wallace receives in *A Wrinkle in Time* by Madeleine L'Engle? "You *must* stay with Meg and Calvin. You must *not* go off on your own. Beware of pride and arrogance, Charles, for they may betray you." *Of course* he's going to go off on his own! *Of course* he's going to become prideful! That is the nature of the warning: It is meant to develop the tension for readers as much as it is meant to be a warning to the character.

BACKSTORY

Backstory is the essential stuff that's happened to the characters before the first page of their story. Part of the backstory in *The Last Book in the Universe* are the Big Shake and the fact that Spaz used to have a family.

- ☐ Hook your reader.
- ☐ Establish the genre, POV, rules of the story, setting, and tone.
- ☐ Introduce your protagonist and the protagonist's voice.
- ☐ Plunge your character into an interesting situation.
- ☐ Promise future conflict.
- ☑ **Parcel out pieces of backstory as needed.**

Remember *WALL•E*? For the first 25 minutes or so, you watched this little robot cleaning up junk piles. You didn't know where the junk came from, but you knew the setting is Earth because of the familiar artifacts he finds and the movie he watches. Only later in the movie did you learn how Earth became so polluted. That's the part that is backstory—how things got the way they were before we met WALL•E.

Because many authors like to begin with a bang, they use a device called *in media res*, or "in the middle of things." This is a good method, even though it requires the author to explain some things and fill in some of the details later. Here's the beginning of "Report on the Barnhouse Effect" by Kurt Vonnegut, Jr., who begins his story "a year and a half" after a major event:

> Let me begin by saying that I don't know any more about where Professor Arthur Barnhouse is hiding than anyone else does. Save for one short, enigmatic message, left in my mailbox on Christmas Eve, I have not heard from him since his disappearance a year and a half ago.

Soon after this, Vonnegut backtracks to explain what the Barnhouse Effect is and then tells the story chronologically from the time the narrator first met Dr. Barnhouse. Since there is no drama when the narrator and Dr. Barnhouse meet, it is best left in the backstory and explained later.

Backstory with a trigger: You learned about a trigger when you studied flashbacks in chapter 11 ("Scenes"). Use a sense, object, or familiar event to tie the current story to the past, as Jhumpa Lahiri does in *The Namesake*. In *The Namesake*, Ashima Ganguli is about to give birth to her first baby, but she is far from her native India. This example shows how to use a trigger to ease into backstory. The backstory is her painful departure from her parents years ago. The trigger is the watch, which connects the two stories. It takes her into her backstory, and it brings her out, along with some help from a bracelet:

> Another contraction begins, more violent than the last . . . . She has been instructed to time the duration of the contractions and so she consults her watch, a bon voyage gift from her parents, slipped over her wrist the last time she saw them amid airport confusion and tears. It wasn't until she was on the plane, . . . as she was drifting over parts of India she'd never set foot in, and then even farther, outside India itself, that she'd noticed the watch among the cavalcade of matrimonial bracelets on both her arms: iron, gold, coral, conch. Now, in addition, she wears a plastic bracelet with a typed label identifying her as a patient of the hospital. She keeps the watch face turned to the inside of her wrist . . . .
> American seconds tick on top of her pulse point.

This backstory of her leaving her family and native land is triggered by Ashima's use of the watch she received at that emotional time.

12.5 All Writers and Discussion

Make a list of five things that happened in Spaz's world (whether to himself or to his setting) before his story began in *The Last Book in the Universe*. Beside each item you list, write the number of the chapter in which you learn it.

End of today's lesson

12.6 Manuscript Track

Evaluate your own beginning by consulting each item on the checklist below. Choose one of your short story or novel manuscripts and fill in the blanks below. Then print off enough copies of your beginning for everyone in your writing group. Critique each other's beginnings with these items in mind:

- ☑ Title
- ☑ First sentences
- ☑ Last sentence of the beginning (the power position)
- ☑ Proof of the genre
- ☑ POV
- ☑ Rules of the story, if applicable
- ☑ Setting
- ☑ Tone
- ☑ Protagonist
- ☑ Voice
- ☑ Interesting situation that culminates in the inciting incident
- ☑ Foreshadowing/promise of future conflict
- ☑ Opening backstory
- ☑ Is your lead's situation worse by the end of the first scene?

ENDINGS

Have you ever finished a book or movie and been thoroughly dissatisfied with the ending? When this occurs, figure out why the ending left a sour taste in your mouth. This is an effective way to educate yourself.

Endings have a different set of expectations than beginnings do, but before getting into that, run your peepers over the endings of the following well-known books.

> Your first chapter sells your book. Your last chapter sells your next book.
> —Mickey Spillane

12.7 All Writers and Discussion

You may be familiar with famous beginnings, but what about the last sentences? Read these endings and guess what famous books they belong to. Then discuss why these endings are appropriate to their stories:

1. "It is a far, far better thing that I do, than I have ever done; it is a far, far better rest that I go to than I have ever known."
2. The bar silver and the arms still lie, for all that I know, where Flint buried them; and certainly they shall lie there for me. Oxen and wainropes would not bring me back again to that accursed island; and the worst dreams that ever I have are when I hear the surf booming about its coasts, or start upright in bed, with the sharp voice of Captain Flint still ringing in my ears: "Pieces of eight! pieces of eight!"
3. Marlow ceased, and sat apart, indistinct and silent, in the pose of a meditating Buddha. Nobody moved for a time. "We have lost the first of the ebb," said the director, suddenly. I raised my head. The offing was barred by a black bank of clouds, and the tranquil waterway leading to the uttermost ends of the earth flowed somber under an overcast sky—seemed to lead into the heart of an immense darkness.
4. He gazed up at the enormous face. Forty years it had taken him to learn what kind of smile was hidden beneath the dark mustache. O cruel, needless misunderstanding! O stubborn, self-willed exile from the loving breast! Two gin-scented tears trickled down the sides of his nose. But it was all right, everything was all right, the struggle was finished. He had won the victory over himself. He loved Big Brother.
5. Tom's most well now, and got his bullet around his neck on a watch-guard for a watch, and is always seeing what time it is, and so there ain't nothing more to write about, and I am rotten glad of it, because if I'd 'a' knowed what a trouble it was to make a book I wouldn't 'a' tackled it, and ain't a-going to no more. But I reckon I got to light out for the territory ahead of the rest, because Aunt Sally she's going to adopt me and sivilize me, and I can't stand it. I been there before.
6. "O Father," said Eppie, "what a pretty home ours is! I think nobody could be happier than we are."

End of today's lesson

WHAT READERS EXPECT FROM ENDINGS

Readers expect the leads to get through the book's climax by bravery, finesse, and by wisdom learned from earlier ordeals, **not by coincidence**. Relying on coincidence ("Oh, I just happen to have the super-secret, magic key with me") cheapens the ending—and the whole story. *Deus ex machina* is the term for coincidences in fiction. It comes from the ancient Greek device of lowering the god character onto the stage by use of machinery. ("God out of the machinery"—get it?) Any power, object, or character that suddenly appears "out of nowhere" feels like cheating, and readers don't trust cheaters.

Readers expect the story to **answer the MDQ** (major dramatic question). Will Captain Ahab ever find relief and get revenge by killing the great white whale? No, definitely not. Will Silas Marner ever recover from his emotional wounds and his miserliness? Yes, conditionally.

Readers expect **the loose ends to be tied up**. *The Last Book in the Universe* wraps up the major relationships in Spaz's life (Billy Bizmo, Bean, and Ryter), but there are still a few characters readers are curious about, which Philbrick deals with this way: He sends a message to Spaz from Lanaya and Little Face.

Readers expect the lead to **face the antagonist**, whether in battle or by facing an inner demon. In thrillers or in novels of adventure and suspense, readers expect to see the lead go toe-to-toe with the antagonist, who has moved from impersonal opposition to very personal opposition. In mysteries, readers want to see the lead find and expose the killer while facing his or her own problems. In romances, readers expect the leads to confront whatever is keeping them apart; they may not be successful, but at least they have confronted it. In a rescue plot, readers expect the lead to confront the kidnaper.

And last, readers expect **the antagonist to be dealt with** in a satisfying way. *Poetic justice* is the term for a comeuppance given in a way that fits the story or character: a murderer dies in a trap he set for someone else; a miser falls into poverty; a vain character is humbled in a public manner, and so forth. Perhaps this type of ending, however, is not appropriate for your story, in which case you will find a satisfying way to resolve the antagonist's character arc. For instance, Spaz faces the antagonist of isolation; he does not deal Billy Bizmo a death blow but learns why Billy is watching out for him as best he can. Billy Bizmo does not become a "good" character, but readers understand his actions better. Also, Spaz has not changed the whole antagonistic system that perpetuated his isolation, but he is doing what he can to ensure that others will find strength. Whatever the case, if the antagonist is a character or a personal failing, readers hope he/she/it is at least partially conquered.

Endings come in different flavors (with examples here):

> The lead achieves his goal and goes home happy. (Cinderella wins her man and lives happily ever after.)
> The lead achieves his goal and is not happy about it. (The Bible's Jonah pouts outside Nineveh after delivering God's message.)
> The lead achieves his goal but at the cost of great sacrifice. (The Bible's Samson finally defeats the Philistines but dies in the effort; *The Hobbit*'s Bilbo Baggins finds the gold but loses some of his possessions and his reputation with the Shire hobbits, among whom he has to live.)
> The lead abandons his goal because he finds something he perceives is better. (The Count of Monte Cristo learns that his plans of revenge will harm those he loves, so he tries to change his plans before it is too late.)
> The lead tries but does not achieve his goal and is not happy about it. (Bernard in Aldous Huxley's *Brave New World* is exiled, and John the Savage hangs himself in despair.)

Many more varieties and combinations of endings exist. What will yours be like?

Happy endings in which the lead has no negative consequences are hard to believe; they feel shallow. On the other hand, negative endings in which the lead does not achieve his goal and is not happy about it or in which he dies short of his goal can leave readers with a "Why did I waste my time reading this?" feeling.

> Those are the facts, and it was quite a job to dig them up. But I did it.
> –the last sentences from "The Facts" by Ring Lardner

Satisfying endings are usually somewhere in the middle (called *ironic*—a combination of positive and negative consequences for the lead). If you write an ending in which your protagonist achieves his goal, make sure it costs him something. The ending of *The Last Book in the Universe* shows Spaz attaining his goal of belonging and finding meaning, but it is not filled with sweetness and cheer.

This journey, this goal, cost Spaz dearly; he gained something of value and lost something of value.

12.8 All Writers

Watch a movie you have not viewed before and are unfamiliar with. When the lead approaches the worst part (think of Inigo, Fezzik, and an almost-dead Westley wondering how to storm the castle in *The Princess Bride*), stop the movie.

Brainstorm ways to get the lead out of the mess and to resolve the MDQ. Then write a possible ending. (It can be a rough sketch; it doesn't have to be full scene with dialogue and action.)

After you have written your ending, turn the movie back on and see how the screenwriters ended the story. Decide which ending you like better—theirs or yours.

End of today's lesson

What you studied in this chapter:

- ✓ What effective beginnings need
- ✓ What effective endings need
- ✓ Reader expectations of beginnings and endings

13: GETTING PUBLISHED

Ah, yes. Getting published.
 Many published authors will tell you that being published does not make you a writer; *writing* makes you a writer. So keep writing!
 In the mean time, let's explore how to get published.

REVISING

 You may be surprised to begin the "how to get published" tips with the topic of revision. After all, that seems to be going backward, not forward. However, your manuscript is your personal representative. If it looks sloppy, is ill-written, or is grammatically deficient, it will speak poorly of you, so make sure your manuscript is as polished as it can be. Why take a chance on disgusting an editor with garbled grammar when you have such a stunningly brilliant story?

> Don't get discouraged because there's a lot of mechanical work to writing . . . . I rewrote the first part of *A Farewell to Arms* at least fifty times.
> –Ernest Hemingway

Comb your manuscript for grammar, punctuation, and spelling mistakes.

Check facts that appear in your story. Did you write that a squirrel backed down a tree or that your character turned on his car's high beams and saw better in the fog? These mistakes and others like them will undermine the credibility of your story.

Check the story elements. Does your main character have an important enough goal to propel her through the story? What is the MDQ and do you answer it sufficiently? Do you show instead of tell? Are the plot points stacked so that the most tense and dramatic ones occur near the end of the story? Is your theme supported by events and imagery? Is your point-of-view strategy effective and consistent throughout the story? These and similar questions will aid you in revising and polishing your story. Take time to review the checklists and points you've already learned in this course.

> I do lots of research for my historical novels. It takes many fat books in order to write a thin one. I often spend as much time researching and planning the book as writing it.
> —Paul Fleischman

Many helpful books on revision for fiction can be found at your local library. Or you might build your writing library by buying one or two to keep on hand. Here is a short list of books to get you started:

› *Self-Editing for Fiction Writers* by Renni Browne and Dave King (Harper Resource)
› *The 38 Most Common Fiction Writing Mistakes (and how to Avoid Them)* by Jack. M. Bickham (Writer's Digest Books)
› *Revision & Self-Editing: Techniques for Transforming Your First Draft into a Finished Novel* by James Scott Bell (Writer's Digest Books)

Double-space your manuscript throughout the whole process—from first draft to polished manuscript. This is important for two reasons: (1) Double-spacing gives you room to correct and polish your work, and (2) Editors expect your submission to be double-spaced to allow room for their notations.

Print on one side of the paper only.

> The art of rewriting and self-editing is what separates the pros from the amateurs.
> —Rodman Philbrick

13.1 All Writers

Print off one full page of any work you've done for this course. Print as many copies as you need for your writing group. Make sure your name is at the top of the page.

Exchange papers in your writing group. Make sure each student does not have his or her own work. Put your name at the top of this new page so the writer will know who proofread it.

Using a colorful pen and the proofreading marks you began using in chapter 2, mark any mistakes you find. Correct them.

End of today's lesson

AVENUES TO GETTING PUBLISHED

In this section, we'll examine a few time-honored methods of getting published. But first, let's take a short look into short stories versus novels.

Some people say that writing short stories will spoil you for the novel; you will not be able to write anything of length or depth.

Others say that writing short stories is good practice for the longer form of novels. You learn how to create characters, how to write with a point-of-view strategy, how to structure your writing with a plot, and so forth, and then transfer that knowledge to a story of novel length. Plus you gain success in the short story form and develop self-confidence, thus breeding more success.

That's the argument. What's the truth?

The truth is that you will most likely become proficient in short stories or novels based on your personality, preferences, and writing habits. And you won't know which form of storytelling is best for you until you write.

Here are some important facts to keep in mind about short stories and novels:

Words: Short stories can run anywhere from 100-15,000 words. Novels are typically from 60,000-90,000 words. Anything in between: novellas.

Focus: Short stories tend to focus on one character and/or one event (one plot line). Novels, because of their length, can handle more characters, more events, more plots, and a longer period of time, if necessary.

Point of View: Short stories generally are from a simple point of view, either first person or third person limited, in which the story is viewed through only one character. Novels generally use one point-of-view strategy, sometimes simple, sometimes not. But some novels cycle among a small group of viewpoint characters or use differing points of view, one character or point of view at a time.

Theme: Short stories focus on one unifying theme. Novels can incorporate more than one or variations of the same one.

Story Time: The events in short stories often take place in a matter of hours or days. The events in novels can happen anywhere from a few hours to a hundred or more years.

Salability: The market for short stories is limited; they are usually published in magazines. Novels are more marketable.

    A few novels are actually collections of short stories written around the same characters or events. *The Things They Carried* by Tim O'Brien focuses on one group of men who fought in Vietnam together. *The Joy Luck Club* by Amy Tan centers around four Chinese women and their Chinese-American daughters living in San Francisco. *Jim the Boy* by Tony Earley is a collection of short stories spanning one year in the life of a ten-year-old boy from North Carolina in the 1930s.
    And then, of course, there are short stories and novels that break the rules. But you can be sure that the authors began simply and learned the ropes before venturing out into experiments.

Okay, back to the avenues by which many writers become published.

Attend a writers' conference or workshop. Many of these exist across the nation with varying degrees of affordability. The benefits of attending a writers' conference are (1) learning practical tools of the trade by attending the many workshops, (2) meeting publishers, editors, and agents, (3) hearing and meeting published authors, and (4) getting to know other writers, their stories, and their successes.

Enter a writing contest. Ever heard of Ellery Queen, the brainy and cultivated crime solver? He was cooked up by Frederick Dannay and Manfred Lee, two cousins who, in the late 1920s, entered a magazine's mystery-writing contest and won. Even though the magazine failed before their story could be published, another publisher gave them a contract, and *The Roman Hat Mystery* was born, written under the pseudonym Ellery Queen.

> When you sell a man a book, you don't sell him twelve ounces of paper and ink and glue. You sell him a whole new life.
> –Christopher Morley, author

More recently, Simon Levack, author of historical thrillers written about a slave in Aztec Mexico, entered the Crime Writers' Association's Debut Dagger Award with a winning first chapter. When he won, he suddenly had to come up with the rest of the story if he wanted to get the book published, which he did.

Plenty of contests exist, and you can find them on the Internet or in the next avenue to getting published (see below).

Submit your work to a publisher by using the information in the current year's *Writer's Market*. This guide, and others like it, is essential to anyone seriously wanting to be published. Other similar resources are *Novel and Short Story Writer's Market, Christian Writers' Market Guide* by Sally E. Stuart (both revised yearly), and www.writersmarket.com (revised daily). These resources list magazines, book publishers, and online publishers who are looking for stories in their specialized fields: sci-fi, romance, thriller, mystery, young adult, historical fiction, spiritual, and so forth. When you follow each publisher's guidelines, you will have a better chance of success.

Some publishers want you to send only a query letter (we'll get to that soon). Others want a chapter of your manuscript (ms or MS) or manuscripts (mss or MSS), along with a synopsis of the story. If they ask for one chapter, send the first one. If they ask for three, send the first three.

> I work all day, morning and afternoon, just about every day. If I sit there like that for two or three years, at the end I have a book.
> –Philip Roth

Some publishers ask for a self-addressed, stamped envelope (SASE) so they can reply to you. If you do not send an SASE, you will not get a reply.

Be sure to follow the publisher's guidelines, which can be found in the market guides or on the publisher's Web site listed in the market guides. Otherwise, your submission will be recycled or thrown away.

Go online to find out what kinds of books are currently on a particular publisher's book list. Does your story fit in with the types of books this company publishes? Have they just published one exactly like yours (in which case yours becomes extraneous)?

The category index in the back of the market guides will aid you in finding a publisher interested in the kind of story you've written. For instance, if your story is of ethnic or multicultural interest, you will find lists of magazine and book publishers looking for stories on this topic. The index is a handy way to narrow down your search.

Use the most current version of any market guide you choose; information is always changing.

Do it yourself. Publish on a site such as CreateSpace.com, owned by Amazon. This is a fairly inexpensive way to get published because books are printed only when they are ordered, cutting down on warehouse and other printing costs. This method is called Print on Demand (POD).

Be persistent. Don't give up. Attend conferences. Enter contests. Keep looking for markets that may be interested in the story you wrote. Study to get better at story writing. Meet other writers and network with them.

As soon as you receive a rejection from one publisher, go to the next publisher on your list and send out a query letter or your story again. It takes anywhere from three to nine months to hear from a publisher, so it makes good sense to juggle a few writing projects and publishers at the same time. If the publisher's time period has passed and you still have not heard from them, write a polite letter to remind them that they have your story and that you are still waiting to hear from them. Include the name of your story and the date you sent it in. If you hear nothing from them, move to the next publisher.

> When I think of the good things still to be written I am glad, for there is no end to them, and I know I myself shall write some of them.
> —William Saroyan, author of *The Daring Young Man on the Flying Trapeze*

Here are some phrases you will find in market guides that may need definitions:

Query letter—your letter to the publisher introducing your story. *Query* simply means *question*, so, in essence, the query letter asks, "I've written this great story. Do you want to read it?"

#10 SASE—a business-size envelope (4 1/8" x 9 ½"), addressed to yourself and stamped, then folded and placed in the envelope that holds your query letter or in the larger manila envelope that holds your submission.

Unsolicited mss—manuscripts that the publisher has not personally asked you for. An editor may ask for your manuscript after she's read your intriguing query letter, in which case it is no longer an unsolicited manuscript. Unsolicited manuscripts may be thrown away or recycled.

Simultaneous submissions—submitting a manuscript to more than one publisher at a time. Some publishers don't care if you do this; others do. You will find specific information about this in each listing of the market guides.

Agented submissions—manuscripts submitted by your agent. In other words, if you don't have an agent, that particular publisher does not want your submission.

Synopsis—a summing up of the story and its pertinent elements (characters, theme, plot, etc.), chapter by chapter, in the present tense. This is not the place to be coy or vague. Publishers need to know what the story is and what happens in it. Keep it interesting to keep them reading.

Author bio—a biography mentioning only information pertinent to getting published. Publishers typically don't care about where you went to elementary school or how many cats you have. They want to know things about you that make you suited to write this book and be published by them: writing courses or degrees, contests you've won, publishing credits (other stories you've had published), and any other information about yourself that gives you a specific advantage to write this story. For instance, if you are the child of an alcoholic and so is your protagonist, this can give your story authenticity. An author bio is generally one paragraph long.

> I was writing stories when I was five . . . don't know what I was doing before that. Just loafing, I suppose.
> –P.G. Wodehouse, author of the Jeeves and Wooster stories

Publishing guidelines—information showing how the publisher wants you to submit your manuscript, if at all. This includes practical information like the name of the acquisitions editor (the person you will send your manuscript or query letter to), the publisher's target audience, how they want the manuscript to look on the paper, recent books they have published and how many they've published in the last year, whether you need an agent, what types of stories they are currently looking for, if they accept simultaneous submissions—really, everything you need to know to contact that publisher. Save yourself some time and energy by checking out any publisher before sending a query or manuscript to them.

Proposal—a packet of information you send the publisher. This generally includes a cover letter, synopsis or outline, sample chapters (consecutive), and author bio. Check with each publisher to see exactly what they want in the proposal. Send a book proposal only if the publisher asks for one.

Slush Pile—the large, overflowing, unmanageable pile your manuscript is put in when it reaches the publisher. Editors get hundreds, sometimes thousands, of manuscripts a year. Make yours stand out by submitting a professional-looking manuscript that is proofread and polished, that contains a great story, and that is targeted to a company that publishes stories like yours.

And now for the promised query letter, which is, basically, your job application. Arthur A. Levine Books' Web site explains a query letter this way:

> A query letter is a one-page description of your manuscript that illuminates its strengths and captures our interest. What is your manuscript about? Why would a reader turn to your book? What makes it original or memorable?

You are selling the editor on your book, hooking her as you explain the story. Competition to be published today is sharp. The query letter is not the place for a dry recitation but should be as full of interest as the blurb on the back cover of a book.

You are also selling the editor on *you*. Your query letter is a reflection of you and your skills; the editor meets you through your letter. Write with correct grammar. Proofread the letter. Let your writing style shine through. Include a short author bio that reflects what makes you eminently suited to write this story.

The query letter follows a business letter format: left justified paragraphs (no paragraph indentation), single-spaced paragraphs, and a double-space between each paragraph to delineate a new paragraph.

On the next page is an imaginary query letter for Nathaniel Hawthorne's *The Scarlet Letter*, were he to write the query today.

Nathaniel Hawthorne
Salem, MA 01234
(555) 555-4321
hawthorneyissues@puritan.com

May 19, 20—

Frank Pierce, Acquisitions Editor
Pierce Publishing
123 Elm Street
Concord, MA 12345

Dear Mr. Pierce:

"All the assembled townspeople leveled their stern regards at Hester Prynne—yes, at herself—who stood on the scaffold of the pillory, an infant on her arm, and the letter 'A' in scarlet, fantastically embroidered with gold thread upon her bosom." You will find Hester's moving story in my completed manuscript of about 83,000 words, *The Scarlet Letter*.

Not so long ago children were forced to wear signs around their necks proclaiming their misdeeds, signs like "I pick my nose." But Hester is not a school child; she is a lonely young woman accused of adultery and forced to wear an embroidered red "A" on her chest in Puritan New England. The story opens in the early days of Boston and examines love, concealment, punishment, and freedom as Hester raises her illegitimate daughter Pearl. Hester is in constant but covert contact with her child's father, the minister Arthur Dimmesdale, who flagellates himself but will not publically acknowledge his relationship to Hester. Hester's lawful husband Roger Chillingworth, long thought dead, finds her early in the story and meticulously wreaks his plan of vengeance on her and Dimmesdale. Though Hester and Dimmesdale's clandestine relationship affects many, their punishment, both public and private, does not have the desired effect, and they continue to love each other; varied punishments do not change their hearts.

The point of view is third-person multiple vision and tells the story from these three characters' perspectives: Hester, Arthur, and Roger. The language and style of the manuscript reflect a time in America when whipping posts were thought appropriate for disobedient children and when women feared to be accused of being witches.

I grew up in the Boston-Salem area and am steeped in the stories and traditions of those former colonial days. Furthermore, I am a descendant of one of the men who sat as a judge in the Salem witch trials; I take the weight of my heritage seriously.

Please contact me if you are interested in the manuscript. I have enclosed an SASE.

Sincerely,

Nathaniel Hawthorne

Nathaniel Hawthorne

Address your query to the editor listed in the market guide. Print your letter on plain white paper using size-12 font. Sign your name above your printed name and include the SASE you mentioned.

13.2 All Writers

Write a query letter for a published novel with which you are familiar. Use the name, address, and editor of a real publisher and pretend the novel has not yet been published and that you are the novel's author.

You will find publishers' information, including addresses and acquisitions editors, on their Web sites or in market guides you find at the library. For this exercise, the market guides do not have to be current.

What will you write to try to get the editor interested in "your" novel?

End of today's lesson

WHAT THE MANUSCRIPT LOOKS LIKE

The first page of your **short story** submission will look like this:

Your Name   about 1,300 words
89 Writing Blvd.
Hopeful, FL 30303
(555) 555-3333
youremail@whatever.com

The Story's Title

by Your Name

    Now you can begin your double-spaced short story. Notice that the margins are at least one inch all around the page. Your work is left justified. Use size-12 font, usually Times New Roman or `Courier`.

    Indent new paragraphs. Do not add an extra double-space between each paragraph. Make a header for all subsequent pages that includes your last name, a key word from your title, and the page number on the top right of the page, something like this: Hawthorne/Stunning/2.

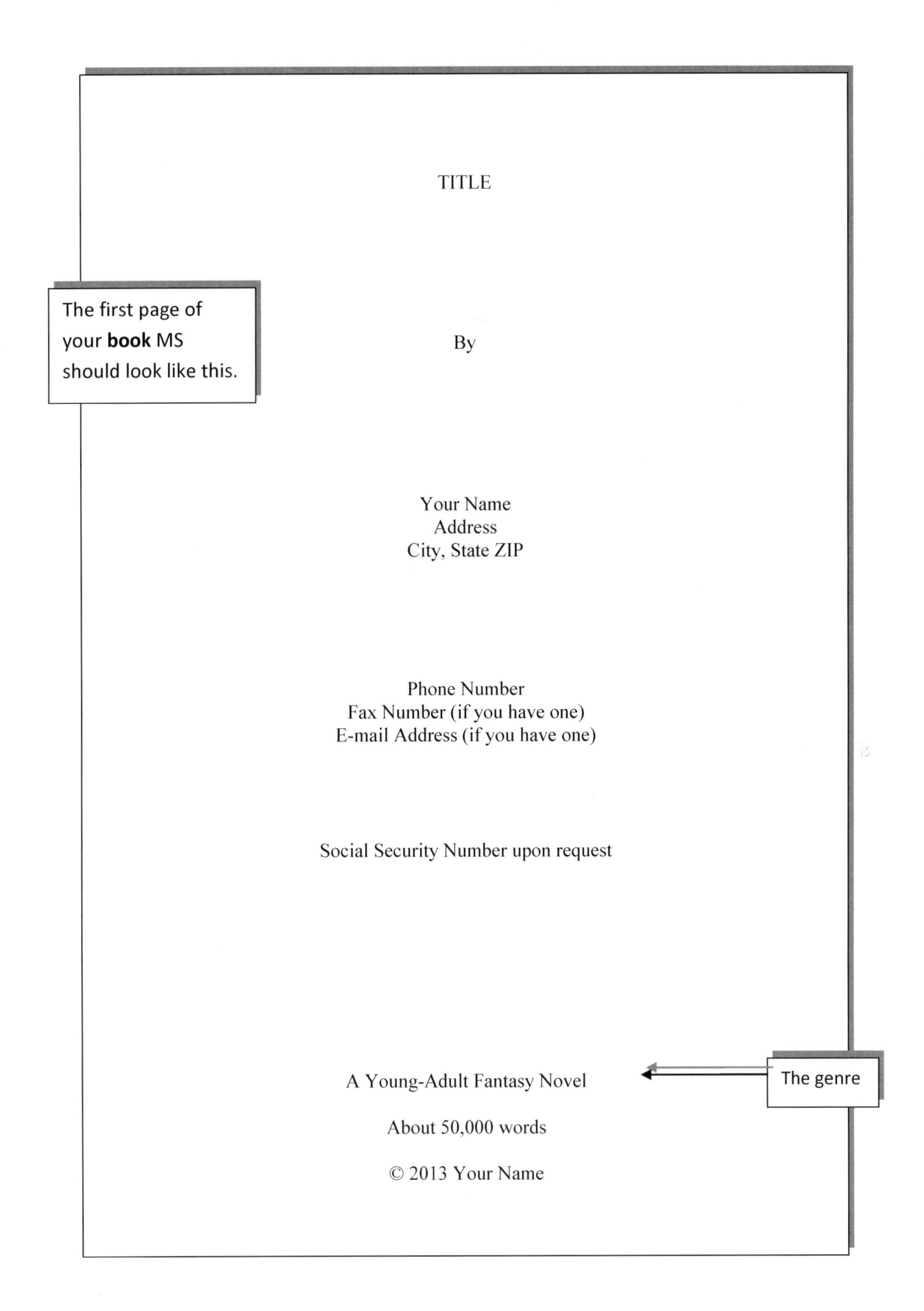

TITLE

By

Your Name
Address
City, State ZIP

Phone Number
Fax Number (if you have one)
E-mail Address (if you have one)

Social Security Number upon request

A Young-Adult Fantasy Novel

About 50,000 words

© 2013 Your Name

> The first page of your **book** MS should look like this.

> The genre

Begin your novel manuscript (the first page of the story) about halfway down the second page and type the chapter number or chapter title, centered. Each page after the title page should have a header with your last name, a key word from your title, and the page number at the top right of the page.

Use size-12 font like Times New Roman or Courier printed on one side of plain white paper of good quality.

More helpful information on all the particulars of getting published can be found in the following resources and in others like them:

> *Sally Stuart's Guide to Getting Published* by Sally Stuart
> *The Complete Idiot's Guide to Getting Published* by Sheree Bykofsky and Jennifer Basye Sander
> *The Complete Idiot's Guide to Book Proposals & Query Letters* by Marilyn Allen and Coleen O'Shea

SHOULD YOU READ WHILE YOU WRITE?

Some writers say they are inspired by other writers and will even begin their writing day by reading an author they particularly admire. Others maintain that when they read another writer while working on their own stories, they end up sounding like that writer.

A lighthearted example of this bleed-over occurs in Ray Bradbury's "A Literary Encounter." When the husband in the story is reading Thomas Wolfe's *Of Time and the River*, he speaks in clipped, one-word sentences and is distant from his wife. Later he switches to Samuel Johnson's *Life of Alexander Pope*, and he says things like this: "A most extraordinary circumstance occurred at the office today," and "A gentleman called to ascertain my health." Eventually, his wife encourages him to read someone else. He does and "bounds into the kitchen" with this greeting: "Hello, beautiful woman! Hello, lovely, wonderful, kind, understanding creature, living in this great wide sweet world!" It turns out he's been reading William Saroyan.

So, to answer the original question: Does it matter if you read other authors while writing your own stories? That depends on you. If the author you absorb makes your work less like your own, stay away from him or her until you are through with your

> I walk around, straightening pictures on the wall, rugs on the floor—as though not until everything in the world was lined up perfectly true could anybody reasonably expect me to set a word down on paper.
> —E. B. White, author of *Charlotte's Web*, before sitting down to write

work. If the author inspires you and spurs you on to greater writing, improving yours exponentially, then, by all means, enjoy him or her.

PEN NAMES

Do you need a pen name, a nom de plume, a pseudonym?

Charles Dodgson, a well-known mathematician, wrote the Alice in Wonderland stories under the name Lewis Carroll, perhaps to separate his mathematical work from his storytelling and poems. Mary Ann Evans, and many other women, wrote at a time when women authors were thought inferior to their male counterparts, so she wrote *Silas Marner* and other classics using the pseudonym George Eliot.

Pen names are used by writers today when they want to write something outside the genre they are best known for. This is a way of keeping name recognition with certain types of books, and it forestalls any disappointment readers might feel when they pick up a book by their favorite author and find it different from what they expected.

Do you need one? It's entirely up to you. If you used a pen name, what name would you choose?

REJECTION LETTERS

If (when) you get a rejection letter, know that you are in good company. According to www.writingclasses.com, Madeline L'Engle's *A Wrinkle in Time* received 29 rejections before it was published, and John Creasy, author of more than 500 mystery novels, received a whopping 743 rejections before his first book was published. Beatrix Potter, author and illustrator of the Peter Rabbit stories, never did find a publisher; she self-published, and we're glad she did.

Have ready a list of potential publishers for your story so that when you get a rejection letter, you can quickly send out your manuscript to the next publisher. This cuts down on moaning and groaning and allows you to use fewer tissues and less crying time in your quest to find a publisher. Getting published is often a long, drawn-out process, so have a plan and use it.

Keep a list or chart of publishers and results so you don't end up sending the same story to the same publisher.

Most of the rejections are form letters. There's really nothing personal about the rejection.

The famous poet Robert Frost says this about writing poetry, but it pertains to writing fiction, as well:

> A poem begins as a lump in the throat, a sense of wrong, a homesickness, a lovesickness.

What gives you a lump in the throat? What feels wrong to you? What do you miss?

Whatever it is, it's your turn to get out there and write about it!

What are you waiting for?

How to Contact This Book's Author

You may e-mail the author at WritingWithSharonWatson@gmail.com or visit www.WritingWithSharonWatson.com.

Bibliography

Chapter 1: Facts About Fiction

Alda, Alan. *Never Have Your Dog Stuffed*. New York: Random House, 2005.
Austen, Jane. *Pride and Prejudice*. New York: Modern Library, 2000.
Bradbury, Ray. *Fahrenheit 451*. New York: Ballantine Books, 1991.
Bulwer-Lytton, Edward George. *Paul Clifford*. http://www.bulwer-lytton.com/.
Chesterton, G. K. "The Flying Stars." http://www.literaturepage.com/read/chesterton-innocence-of-father-brown-67.html.
Crichton, Michael. *Timeline*. New York: Alfred A. Knopf, 1999.
Dickens, Charles. *A Christmas Carol*. New York: The MacMillan Company, 1930.
-----------. *A Tale of Two Cities*. New York: Dover Publications, 1999.
Henry, O. "The Ransom of Red Chief." In *O. Henry's Best Stories*, edited by Lou P. Bunce. New York: Globe Book Company, 1953.
Kafka, Franz. "The Metamorphosis." In *The Story and its Writer*, edited by Ann Charters. Boston: St. Martin's Press, 1995.
LaHaye, Tim and Jerry B. Jenkins. *Nicolae*. Wheaton, Illinois: Tyndale House Publishers, 1997.
Patterson, James. *Maximum Ride: The Angel Experiment*. New York: Little, Brown, 2005.
Philbrick, Rodman. *Freak the Mighty*. New York: Scholastic, Inc., 1993.
Sachar, Louis. *Holes*. New York: Dell Yearling, 1998.
Sparks, Nicholas. *A Walk to Remember*. New York: Warner Books, 1999.

Chapter 2: Point of View

Austen, Jane. *Persuasion*. New York: Oxford University Press, 1998.
Chesterton, G. K. "A Crazy Tale." In *Daylight and Nightmare: Uncollected Stories and Fables*, edited by Marie Smith. New York: Dodd, Mead, 1986.
Crichton, Michael. *Timeline*. New York: Alfred A. Knopf, 1999.
Daningburg, Barbara K. Personal narrative. "The Coop." 2007.
Dickens, Charles. *A Tale of Two Cities*. New York: Dover Publications, 1999.
Early, Tony. *Jim the Boy*. New York: Little, Brown and Company, 2000.
Ferris, Joshua. *Then We Came to the End*. New York: Little, Brown and Company, 2007.
Fitzgerald, F. Scott. *The Great Gatsby*. New York: Charles Scribner's Sons, 1953.
Jackson, Shirley. "The Lottery." In *Adventures in American Literature*, edited by Edmund Fuller and B. Jo Kinnick. New York: Harcourt, Brace & World, Inc., 1963.
James, P. D. *The Children of Men*. New York: Alfred A. Knopf, 1993.
Keagle, Donald P. Personal narrative. "Trapped!" 2007.
Koontz, Dean. *One Door Away from Heaven*. New York: Random House, Inc., 2001.
Lardner, Ring. *You Know Me Al*. New York: Dover Publications, Inc., 1995.

Lee, Harper. *To Kill a Mockingbird*. New York: HarperCollins Publishers, 2002.
Lewis, C. S. *The Magician's Nephew*. New York: Scholastic, Inc., 1995.
Peters, Elizabeth. *Summer of the Dragon*. New York: HarperCollins Publishers, 1979.
Ross, Barnaby [Frederick Dannay and Manfred Lee]. *The Tragedy of Y*. New York: F. A. Stokes, 1941.
Sachar, Louis. *Holes*. New York: Dell Yearling, 1998.
Smith, Alexander McCall. *Tears of the Giraffe*. New York: Random House, Inc., 2002.
Twain, Mark. *A Connecticut Yankee in King Arthur's Court*. San Francisco: Chandler Publishing Company, 1963.

Chapter 3: Fairy Tales

Chesterton, G. K. "The Dragon at Hide-and-Seek." In *G. K. Chesterton: Collected Works, Volume XIV,* edited by Denis J. Conlon. San Francisco: Ignatius Press, 1993.
Gardner, John and Lennis Dunlap. *The Forms of Fiction.* New York: Random House, 1967.
Snicket, Lemony. *The Wide Window*. New York: HarperCollins, 2000.
Tolkien, J. R. R. *The Hobbit*. New York: Ballantine Books, 1982.
West, Jessamyn. "Probably Shakespeare." In *Collected Stories of Jessamyn West*. San Diego: Harcourt Brace Jovanovich, 1987.

Chapter 4: Characters and Characterization

Bradbury, Ray. *Fahrenheit 451*. New York: Ballantine Books, 1991.
Card, Orson Scott. *Ender's Game*. New York: Tom Doherty Associates, LLC, 1991.
Carver, Raymond. "Cathedral." In *Where I'm Calling From*. New York: Random House, Inc.,1989.
Fitzgerald, F. Scott. *The Great Gatsby*. New York: Charles Scribner's Sons, 1953.
Greene, Bette. *Summer of My German Soldier*. New York; Scholastic Inc., 1973.
Grisham, John. *The Rainmaker*. New York: Doubleday, 1995.
Iron Man. DVD. Directed by Jon Favreau. 2008; Hollywood, CA: Paramount Pictures, 2008.
The Italian Job. DVD. Directed by F. Gary Gray. 2003; Hollywood, CA: Paramount Pictures, 2003.
Koontz, Dean. *Dragon Tears*. New York: Putnam, 1993.
Lawson, Robert. *Mr. Wilmer*. Boston: Little, Brown and Company, 1948.
Le Carré, John. *The Constant Gardener*. New York: Scribner, 2001.
Lewis, Beverly. *The Sacrifice*. Minneapolis, Minn: Bethany House Publishers, 2004.
Lewis, C. S. *Prince Caspian*. New York: Scholastic Inc., 1995.
------------. *That Hideous Strength*. New York: Scribner Paperback Fiction, 1996.
London, Jack. "How to Build a Fire." In *Great American Short Stories*, edited by Paul Negri. Mineola, New York: Dover Publications, Inc., 2002.
McDonald, Joyce. *Devil on my Heels*. New York: Delacorte Press, 2004.
McMullan, Margaret. *When I Crossed No-Bob*. Boston: Houghton Mifflin Company, 2007.
Michener, James. *Hawaii*. New York: Random House, 2002.

O'Connor, Flannery. "A Good Man Is Hard to Find." In *The Complete Stories*. New York: Quality Paperback Book Club, 1992.

Peretti, Frank. *The Visitation*. Nashville, Tenn.: Word Publishing, 1999.

Philbrick, Rodman. *Freak the Mighty*. New York: Scholastic, Inc., 1993.

------------. *The Last Book in the Universe*. New York: Scholastic, Inc., 2000.

Queen, Ellery. *Drury Lane's Last Case*. New York: Viking, 1933.

Saki [Hector Munro]. A letter to his sister Ethel M. Munro. In *The Works of Saki*. New York: The Viking Press, n.d.

Smith, Alexander McCall. *Tears of the Giraffe*. New York: Random House, Inc., 2002.

------------. *The No. 1 Ladies' Detective Agency*. New York: Anchor Books, 2002.

Wharton, Edith. *Ethan Frome*. New York: Dover Publications, Inc., 1991.

Wells, H. G. *The Invisible Man*. New York: Dover Publications, Inc., 1992.

Wilde, Oscar. *The Picture of Dorian Gray*. New York: Dover Publications, 1993.

Wodehouse, P. G. *Enter Jeeves: 15 Early Stories*. New York: Dover Publications, 1997.

------------. *How Right You Are, Jeeves*. New York: Harper & Row, 1960.

Zusak, Markus. *The Book Thief*. New York: Alfred A. Knopf, 2005.

------------. "In His Own Words: A Conversation with Markus Zusak." In *The Book Thief*, A Reader's Guide. New York: Alfred A. Knopf, 2007.

Chapter 5: Conflict

Bradbury, Ray. "I Sing the Body Electric." In *The Stories of Ray Bradbury*. New York: Alfred A. Knopf, 1980.

Card, Orson Scott. *Characters and Viewpoint*. Cincinnati: Writer's Digest Books, 1988.

Crichton, Michael. *The Lost World*. New York: Alfred A. Knopf, 1995.

Edgerton, Les. *Hooked*. Cincinnati: Writer's Digest Books, 2007.

Orwell, George. *1984*. New York: New American Library, 1961.

Philbrick, Rodman. *The Last Book in the Universe*. New York: Scholastic, Inc., 2000.

Chapter 6: Dialogue

Blackstock, Terri. *Night Light*. Grand Rapids, Mich.: Zondervan, 2006.

Crichton, Michael. *Airframe*. New York: Alfred A. Knopf, 1996.

Earley, Tony. *The Blue Star*. New York: Little, Brown and Company, 2008.

Harris, Joel Chandler. *The Complete Tales of Uncle Remus*. Boston: Houghton Mifflin, 1955.

Huxley, Aldous. *Brave New World*. New York: HarperPerennial, 1998.

Kimmel, Haven. *A Girl Named Zippy*. New York: Random House, Inc., 2001.

Kipling, Rudyard. "Rikki-tikki-tavi." In *The Jungle Book*. Mineola, New York: Dover Publications, Inc., 2000.

------------. "The Undertakers." In *The Jungle Book 2*. N.p.: Aerie, n.d.

LaHaye, Tim and Jerry B. Jenkins. *Nicolae: The Rise of Antichrist*. Wheaton, Ill.: Tyndale House Publishers, 1997.

McCarthy, Cormac. *The Road*. New York: Alfred A. Knopf, 2006.

McDonald, Joyce. *Devil on my Heels*. New York: Delacorte Press, 2004.

Morrison, Toni. *A Mercy*. New York: Alfred A. Knopf, 2008.

Philbrick, Rodman. *The Last Book in the Universe*. New York: Scholastic, Inc., 2000.

Pratchett, Terry. *Reaper Man*. New York: HarperTorch, 2002.

Snicket, Lemony. *The Slippery Slope*. New York: HarperCollins, 2003.

Tan, Amy. "Rules of the Game." In *The Joy Luck Club*. New York: Penguin Group, 2006.

Yancy, Rick. *The Extraordinary Adventures of Alfred Kropp*. New York: Bloomsbury Publishers, 2005.

Chapter 7: Description

Beagle, Peter. *The Last Unicorn*. New York: Ballantine Books, 1968.

Biggers, Earl Derr. *The Chinese Parrot*. N.p.: Avon, 1951.

Blackston, Ray. *Flabbergasted*. Grand Rapids, Mich.: Fleming H. Revel, 2003.

---------------. *Lost in Rooville*. Grand Rapids, Mich.: Fleming H. Revel, 2005.

Bradbury, Ray. "The Black Ferris." In *The Stories of Ray Bradbury*. New York: Alfred A. Knopf, 1980.

Burroughs, Edgar Rice. *The Chessmen of Mars*. In *Three Martian Novels*. New York: Dover Publications, Inc., 1962.

Carver, Raymond. "A Small, Good Thing." In *Where I'm Calling From*. New York: Random House, 1988.

Cather, Willa. *O Pioneers!* New York: Bantam Books, 1989.

Chandler, Raymond. "Red Wind." In *Collected Stories*, edited by John Bayley. New York: Alfred A. Knopf, 2002.

Conrad, Joseph. *Heart of Darkness*. New York: Dover Publications, Inc., 1990.

Crichton, Michael. *Airframe*. New York: Alfred A. Knopf, 1996.

------------. *Jurassic Park*. New York: Ballantine Books, 1990.

Deighton, Len. *Faith*. New York: HarperCollins Publishers, 1995.

Dickens, Charles. *A Tale of Two Cities*. New York: Dover Publications, 1999.

Dunlap, Susanne. *The Musician's Daughter*. New York: Bloomsbury, 2009.

Earley, Tony. "Aliceville." In *Here We Are in Paradise*. Boston: Little, Brown and Company, 1994.

Grisham, John. *Theodore Boone: Kid Lawyer*. New York: Dutton Children's Books, 2010.

Fitzgerald, F. Scott. *The Great Gatsby*. New York: Charles Scribner's Sons, 1953.

Fleischman, Paul. *Whirligig*. New York: Random House, 1998.

Fleischman, Sid. *The Ghost in the Noonday Sun*. New York: HarperCollins, 1989.

Harris, Joanne. *Five Quarters of the Orange*. New York: HarperPerennial, 2007.

Hawthorne, Nathaniel. *The Scarlet Letter*. New York: Dover Publications, Inc., 1994.

Hesse, Karen. *Out of the Dust*. New York: Scholastic, Inc., 1997.

Hilton, James. *Lost Horizon*. New York: Junior Book Club, 1936.

Kidd, Sue Monk. *The Secret Life of Bees*. New York: Penguin Group, 2002.

Kipling, Rudyard. "Wee Willie Winkie." In *The Man Who Would Be King and Other Stories*, edited by Stanley Applebaum. New York: Dover Publications, Inc., 1994.

Koontz, Dean. *Brother Odd*. New York: Random House, 2006.

Lewis, C. S. *That Hideous Strength*. New York: Macmillan, 1979.

McDonald, Joyce. *Devil on my Heels*. New York: Delacorte Press, 2004.

McMullan, Margaret. *When I Crossed No-Bob*. Boston: Houghton Mifflin Company, 2007.

Peretti, Frank. *This Present Darkness*. Westchester, Ill.: Crossway Books, 1986.

Peters, Elizabeth. *Deeds of the Disturber*. New York: Atheneum, 1988.

Philbrick, Rodman. *The Last Book in the Universe*. New York: Scholastic, Inc., 2000.

Poe, Edgar Allan. "The Fall of the House of Usher." In *Adventures in American Literature*, edited by Edmund Fuller and B. Jo Kinnick. New York: Harcourt, Brace& World, Inc., 1963.

Pratchett, Terry. *The Amazing Maurice and his Educated Rodents*. New York: HarperCollins Publishers, 2001.

Shepherd, Jean. *In God We Trust, All Others Pay Cash*. New York: Broadway Books, 2000.

Smith, Alexander McCall. *Blue Shoes and Happiness*. New York: Random House, 2006.

Wells, Herbert George. *Experiment in Autobiography: Discoveries and Conclusions of a Very Ordinary Brain (Since 1866)*. Boston: Little, Brown and Company, 1962.

------------. "La Belle Dame Sans Merci." In *Select Conversations with an Uncle*. New York: The Merriam Company, 1895.

------------. *The War of the Worlds*. Mineola, New York: Dover Publications, Inc., 1997.

West, Jessamyn. "The Battle of Finney's Ford." In *The Friendly Persuasion*. San Diego: Harcourt Brace & Company, 1973.

Woo, Sung J. *Everything Asian*. New York: Thomas Dunne, 2009.

CHAPTER 8: WORDS, WORDS, WORDS

Beagle, Peter. *The Last Unicorn*. New York: Ballantine Books, 1968.

Bradbury, Ray. "The Veldt." In *The Stories of Ray Bradbury*. New York: Alfred A. Knopf, 1980.

Dickens, Charles. *Great Expectations*. New York: Dover Publications, Inc., 2001.

Fitzgerald, F. Scott. *The Great Gatsby*. New York: Charles Scribner's Sons, 1953.

Gaiman, Neil and Terry Pratchett. *Good Omens*. New York: HarperCollins, 2009.

Hemingway, Ernest. *The Old Man and the Sea*. New York: Charles Scribner's Sons, 1952.

------------. "The Short Happy Life of Francis Macomber." In *The Snows of Kilimanjaro and Other Stories*. New York: Simon & Schuster, 1998.

Irving, Washington. "Rip Van Winkle." In *The Sketch Book*. New York: The New American Library, 1961.

Lindbergh, Anne Morrow. *North to the Orient*. Orlando, Fla.: Harcourt Brace & Company, 1967.

Lowry, Lois. *The Giver*. Boston: Houghton Mifflin, 1993.

MacDonald, George. *Lilith*. Grand Rapids, Mich.: Eerdmans, 2000.

O'Brien, Tim. "Speaking of Courage." In *The Things They Carried*. Boston: Houghton Mifflin, 1990.

Paton, Alan. *Cry, the Beloved Country*. New York: Charles Scribner's Sons, 1948.

Remarque, Erich Maria. *All Quiet on the Western Front*. New York: Fawcett Columbine, 1996.

Shepherd, Jean. *In God We Trust, All Others Pay Cash*. New York: Broadway Books, 2000.

Star Trek II: The Wrath of Khan. VHS. Directed by Nicholas Meyer. Hollywood: Paramount Home Video, 1998.

Thomas, Dylan. "A Child's Christmas in Wales." In *Adventures in Appreciation*, edited by Kathleen T. Daniel and Fannie Safier. New York: Harcourt Brace Jovanovich, 1980.

Twain, Mark. *The Prince and the Pauper*. N.p.: Aerie, n.d.

CHAPTER 9: THEME

Austen, Jane. *Persuasion*. New York: Oxford University Press, 1998.

Cather, Willa. *O Pioneers!* New York: Bantam Books, 1989.

Geisel, Theodor. *Horton Hears a Who*. New York: Random House, 1982.

Glover, Donald E. *C. S. Lewis: The Art of Enchantment*. Athens, Ohio: Ohio University Press, 1982.

Hurley, C. Harold, ed. *Hemingway's Debt to Baseball in* The Old Man and the Sea: *a Collection of Critical Readings*. Lewiston, New York: The Edwin Mellen Press, Ltd., 1992.

Huxley, Aldous. *Brave New World*. New York: HarperPerennial, 1998.

L'Engle, Madeleine. *A Wrinkle in Time*. New York: Farrar, Strauss and Giroux, 1962.

O'Brien, Tim. *In the Lake of the Woods*. New York: Penguin Group, 1994.

O'Connor, Flannery. *Mystery and Manners*, edited by Sally and Robert Fitzgerald. New York: Farrar, Strauss and Giroux, 1969.

Philbrick, Rodman. *The Last Book in the Universe*. New York: Scholastic, Inc., 2000.

Saroyan, William. "Starting with a Tree and Finally Getting to the Death of a Brother." In *Writers [on Writing]: Collected Essays from* The New York Times. New York: Henry Holt, 2001.

Welty, Eudora. *Conversations with Eudora Welty*, edited by Peggy Whitman Prenshaw. Jackson: University Press of Mississippi, 1984.

Wharton, Edith. *Ethan Frome*. New York: Dover Publications, Inc., 1991

CHAPTER 10: PLOT

Alda, Alan. *Never Have Your Dog Stuffed*. New York: Random House, 2005.

Brashares, Ann. *The Sisterhood of the Traveling Pants*. New York: Delacorte Press, 2001.

Fleischman, Paul. *Whirligig*. New York: Random House, 1998.

Hook. VHS. Directed by Steven Spielberg. 1991; Burbank, CA: Columbia TriStar Home Video, 1992.

Philbrick, Rodman. *The Last Book in the Universe*. New York: Scholastic, Inc., 2000.

Pratchett, Terry. *The Amazing Maurice and his Educated Rodents*. New York: HarperCollins Publishers, 2001.

Secondhand Lions. DVD. Directed by Tim McCanlies. 2003; Los Angeles: New Line Home Entertainment, 2004.

The Wizard of Oz. DVD. Directed by Victor Fleming. 1999; Burbank, CA: Warner Home Video, 1999.

CHAPTER 11: SCENES

Bickham, Jack. *Scene and Structure*. Cincinnati: Writer's Digest Books, 1993.

Chekhov, Anton. "The Bet." In *Adventures in Appreciation*, edited by Kathleen T. Daniel and Fannie Safier. New York: Harcourt Brace Jovanovich, 1980.

Davis, J. Madison. *Novelist's Essential Guide to Creating Plot*. Cincinnati: Writer's Digest Books, 2000.

Dickens, Charles. *A Tale of Two Cities*. New York: Dover Publications, 1999.

Eliot, George [Mary Anne Evans]. *Silas Marner*. New York: Mineola, 1996.

Fleischman, Sid. "The Ouch Factor." In *The Writer's Handbook 2001*, edited by Sylvia K. Burack. Boston: The Writer, Inc., 2001.

The Fugitive. DVD. 1993. Directed by Andrew Davis. Burbank, Calif.: Warner Home Video, 2001.

Golding, William. *Lord of the Flies*. New York; Capricorn Books, 1959.

Haddon, Mark. *The Curious Incident of the Dog in the Night-Time*. New York: Vintage Contemporaries, 2003.

Ishiguro, Kazuo. *The Remains of the Day*. New York: Alfred A. Knopf, 1989.

Lee, Harper. *To Kill a Mockingbird*. New York: HarperCollins Publishers, 2002.

Lewis, C. S. *The Magician's Nephew*. New York: Scholastic, Inc., 1995.

MacDonald, John D. *Cape Fear*. New York: Fawcett Gold Medal, 1991.

McKee, Robert. *Story*. New York: HarperCollins Publishers, 1997.

Meyer, Stephenie. *Twilight*. Boston: Little, Brown and Company, 2005.

"Mr. Monk and the Candidate." *Monk*. DVD. 2002. Universal City, Calif.: Universal Studios, 2003.

Philbrick, Rodman. *The Last Book in the Universe*. New York: Scholastic, Inc., 2000.

Rosenfeld, Jordan E. *Make a Scene*. Cincinnati: Writer's Digest Books, 2008.

Sense and Sensibility. DVD. 1995. Directed by Ang Lee. Culver City, Calif.: Columbia Tristar Home Video, 1999.

CHAPTER 12: BEGINNINGS AND ENDINGS

Conrad, Joseph. *Heart of Darkness*. New York: Dover Publications, Inc., 1990.

Dickens, Charles. *Great Expectations*. New York: Dover Publications, Inc., 2001.

------------. *A Tale of Two Cities*. New York: Dover Publications, 1999.

Eliot, George [Mary Anne Evans]. *Silas Marner*. New York: Mineola, 1996.

Fish, Robert L. *The Bridge that Went Nowhere*. New York: Putnam, 1968.

Henry, O. "Springtime à la Carte." In *O. Henry's Best Stories*, edited by Lou P. Bunce. New York: Globe Book Company, 1953.

Ishiguro, Kazuo. *The Remains of the Day*. New York: Alfred A. Knopf, 1989.

Lahiri, Jhumpa. *The Namesake*. New York: Houghton Mifflin Company, 2003.

McCaughrean, Geraldine. *The Pirate's Son*. New York: Scholastic Press, Inc., 1998.

O'Dell, Scott. *The King's Fifth*. Boston: Houghton Mifflin Company, 1994.

Orwell, George. *1984*. New York: New American Library, 1961.

Philbrick, Rodman. *The Last Book in the Universe*. New York: Scholastic, Inc., 2000.

Raskin, Ellen. *The Westing Game*. New York: Avon Flare, 1978.

Rosenberg, Joel C. *Dead Heat*. Carol Stream, Ill.: Tyndale House Publishers, 2008.

Stevenson, Robert Louis. *Treasure Island*. New York: Dodd, Mead, 1956.

Twain, Mark [Samuel Clemens]. *The Adventures of Huckleberry Finn*. New York: Grosset & Dunlap, 1948.

Vonnegut, Kurt Jr. "Report on the Barnhouse Effect." In *Welcome to the Monkey House*. New York: Delacorte Press, 1968.

Wells, H. G. *The War of the Worlds*. Mineola, New York: Dover Publications, Inc., 1997.

CHAPTER 13: GETTING PUBLISHED

Bradbury, Ray. "A Literary Encounter." In *We'll Always Have Paris*. New York: William Morrow, 2009.

Hawthorne, Nathaniel. *The Scarlet Letter*. New York: Dover Publications, Inc., 1994.

Bibliography

Made in the USA
Columbia, SC
26 July 2020